7-841

A SEASON
OF
VOTING

A SEASON OF VOTING

The Japanese Elections of 1976 and 1977

Edited by Herbert Passin

American Enterprise Institute for Public Policy Research
Washington, D.C.

Library of Congress Cataloging in Publication Data

Main entry under title:
A Season of voting.

(AEI studies;240)
Includes index.
1. Elections—Japan.   2. Voting—Japan.   3. Japan—
Politics and government—1945–   I. Passin, Herbert.
JQ1692.S35   329'.023'5204   79–15712
ISBN 0–8447–3343–1

AEI Studies 240

CONTENTS

PREFACE   *Herbert Passin*

1 **JAPANESE POLITICS TODAY**   *Herbert Passin*   **1**

The LDP and the Parliamentary System   1
The Japanese Electoral System   3

Part One
THE 1976 HOUSE OF REPRESENTATIVES ELECTION

2 **THE CONSERVATIVES IN CRISIS**   *Michael Blaker*   **13**

The Lockheed Election   14
The New Liberal Club   18
Candidate Selection   21
The 1976 Election Results   25
Summary and Conclusions   38

3 **THE OPPOSITION**   *Gerald L. Curtis*   **43**

The Japan Socialist Party   44
The Democratic Socialist Party   54
The Kōmeitō   59
The Japan Communist Party   66
Opposition Party Cooperation   69
Campaign Issues   74

4 HISTORICAL STATISTICS *Nisihira Sigeki* 81
    Changes in National Election Results 81
    Party Voting Percentages by Electoral Districts 86
    Voting Rates by Degree of Urbanization 89
    Distribution of Seats by Size of Constituency 93
    Vote Share by Size of Municipality 100
    Characteristics of the Parties 105
    A Comparison with the Political Parties of Europe 109

Part Two
1977 HOUSE OF COUNCILLORS ELECTION

5 THE HOUSE OF COUNCILLORS *Herbert Passin* 115
    A Note on the Upper House 115
    The Political Environment 117
    The Elections 118
    The Results 133
    Representativeness and Reform 136

Part Three
OVERVIEW

6 FINANCING POLITICS *Katō Hirohisa* 141
    The LDP and Money 144
    Opposition Party Funds 148
    Revision of the Public Office Election Law 152
    Revision of the Political Funds Regulation Law 154
    Public Attitudes toward the High Cost of Elections 157

7 THE SIGNIFICANCE OF THE ELECTIONS
    Herbert Passin 160
    The LDP Defeat 161
    The Operation of the Diet 163
    Winners and Losers 166
    Public Opinion and the Elections 168
    New Political Forces 176
    Campaign Issues 178
    Political Developments 179

APPENDIX: Japanese Ballots, 1974   189

CONTRIBUTORS   191

INDEX   193

ABBREVIATIONS

DSP   Democratic Socialist party (Minshushugi Shakaitō)
JCP   Japan Communist party (Nippon Kyōsantō)
JSP   Japan Socialist party (Nihon Shakaitō)
KMT   Kōmeitō (Clean Government party)
LDP   Liberal Democratic party (Jiyū-Minshutō)
NLC   New Liberal Club (Shin Jiyū Kurabu)
PFL   Progressive Freedom League (Kakushin Jiyū Rengō)
SCL   Socialist Citizens League (Shakai Shimin Rengō)
WP   Women's party (Nippon Joseitō)

NOTE: Japanese personal names are presented in Japanese order—the family
name first and the given name last.

PREFACE

That Japan is the second largest industrial power in the world is by now recognized by most moderately well-informed people. But many are not aware that it is also the world's third largest democracy. The first is India, then the United States; among the advanced industrial democracies, Japan is second, the same rank it holds as an economic power.

But this has not always been so. Until World War II Japan had a parliamentary and cabinet system that in many superficial respects resembled the British system. But it was in no sense a democracy. The rights of the people were severely proscribed, the elected parliament had only limited powers, the cabinet was responsible to the emperor, not to the parliament, and the ministers of the army and navy were responsible not to the prime minister but to their respective services. A system so hedged-in could scarcely qualify as a parliamentary democracy. It should not be forgotten, however, that neither prewar Germany (except for the brief flowering of the Weimar period) nor Italy was a democracy. Nor was India, for that matter, since it was still a colony. Democracy in the Western sense was entirely limited to Western Europe and the relatively autonomous British dominions of Canada, Australia, and New Zealand.

The full-scale democratic political system in Japan today is the product of World War II. The American Occupation, as part of its program to assure that Japan would never again become a military threat to the rest of the world, placed its primary emphasis on the democratization of the country. "Democratization" meant many things —from retraining the police to land reform, from coeducation to a new constitution based on Western concepts of human rights and popular sovereignty, from the encouragement of square dancing to the dissolution of the zaibatsu cartels, from the midmorning coffee break to the enfranchisement of women. But one thing it surely meant was the complete reorganization of the political system to reflect the Occupation's concept of what a responsible parliamentary democracy should be.

Curiously, despite the fact that the changes were imposed by a foreign occupying power, they struck deep roots and held firmly. Since the end of the war Japan has had thirteen general elections for the House of Representatives and eleven triennial elections for the House of Councillors. The turnout for these elections is normally between 70 and 75 percent of the electorate, higher than for American elections by a significant margin. The elections have been hard fought and their outcomes, on the whole, accepted as legitimate. Challenges have always been by the legal procedures available in a democratic society; there has never been the slightest hint of extraparliamentary methods.

This bespeaks a high degree of democratic stability, a mark of how firmly democracy has struck roots. Perhaps, however, this very lack of sensation, drama, and excitement accounts for the fact that Japanese elections appear to have very little news value in the American media. My principal source of daily news is the *New York Times*. During the British elections of May 1979, I found myself very well served by the news coverage. Reporting was in considerable depth, so that I was able to follow not only the general course of the campaign but also the local trends in Scotland and Wales, the key issues, the reasons for public disenchantment with Labour, and even Jeremy Thorpe's desperate campaign. This is as it should be.

But when I tried to follow the elections in Japan, which is twice the size of Britain, much more powerful economically, and, as our regional ally, at least as important in Asia as Britain is in Europe, I could not do so. The *Times* gave a brief summary of the results of the 1976 and 1977 national elections and not a word about the equally significant outcome of the spring 1979 local elections.

At about the time of the British elections, Prime Minister Ōhira made a visit to the United States. One would think that the visit of the prime minister of one of our principal allies in the world, and our most important Asian ally, would rate some front-page attention. But while the British election campaign was receiving meticulous coverage, the *New York Times* did not carry a single front-page story on Mr. Ōhira. The only two items about the visit that I saw were on page 14 of the business section and page 1 of the metropolitan section. The imbalance in attention is hard to comprehend.

The contrast with the coverage of British elections or with the visit of Teng Hsiao-ping could not be greater.

This lack of attention to Japan is to some extent a reflection of the current state of public interest. But lack of attention, in turn, reinforces public disinterest. The only way to break the vicious circle is to keep firmly in mind that Japan's size, economic weight, and political relation to us make it one of our most important allies—if not the most important.

This book is a study of Japan's political system as seen through the two latest national elections. The first was for the House of Representatives in 1976, the second for the House of Councillors in 1977. Since the main body of the study was completed, Japan has had another major round of elections, the local elections for governors, mayors, and prefectural, city, town, and village assemblymen. The results were entirely consistent with the general directions detected earlier and predicted by all the contributors to this volume: the conservatives, rather than continuing their decline, made a major turnabout.

The book is divided into three main parts. Part I deals with the 1976 House of Representatives election. Michael Blaker analyzes the conservative side, the governing Liberal Democratic party, the recently defected New Liberal Club, and the independent conservatives. Gerald Curtis deals with the opposition parties. Nisihira Sigeki analyzes electoral trends through the historical statistics of lower-house elections.

Part II is my analysis of the 1977 House of Councillors election.

Part III is an examination of some overall issues in the elections. Katō Hirohisa analyzes the problem of political funding, which has become as much of an issue in Japan as it has in the United States. In the final chapter, I attempt to evaluate the significance of the recent round of elections.

We have had the benefit of a great deal of cooperation and advice from many Dietmen, academics, and journalists. I take this opportunity to thank them all, in particular Sakagami Norio, of Gakugei University, whose help was indispensable in digesting the vast amount of statistics generated by the elections, and Miyagawa Takayoshi, director of the Seiji Kōhō Center, who made not only his center and its materials available but his experience and wise advice as well.

In general, the authors are in substantial agreement in their interpretations, but the reader may well find some differences in emphasis and nuance. No attempt has been made to impose a uniform editorial line, even in the few cases where the interpretations appear to disagree. It was felt that the reader would obtain a livelier feeling for Japanese politics if these distinctive views were left in place.

Thirty-five years ago Japan was, along with Nazi Germany and Fascist Italy, a prime example of authoritarianism, military rule, and even—to some—fascism. Today, it is the third largest parliamentary democracy in the world and a very stable and prosperous one. We Americans would do well to understand its politics a little more deeply than we have done in the past.

HERBERT PASSIN

JAPAN: PRINCIPAL CITIES

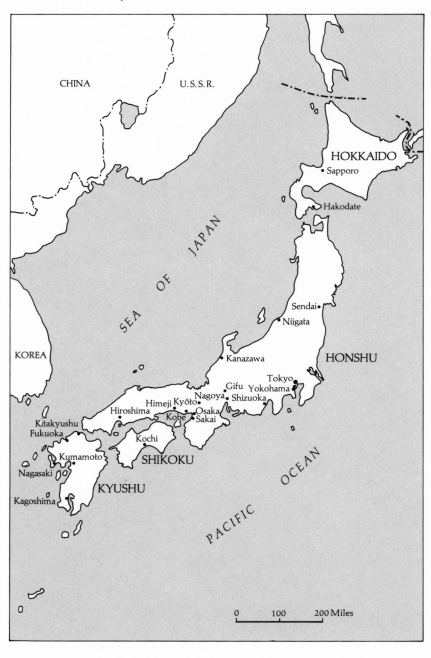

CHINA

U.S.S.R.

HOKKAIDO

• Sapporo

• Hakodate

SEA OF JAPAN

KOREA

Sendai •
• Niigata

• Kanazawa

HONSHU

Tokyo •
Gifu Yokohama
Nagoya • Shizuoka
Himeji Kyōto
Hiroshima Osaka
Kobe • Sakai

Kitakyushu
Fukuoka

Kochi

Kumamoto

SHIKOKU

Nagasaki

Kagoshima

KYUSHU

PACIFIC OCEAN

0   100   200 Miles

1

Japanese Politics Today

Herbert Passin

Since the end of World War II, the Japanese political scene has been remarkably stable. Except for the one-year socialist-conservative coalition in 1947–1948, Japan has been governed by conservatives. The Liberal Democratic party (LDP) was established in 1955 as the unified party of the conservatives and has been in office continuously ever since. Now, for the first time, this stability is in serious question. To be sure, it was always based upon a tightly drawn equilibrium, but the unquestioned dominance of the LDP made possible a steady and predictable relation among the key elements of power—the Diet (dominated by the LDP), the bureaucracy, and business.

The LDP and the Parliamentary System

Although this triad tended to dominate the center of the decision-making process, representatives of the other elements of the social-political scene were not entirely without influence. The labor movement (despite its divisions), the opposition parties, the civic movements, and the national press were often able to exert influence on the decision-making process in a variety of ways. The mobilization of large numbers of people for or against an action, the organization of interest groups, and the use of public exposure, economic threats, and street demonstrations often forced the modification of government programs even if unable to block them outright.

But the relations among the actors, both major and minor, were relatively predictable. One could usually depend upon the LDP to carry through a program, even if it were unpopular and even if it took longer than usual to adjust all the different elements, to neutralize the opposition or to reduce its resistance by timely concessions, and to accommodate the demands of pressure groups. The position of

1

the Self-Defense Forces illustrates both the power of the LDP and the limitations on that power: the Self-Defense Forces can function only within the limits of the tacit budget of 1 percent of gross national product; if the government tried to go seriously beyond this, the limits of its unstated understanding with the opposition would immediately become apparent.

The LDP's record is on the whole remarkable when the political stability of Japan over the past twenty years is compared with that of the other major industrial democracies. The LDP has not only remained continuously in power since 1955 but it has won a clear majority of seats in every election except 1976, when it gained its majority by the accession of several independently elected conservatives. Although it has failed to win a popular majority since 1976, its nearest rival, the Japan Socialist party (JSP), usually obtains half or less than the number of LDP votes. In other words, although the LDP no longer commands an unambiguous majority of the vote on its own, it is still a giant surrounded by pygmies. The gap between the LDP and the second largest party in terms of popular votes is much greater (42 to 21 percent)[1] than between the two leading parties in any other major industrial democracy.[2]

During this same period, the United Kingdom and Germany have seen changes of government—between the Conservative and Labour party in the United Kingdom and the Christian Democratic Union (CDU) and Socialist party (SPD) in Germany. Moreover, in no case did the governing party in the United Kingdom win a majority of the popular vote, even though it managed to win a majority of seats. In Germany, the only time a governing party won a clear majority of votes was in 1957, when the CDU won 54.3 percent. The SPD not only has never won a popular majority on its own, but it has always had to depend upon its alliance partner, the Free Democratic party (FDP), to eke out its parliamentary majority. Contrast this with the stability of the LDP, which has always managed to win a majority of seats in the lower house, in spite of its declining popular majority.

In Italy and France, to be sure, the same ruling party has been in

---

[1] December 1976 lower-house election.

[2] In the United Kingdom in the second election of 1974 the difference was 39 to 36 percent. In France in 1973, 24 percent of the Union of Democrates for the Republic plus the Independent Republicans' 7 percent gave a total of 31 percent, as against the nearest competition, the socialist coalition, of 22 percent. In the 1976 elections in West Germany the Christian Democratic Union outpolled the Socialist party 49 to 43 percent, but the Free Democratic party's 8 percent gave the governing coalition a majority. In Italy's 1976 election the Christian Democrats won 39 percent and the Communists 34 percent (see Table 4–17).

power over the past twenty years. The record, however, is not as impressive as the LDP's. The Gaullist party, despite the overwhelming charisma of its leader, never won a popular majority. And in Italy, the Christian Democratic party (DC) has managed to form a succession of governments by adroit coalition politics, in spite of the fact that throughout the period it never once won a majority of the popular vote or commanded a majority of seats.

The LDP's comfortable position has so far allowed Japan to maintain a high degree of consensus among the major forces on national policy issues, to hold opposition down to tolerable levels, and to be reasonably sure of carrying through important programs. Whether it will continue to do so is the subject of this book.

The Japanese Electoral System

In 1976 and 1977, within a short seven-month period, Japan held two important national elections. The first was for the House of Representatives and the second for the House of Councillors. To understand the significance of these elections and to follow these discussions, the reader needs an explanation of several features of the Japanese electoral system.

At present, the Japanese people elect six different kinds of public officers: members of the House of Representatives; members of the House of Councillors; prefectural governors; prefectural assemblymen; municipal mayors (cities, towns, and villages); and municipal assemblymen. Except for governorships and mayoralities, all these posts have always been elective.[3]

Japan's national legislature, the Diet, consists of two chambers: the House of Representatives, or lower house, and the House of Councillors, or upper house. The House of Representatives has been in continuous existence since 1889, when the first national elections were held, but the House of Councillors started only after World War II, in 1947. The councillors replaced the prewar House of Peers, which was an appointed body on the order of the English House of Lords, but more powerful. Although the House of Representatives is called the "lower house," it is in fact more powerful than the Councillors, just as the British House of Commons has become more powerful than the "upper" House of Lords. This change came to Japan as a result of the American Occupation, but the older terminology lingers on, a holdover from the days when the House of Representatives

---

[3] See the Public Office Election Law, enacted in 1950, during the American Occupation.

TABLE 1–1

ELECTION SYSTEMS FOR THE HOUSE OF REPRESENTATIVES, 1889–1976

Year of Passage of Relevant Law	Desig- nated Number of Seats	Constituencies		Suffrage	Number of Elections Under Relevant Law
		Number	Seats in each		
1889	300	257	1–2	Taxpaying males, 25 years and over	6
1900	369	97	1–13	Same	7
1902	381	109	1–12	Same	7
1919	464	374	1–3	Same	2
1925	466	122	3–5	All males, 25 years and over	6
1946	468	54	1–14	All adults, 20 years and over	1
1947	466	117	3–5	Same	3
1953[a]	467	118	1–5	Same	5
1964	486	123	1–5	Same	2
1972[b]	491	124	1–5	Same	1
1976	511	130	1–5	Same	1

[a] Addition of Amami-Oshima district, one seat.
[b] Addition of Okinawa, two seats.

was considered to represent the "people" and the House of Peers, the emperor and the nation as a whole.

Since 1889 there have been thirty-four general elections for the House of Representatives, thirteen of them after World War II. Table 1–1 shows the changes in election methods for the lower house during its ninety-year history. Since 1925 the number of electoral districts has varied from 117 to 130.[4] All except one, Amami-Oshima, elect between three and five seats. The Amami-Oshima district, a small island group that lies between Kagoshima, the southernmost prefecture on the main islands, and Okinawa, was first established in 1955 and elects only one member.

No matter how many seats are elected from a district, each voter has only one vote, and the winners are those who receive the largest number of votes. The Japanese characterize the English and American

---

[4] Except for 1946, when a special emergency election was called on orders of the American Occupation.

electoral districts, which elect only one member, as "small" and the Japanese district as "medium." In the American-style small-constituency system, the winner usually takes the majority of votes or, if there are more than two candidates, a large plurality. In Japan's medium-constituency system, a majority is virtually unheard of, and winning with 10 precent of the votes is not uncommon.

At present, there are 511 representatives, but this number has been increasing slowly (see Table 1–1). The principal reason for the increase in seats is the need to accommodate the demand for more equal representation. In the United States, population change is adjusted by regular redistricting but with no change in the number of representatives. In Japan, however, from time to time the number of representatives is increased in the districts with population growth.

The maximum term of office for a representative is four years, but the House may be dissolved by Diet vote or by cabinet decision before that time. The postwar average has been two and a third years, and the 1976 election, with which this book is concerned, was the only one in the postwar period held after a full four-year term.

The House of Councillors was established in 1947, during the American Occupation, as the successor to the House of Peers. It consists of 252 members, 152 of whom are elected from the local (prefectural) constituencies and 100 elected at large from the so-called national constituency. Japan is divided into forty-seven prefectures, which correspond approximately to states in the United States, and each one constitutes an electoral district for the upper house, just as our states do for Senate elections. Twenty-six of the prefectures elect a single member, the rest between two and four apiece (see Table 5–1). A councillor's term of office is six years, and half the seats are elected every three years. Since the end of World War II, there have been eleven triennial elections for the upper house. The next one is scheduled for 1980.

In the discussions that follow, it is necessary to distinguish between the electorate, the voters, and the valid votes. For example, in the 1976 lower-house elections, there were 77,926,588 registered voters; they are the electorate. Only 73.45 percent, however, or 57,236,622, actually voted. Since in any election some ballots are inevitably cast improperly, the total number of valid votes is below the total number of votes cast. In the case in point, there were 56,612,764 valid votes, or 72.65 percent of the electorate (98.9 percent of the total votes cast).

Voters must be twenty years of age or over. Representatives must be at least twenty-five years of age, councillors thirty.

Candidates run either on a party ticket or as independents. An officially endorsed candidate (kōnin) is the party candidate, and official endorsement carries with it financial and organizational support. Some independents may receive a party's recommendation (suisen), but while this brings them moral support it does not usually entail financial or organizational backing.

The authors in this volume use different criteria for classifying electoral districts by degree of urbanization. Baker and Curtis use the system devised by the newspaper, the Asahi Shinbun, which classifies lower-house electoral districts into four types: metropolitan, urban, semiurban, and rural (see Table 1–2). Nisihira and I use a five-point

TABLE 1–2

HOUSE OF REPRESENTATIVES ELECTORAL DISTRICTS, BY DEGREE OF URBANIZATION, Asahi Shinbun CLASSIFICATION

Degree of Urbani- zation	Number of Districts	Percent of Electorate	Percent of Valid Votes	Number of Seats	Percent of Seats
Metropolitan[a]	25	25.2	22.0	100	19.6
Urban[b]	34	31.8	32.0	136	26.6
Semiurban[c]	46	30.7	32.5	185	36.2
Rural[d]	25	12.3	13.5	90	17.6
Total	130	100.0	100.0	511	100.0

NOTE: The numbers following the names in the following notes identify the electoral districts in the specified locale; thus "Saitama 1" refers to the Saitama First District.

[a] Metropolitan districts: Saitama 1; Tokyo 1–10; Kanagawa 1, 2, 4; Aichi 1, 6; Kyōto 1; Osaka 1–4, 6, 7; Hyōgo 1, 2.

[b] Urban districts: Hokkaidō 1, 3; Miyagi 1; Fukushima 1; Tochigi 1; Saitama 2, 5; Chiba 1, 4; Tokyo 11; Kanagawa 3; Niigata 1; Shizuoka 1–3; Aichi 2–4; Gifu 1; Miye 1; Ishikawa 1; Kyōto 2; Osaka 5; Hyōgo 3, 4; Nara; Wakayama 1; Kagawa 1; Okayama 1; Hiroshima 1, 2; Fukuoka 1, 2, 4.

[c] Semiurban districts: Hokkaidō 2, 4, 5; Aomori 1; Iwate 1; Akita 1; Yamagata 1; Fukushima 2; Ibaragi 1, 2; Tochigi 2; Gumma 1–3; Saitama 3, 4; Kanagawa 5; Niigata 3; Nagano 1, 3, 4; Aichi 5; Gifu 2; Miye 2; Wakayama 2; Toyama 1, 2; Fukui; Shiga; Kagawa 2; Tokushima; Ehime 1, 2; Kōchi; Okayama 2; Hiroshima 3; Tottori; Yamaguchi 1, 2; Fukuoka 3; Nagasaki 1; Kumamoto 1; Ōita 1; Miyazaki 1; Kagoshima 1; Okinawa.

[d] Rural districts: Aomori 2; Iwate 2; Akita 2; Yamagata 2; Miyagi 2; Fukushima 3; Ibaragi 3; Chiba 2, 3; Niigata 2, 4; Nagano 2; Yamanashi; Ishikawa 2; Hyōgo 5; Ehime 3; Shimane; Saga; Nagasaki 2; Kumamoto 2; Ōita 2; Miyazaki 2; Kagoshima 2, 3; Amami-Ōshima.

classification, based upon the percentage of the labor force engaged in the primary industrial sector (agriculture, forestry, and fishery; see Tables 1–3 and 1–4). Nisihira and I also use three other measures:

TABLE 1–3

House of Representatives Electoral Districts, by Degree of Urbanization based on Labor Force, 1969, 1972, 1976

Degree of Urbanization[a]	Number		1969 Number	1969 Percent	1972 Number	1972 Percent	1976 Number	1976 Percent
Metropolitan (0–9%)[b]	34	Seats	102	21.0	114	23.2	134	26.2
		Votes		35.5		35.8		35.6
Urban (10–19%)[c]	20	Seats	67	13.8	78	15.9	80	15.6
		Votes		16.0		16.3		16.8
Intermediate (20–29%)[d]	36	Seats	92	18.9	143	29.1	145	28.4
		Votes		25.4		25.2		25.4
Semirural (30–39%)[e]	26	Seats	140	28.8	106	21.6	101	19.8
		Votes		15.9		15.6		15.4
Rural (40% and over)[f]	14	Seats	85	17.5	50	10.2	51	10.0
		Votes		7.2		7.1		6.8
Total	130		486		491		511	

[a] The degree of urbanization is based on the percentage of the labor force in the primary industrial sector (agriculture, forestry, and fishery).
[b] Metropolitan districts: Hokkaidō 1; Saitama 1, 5; Chiba 1, 4; Tokyo 1–11; Kanagawa 1–5; Aichi 1, 6; Kyōto 1; Osaka 1–7; Hyōgo 1, 2; Fukuoka 2.
[c] Urban districts: Saitama 2; Niigata 1; Ishikawa 1; Gifu 1; Shizuoka 1–3; Aichi 2–4; Kyōto 2; Hyōgo 3, 4; Nara; Wakayama 1; Hiroshima 1, 2; Kagawa 1; Fukuoka 1, 4.
[d] Intermediate districts: Hokkaidō 2–5; Miyagi 1; Fukushima 3; Ibaragi 2; Tochigi 1, 2; Gumma 1–3; Saitama 3, 4; Toyama 1, 2; Fukui; Yamanashi; Nagano 3; Gifu 2; Aichi 5; Miye 1; Shiga; Okayama 1, 2; Hiroshima 3; Yamaguchi 1, 2; Kagawa 2; Ehime 1, 2; Fukuoka 3; Nagasaki 1; Kumamoto 1; Kagoshima 1; Okinawa.
[e] Semirural districts: Aomori 1; Iwate 1; Akita 1; Yamagata 1; Fukushima 1; Ibaragi 1; Chiba 3; Niigata 2–4; Ishikawa 2; Nagano 1, 2, 4; Miye 2; Hyōgo 5; Wakayama 2; Tottori; Shimane; Tokushima; Kōchi; Saga; Nagasaki 2; Ōita 1, 2; Miyazaki 1.
[f] Rural districts: Aomori 2; Iwate 2; Miyagi 2; Akita 2; Yamagata 2; Fukushima 2; Ibaragi 3; Chiba 2; Ehime 3; Kumamoto 2; Miyazaki 2; Kagoshima 2, 3; Amami-Ōshima.

population density (Table 1–5), size of municipality (see Table 4–15), and the nine largest prefectures versus the rest see Table 5–10). Each has its own distinctive uses. All of them, however, yield approximately the same results, so that there has been no need to adjust them.

TABLE 1–4

House of Councillors Local Constituencies, by Degree of Urbanization, 1977

Degree of Urbani- zation[a]	Number of Districts	Percent of Electorate	Percent of Valid Votes	Number of Seats	Percent of Seats
Metropolitan[b]	5	29.9	27.6	14	18.4
Urban[c]	6	24.1	23.6	16	21.1
Intermediate[d]	11	14.6	15.0	12	15.8
Semirural[e]	10	14.6	15.5	15	19.7
Rural[f]	15	16.8	18.3	19	25.0
Total	47	100.0	100.0	76	100.0

[a] The degree of urbanization is based on the proportion of the labor force in the primary industrial sector (agriculture, forestry, and fishery).
[b] Metropolitan prefectures: Tokyo, Kanagawa, Kyōto, Osaka, and Hyōgo.
[c] Urban prefectures: Hokkaidō, Saitama, Chiba, Aichi, Hiroshima, and Fukuoka.
[d] Intermediate prefectures: Aomori, Miyagi, Ishikawa, Shizuoka, Nara, Wakayama, Yamaguchi, Ehime, Kōchi, Nagasaki, and Okinawa.
[e] Semirural prefectures: Gumma, Niigata, Gifu, Mie, Okayama, Kagawa, Kumamoto, Ōita, Miyazaki, and Kagoshima.
[f] Rural prefectures: Iwate, Akita, Yamagata, Fukushima, Ibaragi, Tochigi, Toyama, Fukui, Yamanashi, Nagano, Shiga, Tottori, Shimane, Saga, and Tokushima.

TABLE 1–5

House of Representative Electoral Districts, by Degree of Population Density, 1969, 1972, 1976

Degree of Population Density[a]	Number of Districts		1969		1972		1976	
			Number	Percent	Number	Percent	Number	Percent
High (90–100%)[b]	18	Seats	54	11.1	60	12.2	72	14.1
		Votes		20.9		20.6		17.1
Midhigh (70–89%)[c]	11	Seats	29	6.0	44	9.0	45	8.8
		Votes		11.0		11.6		13.7
Intermediate (50–69%)[d]	14	Seats	39	8.0	49	10.0	55	10.7
		Votes		11.5		11.6		13.7
Midlow (30–49%)[e]	50	Seats	173	35.6	196	39.9	196	38.4
		Votes		35.8		35.9		35.3
Low (0–29%)[f]	37	Seats	191	39.3	142	28.9	143	28.0
		Votes		20.8		20.3		20.2
Total	130		486		491		511	

[a] Based upon proportion of population in densely inhabited districts (DIDs). For explanation, see Chapter 4, note 6.

[b] High-density districts: Tokyo 1–10; Kanagawa 1; Aichi 1, 6; Osaka 1, 2, 4; Hyōgo 1; Kyōto 1.

[c] Midhigh-density districts: Hokkaidō 1; Saitama 2; Chiba 1; Tokyo 11; Kanagawa 2, 4; Osaka 3, 5–7; Hyōgo 2.

[d] Intermediate-density districts: Hokkaidō 3, 4; Miyagi 1; Saitama 5; Chiba 4; Kanagawa 3, 5; Niigata 1; Shizuoka 1; Kyōto 2; Hiroshima 1; Fukuoka 1, 2, 4.

[e] Midlow-density districts (40–49%): Hokkaidō 2, 5; Aomori 1; Saitama 1; Ishikawa 1; Gifu 1; Shizuoka 2; Aichi 5; Hyōgo 3; Wakayama 1; Hiroshima 2, 3; Yamaguchi 1; Ehime 1; Nagasaki 1; Kumamoto 1; Kagoshima 1; Okinawa; (30–39%): Iwate 1; Akita 1; Yamagata 1; Fukushima 1; Ibaragi 2; Tochigi 1; Gumma 1, 2; Saitama 3, 4; Niigata 3; Toyama 1, 2; Fukui; Nagano 1, 3; Shizuoka 3; Aichi 2–4; Hyōgo 4; Miye 1; Nara; Okayama 1; Yamaguchi 2; Kagawa 1; Ehime 2; Kōchi; Fukuoka 3; Ōita 1, 2; Miyazaki 1.

[f] Low-density districts: Aomori 2; Iwate 2; Miyagi 2; Akita 2; Yamagata 2; Fukushima 2, 3; Ibaragi 1, 3; Tochigi 2; Gumma 3; Chiba 2, 3; Niigata 2, 4; Ishikawa 2; Yamanashi; Nagano 2, 4; Gifu 2; Miye 2; Shiga; Hyōgo 5; Wakayama 2; Tottori; Shimane; Okayama 2; Tokushima; Kagawa 2; Ehime 3; Saga; Amami-Ōshima; Nagasaki 2; Kumamoto 2; Miyazaki 2; Kagoshima 2, 3.

PART ONE

The 1976 House of Representatives Election

2

The Conservatives in Crisis

Michael Blaker

The 1976 lower-house election was the thirteenth contest of the postwar era, and many observers thought it would be the most pivotal. An unprecedented four years had passed since the previous election, and it was expected that the December balloting would further erode conservative strength and might even topple the Liberal Democratic party's long-held Diet majority. Indeed, the single most conspicuous trend in Japanese national elections since 1955 has been the steady deterioration of the LDP's performance at the polls. As Table 2–1 shows, while the Japanese electorate has grown, the number of LDP votes has remained relatively constant, at approximately 23 million, since 1958. The party's share of the national vote has slowly dwindled, from 57.8 percent in 1958 to 54.7 percent in 1963 to 46.9 percent in 1972. In terms of Diet seats held, the LDP enjoyed a comfortable majority until 1972, when it captured only 271 of the 491 total seats. Thus, the LDP's loosening grip on a legislative majority in both the House of Councillors and the House of Representatives seemed to point toward its eventual displacement as the majority party in the Diet and the government party of Japan. A key question was whether 1976 would be the year this would happen, or whether the LDP would be able to stem or reverse the trend.

A significant factor in the 1976 election was the large number of uncommitted of "floating" voters—those who answer either "no preference" or "don't know" in public opinion polls on party support. In all polls the ranks of the uncommitted have swelled in recent years in both rural and urban areas. Generally the floating vote is roughly 20 percent outside the cities and 30–35 percent in urban areas. One

NOTE: I would like to thank Anita M. O'Brien and Suzanne Seear Brown for assisting with the preparation of the statistical data used in this study.

13

TABLE 2–1

LIBERAL DEMOCRATIC PARTY SHARE OF VOTE IN HOUSE OF
REPRESENTATIVES ELECTIONS, 1958–1972

Election	Percentage of Votes	Seats Won	LDP Votes	Total Valid Votes Cast[a]
1958	57.8	287	22,976,846	40,045,216
1960	57.6	296	22,740,271	39,925,481
1963	54.7	283	22,423,915	41,016,540
1967	48.8	277	22,447,838	45,996,574
1969	47.6	288	22,381,570	46,989,893
1972	46.9	271	24,563,199	52,425,265

[a] The actual electorate is larger, but nonvoting and invalid ballots reduce the number of valid votes cast.
SOURCE: Ministry of Home Affairs statistics.

poll taken in a densely populated district just before the December 1976 election revealed 41 percent of its sample to be nonpartisan.[1]

For the LDP, the chief lesson of the two preceding elections—the 1972 general election and the 1974 House of Councillors election[2]—was that if the party was to halt the erosion of its strength it had to attract more votes in metropolitan and urban districts. It would have to appeal to the growing nonpartisan or undecided vote, while maintaining its generation-long domination of the rural and semirural districts.

The Lockheed Election

Apart from these longer-term trends, two specific and related events influenced the LDP as it geared up for the 1976 election. The first was the Lockheed bribery case; the second was the establishment of the New Liberal Club. The expected voter backlash against the LDP over the Lockheed scandal riveted public and media attention. The "Lockheed election" was the first national test of popular sentiments about the affair since it had erupted ten months earlier.

The revelations had begun in February 1976 with testimony by former Lockheed Aircraft Corporation President Carl Kotchian and

[1] Tama New Town poll, in *Mainichi Shinbun*, November 24, 1976.
[2] For the 1974 Councillors election, see Michael K, Blaker, ed., *Japan at the Polls* (Washington, D.C.: American Enterprise Institute, 1976).

14

others before the U.S. Senate Foreign Relations Subcommittee on Multinational Corporations. This testimony and supporting documents issued by the committee revealed that certain Japanese officials and businessmen had accepted payments from Lockheed to promote the company's business prospects in Japan.[3] A major figure named as a recipient of illegal funds was backstage wheeler-dealer Kodama Yoshio, who was allegedly paid $7 million to serve as Lockheed's secret agent in Japan and to persuade All-Nippon Airways to buy the Lockheed Tristar jet.[4]

Immediately following the initial disclosures, Prime Minister Miki Takeo appeared before the Diet Budget Committee and promised a thorough investigation. He sent a personal letter to President Ford requesting information on the scandal, and after an exchange of letters between the two leaders the Japanese Justice Ministry and the U.S. Department of Justice reached a settlement designed to facilitate the inquiry. The agreement, based on the premise of keeping all documents confidential, drew heavy criticism from Japanese opposition parties as a "cover-up." For nearly six weeks the opposition boycotted the Diet.

Charges were filed in May against Kodama for having received payoffs from Lockheed. He was subsequently arrested, along with executives of the Japanese trading firm Marubeni Corporation and of All-Nippon Airways. An aggressive pursuit of the investigation was inhibited, however, by intra-LDP rivalries. Miki had enjoyed an unusual degree of public support, largely because of his reputation for personal honesty and integrity. But his position in the LDP was weak. Chosen as a compromise candidate by party chieftains late in 1974, Miki continued in office through the backing of an uneasy coalition. His faction ranked fourth in size and was considerably smaller than those of other LDP leaders. Thus his dilemma: as party leader he had to contain the potentially explosive effect of Lockheed on the LDP, but his own personality, sense of responsibility as prime minister, and sensitivity to public feelings compelled him to investigate those implicated in the scandal. But if high party officials were involved, a vigorous investigation could hurt the LDP and possibly ruin Miki's chances of retaining the prime ministership. Despite his favorable public image, Miki could not maintain his position within the party without the support of major LDP faction leaders.

---

[3] An excellent discussion of the Lockheed incident can be found in Hans H. Baerwald, "Lockheed and Japanese Politics," *Asian Survey* (September 1976), pp. 817–829.

[4] Kodama was convicted as a war criminal after World War II and spent several years in prison; see his *Sugamo Diary* (Tokyo: Radiopress, 1960).

A stalemate developed. LDP President Shiina Etsusaburō (ironically, the man behind Miki's appointment to the prime ministership two years before) conferred frequently over the summer with top party leaders Tanaka Kakuei, Ōhira Masayoshi, and Fukuda Takeo about how to force Miki from office. Miki's only weapon against those seeking his ouster was public opinion. But with the Lockheed investigation apparently stalled, Miki's popularity dipped from 45 percent when he assumed office to 26 percent a month after the scandal erupted.[5]

While most people anticipated further revelations concerning Lockheed,[6] few realized the extent to which the scandal had penetrated the LDP until August, when former Prime Minister Tanaka and five other party leaders were arrested and indicted. Tanaka, who previously had denied any personal involvement in the affair, was charged with having accepted a bribe of $1.67 million in Lockheed funds through Marubeni. Indicted with him were former LDP Secretary-General Hashimoto Tomisaburō, former Vice-Minister of Transport Katō Mutsuki, LDP Aeronautics and Maritime Affairs Committee Chairman Fukunaga Kazuomi, and Party Affairs Bureau Chief Satō Takayuki. These arrests pierced the very heart of the conservative party, creating the worst crisis in its history.

Tanaka's arrest and withdrawal from the party precipitated a renewed hue and cry within the LDP for Miki's ouster. This time the anti-Miki charge was led by former LDP Secretary-General Hori Shigeru and lower-house Speaker Funada Naka. At a party gathering in October, to which Miki was pointedly not invited, the 245 Diet members present voted unanimously for Miki's removal and Fukuda's accession to the prime ministership. But Miki ignored the rebuff and, as he had done so often since the Lockheed scandal first surfaced in February, used public opinion to shore up his position in the party. Thus he was able to keep hold of the reins of office in the face of persistent and at times frantic attempts to depose him.

Despite his proven political resiliency, time was running out for Miki. All year the party had balked at dissolving the Diet and holding an election. Fearful of a hostile public reaction, the Tanaka faction was especially opposed to an early election. But the law required that an

---

[5] *Asahi Shinbun*, July 8, 1976.

[6] The newspapers were full of possible names. One was Nakasone Yasuhiro, then LDP secretary-general. To parry the large number of questioning telephone calls to his election district headquarters, Nakasone hit upon the novel device of using a recorded message with a blanket denial of any personal connection with the scandal.

election be held before December 10 and, having been postponed almost as long as legally possible, it was finally scheduled for December 5. Miki, labeled a "kite without a string" by some critics who considered his leadership uninspired, led the beleaguered LDP into the election, postponing a party convention and a possibly ruinous intraparty showdown.

Public Reaction to Lockheed. Public opinion surveys provide some clues about Japanese attitudes toward the Lockheed aircraft payoff scandal. They all placed high prices and social welfare at the forefront of Japanese concerns, with Lockheed relegated to second or third position.[7] Many respondents in all surveys blamed the Japanese political system and especially the collusion of moneyed interests and politics for making such corruption "inevitable." Another dimension of cynicism was evident in one poll, in which 58 percent of those polled expressed the belief that Lockheed would not alter the course of politics in Japan. Most respondents in various polls criticized Miki's handling óf the investigation.

Most relevant to the 1976 election were the surveys finding that even though most Japanese (from 53 to 70 percent) opposed as unethical the reelection candidacies of Lockheed-tainted politicians, and despite the high degree of public concern with Lockheed, few responding expected their own votes to be swayed by the scandal. In a national survey sponsored by the *Tokyo Shinbun* only 2.4 percent of those questioned stated that their votes would be decided by Lockheed. In a poll by *Yomiuri Shinbun* respondents doubted that the incident would affect the outcome of the election. Public opinion polls, in short, suggested that Lockheed would have a limited national impact when Japan went to the polls on December 5.

Niigata's Third District and the Tanaka Candidacy. Having quit the LDP, Tanaka announced that he would seek election to the House of Representatives as an independent in Niigata's Third District. He had been elected eleven times there during his climb to the prime ministership. In 1972 he had polled 42 percent of the district vote, swamping all adversaries with his 182,000 votes, the third highest total of any candidate in the country in that election.

Despite his Lockheed-related woes, Tanaka's victory in 1976 was never really in doubt. He had served his constituents well during his

---

[7] This summary reflects all opinion surveys by leading newspapers during the three-month period preceding the election. See especially *Asahi Shinbun*, March 27 and October 9, 1976; *Yomiuri Shinbun*, November 2 and 7, 1976; and *Tokyo Shinbun*, November 14, 1976.

thirty-year political career, channeling funds for a dazzling array of construction projects—bridges, schools, roads, and eleven tunnels (including the Kakuei Bridge and the Tanaka Tunnel)—all politically significant and visible symbols of Tanaka's clout. His constituents, remembering his record, were fiercely loyal. His supporters' organization, the Etsuzankai, boasted 98,000 members—one-fifth of the voting population of the district and more than any other such organization in Japan.

Tanaka moved quickly after his resignation from the LDP to capitalize on his massive local support. As he declared in the first issue of *Etsuzan*, the monthly tabloid issued in Niigata to promote his candidacy, "I was born, raised, and have devoted myself to this district. Now I need your help in overcoming the worst crisis I have ever faced."[8] Niigata residents were aroused and responded enthusiastically to the appeal. There was only scattered opposition to his candidacy. The Etsuzankai and Tanaka's support group in Tokyo scrambled after votes and money with great zeal. At Tokyo headquarters the technique was to ask potential contributors for ¥2,000[9] and, if that was not forthcoming, to request half that sum. If the lesser amount was rejected, the potential donor would be reminded that "we cannot forget what he has done." These appeals were more to demonstrate solidarity with the Tanaka cause than anything else, for Tanaka's organization scarcely needed a special effort. The depth of Etsuzankai support for Tanaka is indicated by a poll finding that members firmly backed the discredited former prime minister even though only 8 percent believed Tanaka to be innocent of the charges brought against him. Even non-Etsuzankai residents of Niigata were strongly behind Tanaka. In an *Asahi Shinbun* survey of attitudes toward Tanaka in the district, 60 percent responded either "it's too bad for him," or "I believe him," or "he made a contribution to the [Niigata] area." In a *Mainichi Shinbun* sample, 74 percent ignored or downplayed his alleged transgressions, pointing out instead his achievements as a hardworking, effective politician dedicated to his district.[10]

The New Liberal Club

On top of various Lockheed-related troubles, the LDP received another blow from within party ranks five months before the election.

---

[8] *Etsuzan*, October 19, 1976, as cited in *Mainichi Shinbun*, November 22, 1976.

[9] The yen was worth about US$8 at the time.

[10] *Mainichi Shinbun*, October 21 and 27, 1976; *Asahi Shinbun*, November 6, 1976.

Citing unhappiness with Miki's handling of the Lockheed investigation, Kōno Yōhei and five other LDP Diet members dramatically withdrew from the party on July 1 to form a new conservative organization.

During the generation of conservative hegemony in Japanese politics since the two main conservative groups merged to form the LDP in 1955, the disparate factions and personalities in the party had managed to coexist despite their differences. No discord or rivalry in the conservative camp had escalated to the point of splitting the party. One chronic source of intraparty friction was reform of the party itself, and the Lockheed scandal widened internal divisions over this issue. Despite repeated promises to reform, the party had not moved far in that direction by 1976, even though it seemed that a renovation of its campaign financing methods and organizational structure was needed to restore flagging public confidence.

The alleged failure of the LDP to reform itself provided the impetus for the defection of Kōno and his supporters. The fledgling group took the rather awkward-sounding name of Shin Jiyū Kurabu, or New Liberal Club, which expressed the image it was seeking to build—one of freshness, reformism, and informality. It was a "club" in the important sense that until it secured twenty-five lower-house and ten upper-house seats, it could not be a party with the right to introduce legislation. Thus newness, reform, and collegiality were the impressions sought by the NLC's founders, who were given by some the less complimentary label of the "Kōno Six."

The NLC occupied the limelight in the Japanese media only briefly. Scarcely a month after the party was founded, Tanaka was arrested and the NLC was washed from the center of the political stage by the tide of Lockheed revelations. Poor timing, however, was the least of the NLC's worries as it made its political debut. First, the group faced formidable obstacles in building its organizational base and in securing the funds necessary to perform well in the election. Unlike the other political parties, the NLC had no organizations supporting it. It started out with the motto "clean politics" and promised to rely on individual, not corporate, contributions for its campaign financing.[11] By early November, however, the club had begun to solicit corporate money. At that time roughly one-seventh of the NLC's officially disclosed contributions were corporate (¥23 million of ¥150 million). According to the NLC secretary-general, Nishioka Takeo, such contributions were to be restricted to ¥1 million per company. In the end, of all contributions to the NLC, aside from loans

---

[11] For details, see Katō, Chapter 6 in this volume.

19

and government-paid expenditures, more than a third came from corporations. The NLC's lack of success in raising sufficient funds by individual contributions was a sensitive issue to the group's leaders. As Nishioka defended the situation, "Although our coffers are empty, that is better than depending on factional contributions like the LDP."[12]

Another problem the NLC faced was its limited appeal to the voting public, despite a projected image of reform, youth, and vigor. Opinion polls taken during the August–December period registered the NLC's national support base at a tiny 1–4 percent.[13] Popular support was not only thin but also frail, derived mainly from nonpartisan voters and those alienated from other parties, especially the LDP and the Japan Communist party (JCP). A substantial number of the NLC's backers, in short, supported the group only because they disliked another party. Typically, NLC supporters were young (in their twenties or thirties), urban, and unhappy with politics and politicians.

But the chief problem confronting the NLC was how to carve out an independent, identifiable position and to avoid being cast simply as an anti-LDP splinter group. From the outset NLC leaders insisted they had not created a "mini-LDP" and stressed the differences between the two parties. NLC leaders argued that their group was a moderate-conservative alternative to the LDP and the other parties, the champion of clean elections, "understandable politics," and decisive action rather than endless Diet debate.[14] Their aim was to restore public faith in the political process. The NLC, according to the polls, seemed successful in projecting this image. Nearly 40 percent of one sample of supporters liked the club's "political posture."[15]

Posturing and slogans aside, the NLC's policy platform was sparse. Officially it had four pillars: reform of the educational system, chiefly the overhaul of the college entrance examination system; expansion of social welfare programs, especially for the elderly and women; a larger—by ¥1 trillion—budget and lower taxes,[16] designed to raise personal consumption and stimulate the economy; and a revamping of the local government system to make it more responsive to the people. Educational reform was the core of the NLC policy

---

[12] *Nihon Keizai Shinbun*, November 11, 1976.

[13] For example, *Yomiuri Shinbun*, November 2, 1.2 percent; *Tokyo Shinbun*, November 14, 2.1 percent; NHK, 4.2 percent; *Asahi Shinbun*, December 3, 2.5 percent.

[14] Kōno Yōhei, "Jimintō yosaraba," *Bungei Shunjū* (August 1976), pp. 94–102.

[15] *Yomiuri Shinbun*, November 2, 1976.

[16] NLC spokesmen never convinced skeptics how this marvelous feat was to be accomplished.

recommendations, to such a degree, in fact, that the group was criticized as a one-issue party.[17] Nonetheless, education was a major concern to many voters in their twenties and thirties with school-age children. These voters, along with the urban uncommitted and anti-LDP vote, became the major targets of the NLC's 1976 campaign.

Candidate Selection

The selection of candidates in Japan's multimember electoral district system requires careful calculations. In effect there are 130 individual local elections in each of which three to five Diet members are elected.[18] The NLC's strategy for the 1976 election was designed to capitalize on its few strengths. It endorsed twenty-five candidates, the minimum necessary to qualify as a political party. They were younger than LDP candidates but about the same age as those from the Kōmeitō (KMT) and the JCP, and every effort was made to ensure that they were untainted by political scandal. Their backgrounds resembled those of LDP candidates—secretaries to Diet members (25 percent); former bureaucrats (16 percent); local politicians (12 percent); and the "self-employed," meaning doctors, lawyers, and the like (12 percent)— although there was a smaller percentage of former government officials than among the LDP candidates.[19] Its popularity was so low that the NLC could not hope to field successfully more than one candidate in a given district. Most, and the strongest, of its candidates were running in the metropolitan and urban constituencies.

For the LDP, candidate selection was far more complex. Merely determining how many candidates to run was difficult, especially in view of the party's dwindling vote. Endorsing fewer candidates raises the chances of winning a larger percentage of the rate, with the safest strategy being to run just one candidate. This strategy would, however, yield only 130 seats, scarcely more than half the 256 required for a bare majority. A national party, with ambitions to rule the country, must be able to win more than one seat in many districts. The directly contrary strategy, which is of course the riskiest, is to attempt to monopolize all of the seats in a given district. In practice, the LDP has followed an approach somewhere between these two extremes—running two candidates in three-member districts (or three in rural and semiurban districts); three candidates in four-member districts; and

---

[17] Among the public the NLC was perceived as the least policy-oriented party (*Yomiuri Shinbun*, November 2, 1976).
[18] Except Amami-Ōshima, which elects just one Diet member.
[19] *Mainichi Shinbun*, November 16, 1976.

two, three, or four candidates in five-member districts, depending on urban-rural district variations.

In recent elections the average winning LDP candidate has received about 19 percent of the vote, regardless of district type. On the average, therefore, the party needs 38 percent of the vote to run two candidates successfully, 57 percent for three winners, and so forth. It is possible to win with lower percentages of the vote, of course, depending on how many opposition candidates run and the distribution of the LDP's vote among its own candidates. But these percentages are generally necessary for success. As support for the LDP among the Japanese voting public has ebbed, the LDP's share of the vote has dropped in most districts to levels where the party cannot reasonably expect to run as many candidates as before.

Running more candidates does tend to arouse voter interest in the LDP's campaign and to draw more conservative voters to the polls. Therefore, the LDP's endorsement calculation was based in part on whether running more candidates would swell the conservative vote and, if so, whether the increase would be enough to support another LDP contender.

The LDP's approach to candidate selection in 1976 was partially influenced by the entry of NLC candidates in the election. In particular, competition from the NLC dictated caution in the metropolitan and urban districts where the new party was expected to perform well. In the five constituencies in which NLC incumbents were running, the LDP Election Policy Committee decided to endorse only incumbents, believing it pointless to name unfamiliar candidates to challenge these former LDP Diet members. Overall, in the NLC-contested districts the LDP ran just fifty-one candidates, down from sixty in 1972. Nearly all these districts were metropolitan or urban.

In a handful of other districts the LDP was hesitant to make endorsements for another reason—Lockheed. Hoping to avert the embarrassment of endorsing persons who might later be linked to the scandal, the committee decided to await all Lockheed disclosures before releasing its final choices. Accordingly, it had issued only a provisional list before the July–August unveiling of LDP figures tied to the bribery scandal. After that the party faced the dilemma of what to do in the seven districts where Lockheed-associated LDP politicians were slated to run. Four of these Dietmen allegedly involved but not indicted in the affair were permitted to run under the party's banner. The other three, Hashimoto Tomisaburō (Ibaragi First) and indicted representatives Satō Takayuki (Hokkaidō Third) and Tanaka Kakuei

(Niigata Third) resigned from the LDP and ran as independents.[20] For Tanaka's home district, LDP Tokyo headquarters rejected not only party endorsement but also the local organization's proposal for a party recommendation. Although Tanaka ultimately ran without the LDP's imprimatur, he had the "tacit recommendation" of the local chapter.[21]

Another factor complicating LDP candidate endorsement in 1976 was that a number of districts were redrawn for the 1976 election.[22] The effect was to increase by twenty the Diet seats in a number of densely populated metropolitan districts. The LDP cautiously ran only one more candidate in 1976 than it had in the previous election in these districts.

Neither Lockheed, nor the NLC threat, nor the wish to field a more palatable candidate for the independent voter shaped LDP endorsement strategy as much as did the outcome of the 1972 election. The main lesson there had been that the party had to retrench in order to stay in power. Table 2–2 illustrates the overall situation facing the LDP after the 1972 lower-house election. The LDP had fared worst in the three-member districts where it had run three candidates. The party's overall percentage of the vote would not permit endorsement of as many candidates in 1976 as in 1972, especially in the metropolitan and urban districts. This was particularly true in four- and five-member districts in which the party had endorsed three candidates in 1972. The 1972 results, in short, pointed clearly toward a more cautious strategy in 1976.

In terms of the type of LDP candidates finally chosen for the 1976 election, there was no departure from past practice. Few women were endorsed, preference was given to incumbents, and, despite statements that the party would seek out younger candidates, the average LDP candidate was older than in previous years. In terms of career background, the proportions were roughly the same as in past

---

[20] Unindicted officials, called "gray officials" or *haiiro kōkan*, and their districts were: Katō Mutsuki, Okayama Second; Fukunaga Kazuomi, Kumamoto Second; Nikaidō Susumu, Kagoshima Third; and Sasaki Hideyo, Hokkaidō Second. Despite strong backing in his district, Sasaki withdrew from the race shortly before the election, citing public opinion and the possible negative impact his candidacy might have on the LDP. Satō, Tanaka, and Hashimoto were dubbed "black officials" or *kuroi kōkan*.

[21] *Mainichi Shinbun*, November 9, 1976.

[22] In Kanagawa the number of districts increased from three to five, adding five seats; Tokyo Tenth District gained one more seat, and Aichi First and Sixth, one seat each; Tokyo Seventh, Osaka Third, and Chiba First divided into two districts each, adding three seats each for a total of nine; Saitama First divided into two districts, with two additional seats; and Hyōgo First gained one seat.

TABLE 2–2

NUMBER OF CANDIDATES, LOSING CANDIDATES, AND PERCENTAGE OF VOTE
BY URBANIZATION OF DISTRICT, LIBERAL DEMOCRATIC PARTY,
1972 HOUSE OF REPRESENTATIVES ELECTION

Number of LDP Candidates per District	Number of Districts	Total LDP Candidates	Vote Percentage[a] (Number of Losers) by District Type[b]				
			Metropolitan	Urban	Semi-urban	Rural	All districts
Three-member districts							
1	6	6	24(2)	—	—	—	24(2)
2	16	32	33(2)	51(0)	52(4)	53(0)	48(6)
3	21	63	28(0)	59(6)	66(9)	74(6)	65(21)
Subtotal	43	101	28(4)	55(6)	61(13)	65(6)	53(29)
Four-member districts							
1	1	1	20(0)	—	—	—	20(0)
2	11	22	35(3)	28(1)	43(0)	—	36(4)
3	23	69	—	51(4)	62(4)	58(2)	57(10)
4	4	16	—	64(1)	66(2)	71(1)	67(4)
Subtotal	39	108	34(3)	50(6)	60(6)	60(3)	52(18)
Five-member districts							
1	0	0	—	—	—	—	—
2	11	22	28(3)	35(1)	30(0)	—	30(4)
3	16	48	34(2)	45(2)	50(3)	—	48(7)
4	11	44	—	53(6)	54(0)	63(1)	57(7)
5	3	15	—	—	69(2)	79(1)	66(3)
Subtotal	41	129	28(5)	46(9)	50(5)	66(2)	47(21)
Total	123[c]	338	29(12)	47(21)	54(24)	61(11)	47(68)

Dash (—): No LDP candidate in this category.
[a] Vote percentages are average figures.
[b] Districts are classified by degree of urbanization according to the system used by the *Asahi Shinbun* (see Table 1–2).
[c] Table excludes Amami-Ōshima, a one-member district where the LDP ran one candidate unsuccessfully.
SOURCE: Adapted from Ministry of Home Affairs statistics.

elections. Twenty-eight percent of all LDP candidates were former officials, 24 percent were local politicians, 15 percent were former aides to Diet members, 12 percent had a business background, and 21 percent had other experience. A similar distribution was evident with the fifty-four new candidates designated, of whom 26 percent were former bureaucrats, 25 percent were local politicians, 25 percent were former Diet members' aides, plus various others. A higher percentage of LDP candidates (17 percent) were running for the first time in 1976 than in any recent election. The party endorsed the fewest candidates of any election since its inception, continuing a trend (see Table 3–1). Nineteen fewer candidates were endorsed in 1976 than in 1972, largely because of the party's retrenchment policy.

More specifically, while the party had run only a single candidate in seven districts in 1972, in 1976 it did so in twenty districts, all but one of which were metropolitan or urban. In 1972 the LDP went after every seat in twenty-eight districts; in 1976 it made the attempt in just sixteen. It was the LDP's heavy losses in the rural and semiurban three-member districts that convinced party leaders to retrench and endorse one less candidate in many such constituencies for 1976. Furthermore, the party attempted less often to capture all seats in a given district, and it adopted a more defensive posture in metropolitan and urban districts.

The 1976 Election Results

Shaken by the Lockheed revelations, the defection of the New Liberal Club, and the bitter intraparty leadership struggle between Miki and Fukuda, the LDP entered the December election with an accumulation of disadvantages. But other signs were more encouraging. First, scattered election results during the year had favored the LDP. After the Lockheed incident broke in February, the LDP emerged victorious in by-elections for the House of Councillors in Akita, Ōita, and Nagasaki prefectures, in the mayoral election in Fukuoka, and in local gubernatorial contests in Gumma, Fukushima, and Yamaguchi prefectures. Further, most public opinion surveys agreed that the LDP would take from 252 to 256 seats, with the opposition parties relatively unchanged and the NLC winning between nine and twelve seats.[23] Miki's optimistic projection varied between 271 and 275 seats for the LDP, a figure he lowered to 265 shortly before the balloting.

[23] *Asahi Shinbun*, December 1, 1976; *Yomiuri Shinbun*, November 29, 1976; *Mainichi Shinbun*, November 30, 1976.

Also, an *Asahi* survey in October showed Miki's popularity had climbed again—to just over 35 percent because he was "trusted." The same newspaper poll found LDP public support higher, while the opposition, notably the Japan Socialist party (JSP), had fallen in popularity.[24]

The New Liberal Club. When the votes were tabulated in the 1976 balloting, the biggest and most surprising winner was the NLC (see Table 2–3). Seventeen of its twenty-five candidates were successful. In overall statistical terms, of course, the NLC's appearance on the stage of Japanese politics may not appear especially significant. The club's popularity was minuscule: its twenty-five candidates represented only 2.8 percent of the total candidates, they received just 4.2 percent of the total votes cast, and the seventeen seats they won constituted only 3.3 percent of the seats in the newly elected Diet. But these numbers give a distorted picture of the party's showing in the election. In Japan's multimember district electoral system, generalizations for the entire system are often flawed because only the LDP, the JSP, and the JCP run candidates in all districts. Thus, to say that the Kōmeitō (KMT) received 10 percent of the national vote may suggest its strength nationally, but it gives a very misleading indication of the strength of individual candidates in particular districts. The KMT may have run candidates in only half the districts—and each candidate may have received an average of 18 percent of the vote. Thus, in order to evaluate fairly the performance of New Liberals in the 1976 election, it is necessary to concentrate on the twenty-five districts in which the NLC offered candidates and to compare them with districts in which the party did not compete. Because two of the twenty-five districts (Saitama Fifth and Tokyo Eleventh) had been redrawn before the election, the outcome in them cannot be compared with previous election results and is omitted from comparative calculations. Excluded also are the two districts in which the NLC recommended candidates but did not actually endorse them as official candidates.

When the 1976 election results are analyzed by looking at only those districts where the NLC ran candidates, the club's stunning performance is clear: it ran second to the LDP with a startling 18 percent of the vote. The NLC turned out to be essentially an urban phenomenon, performing best in the metropolitan and highly urbanized districts. In the metropolitan districts all the club's candidates won, averaging 23 percent of the vote—the highest per candidate figure

[24] *Asahi Shinbun*, October 9, 1976.

TABLE 2-3

Votes and Seats Won, by Party, in 1969, 1972, and 1976
House of Representatives Elections

Party	Year	Vote (percent)	Seats Number	Seats Percent
LDP	1969	47.6	288	59.3
	1972	46.9	271	55.2
	1976	41.8	249	48.7
JSP	1969	21.4	90	18.5
	1972	21.9	118	24.0
	1976	20.7	123	24.1
KMT	1969	10.9	47	9.7
	1972	8.5	29	5.9
	1976	10.9	55	10.8
JCP	1969	6.8	14	2.9
	1972	10.5	38	7.7
	1976	10.4	17	3.3
DSP	1969	7.7	31	6.3
	1972	7.0	19	3.9
	1976	6.3	29	5.7
NLC	1969	—	—	—
	1972	—	—	—
	1976	4.2	17	3.3
Other parties	1969	0.2	0	0.0
	1972	0.3	2	0.4
	1976	0.1	0	0.0
Independents	1969	5.3	16	3.3
	1972	5.1	14	2.9
	1976	5.7	21	4.1

Dash (—): Not applicable.
Source: Adapted from Ministry of Home Affairs statistics.

of any party. In urban districts, three-fourths of the NLC's candidates were successful, and their average 19 percent of the vote nearly tied them with the JSP for second place behind the LDP. While only three of nine NLC hopefuls in semiurban and rural districts won seats, with the nine candidates averaging slightly over 10 percent of the vote, the NLC still fared better than the JCP and roughly on a par with the KMT and the Democratic Socialist party (DSP).

What impact did the entry of NLC candidates have on the overall results of the 1976 election? It appears to have increased the number of voters. The percentage of votes cast in districts with NLC candidates was 6.2 percentage points more than in 1972, compared with a 2.9 point rise in all other districts.[25] In only four NLC-contested districts did the voting rate decline, and, interestingly, these were all rural or semiurban districts with weak NLC candidates. Elsewhere, NLC candidates increased the vote, particularly in those districts in which popular NLC contenders were standing for election. In short, NLC candidates sparked voter interest.

It is harder to evaluate whether the NLC's entry into these twenty-five districts brought more conservative voters to the polls, although it appears to have done exactly that, if one assumes the NLC was widely viewed as a reformist but nonetheless conservative party. In the NLC-contested districts, if NLC, LDP, and conservative-related independent votes are counted as conservative, the conservative vote climbed from 48.2 percent in 1972 to 53.1 percent in 1976. This increase suggests that it was the conservatives rather than progressives who reaped the benefits of the higher voting rate and the heightened competition among conservative candidates in the 1976 election.

Which parties suffered from NLC competition? In terms of voting percentages, the principal victim was without doubt the LDP. In the NLC-contested districts, the LDP's share of the vote plummeted over 13 percentage points from 1972, as shown in Table 2–4. Even adding votes for conservative-related independents to LDP totals scarcely alters the picture.

The impact of the NLC on the various parties in the 1976 election can be seen by comparing party performance in the districts in which the NLC competed with those in which it did not, and contrasting those figures with the 1972 election results (Table 2–4). The DSP and the KMT appear not to have suffered much from the rise of the NLC. If anything, they appear to have gained more in the contested than in the uncontested districts. With 1972 taken as 100, the DSP went up to 110 in the uncontested districts, but to 196 in the contested districts. The KMT went up to 115 in the uncontested and to 149 in the contested districts.

To what extent did the NLC's performance in the 1976 election rest upon its ability to win over the uncommitted voter? A rough idea of how well the NLC and other parties did in attracting the floating vote can be gained from Table 2–5, which presents data on the relation between each party's preelection popularity (its popular support

---

[25] The voting percentage in districts *without* NLC candidates was 70.7 in 1969, 73.7 (up 3.1) in 1972, and 76.7 (up 2.9) in 1976. The voting percentage in districts *with* NLC candidates was 69.5 in 1969, 72.6 in 1972 (up 3.1), and 78.8 (up 6.2) in 1976.

TABLE 2–4

VOTE PERCENTAGES, BY PARTY, IN DISTRICTS WITH AND WITHOUT
NEW LIBERAL CLUB CANDIDATES, 1972 AND 1976
HOUSE OF REPRESENTATIVES ELECTIONS

Party	NLC-Contested Districts			Non-NLC Districts		
	1976	1972	Change	1976	1972	Change
LDP	32.4	45.4	−13.0	48.3	52.7	−4.4
JSP	17.2	19.9	− 2.7	21.7	21.8	−0.1
JCP	8.2	10.0	− 1.8	10.0	9.7	+0.3
DSP	18.4	12.9	+ 5.5	15.1	13.8	+1.3
KMT	15.8	14.0	+ 1.8	16.9	14.7	+2.2
NLC	17.9	—	+17.9	—	—	—

Dash (—): Not applicable.
NOTE: Figures are averages of each party's percentage of the vote and therefore do not total 100 percent. Moreover, calculations are limited to data from districts where all five parties ran candidates in both elections.
SOURCE: Calculated from Central Election Management Committee figures.

rate) and its percentage of the vote in the ten districts where all six parties ran candidates in 1976. The total difference between support rates and vote percentages is slightly over 40 percent—a figure that can be taken as an approximation of the average floating vote in these ten constituencies. Moreover, the difference for each party can be considered a general measure of its average share of the uncommitted vote.

When figures for these districts are compared with similar national data on party support levels and votes received, one finds that the KMT and the JCP did about the same, the DSP exceeded its national average by several percentage points, the JSP received slightly less, and the LDP much less. In these ten districts it received a negative percentage of the floating vote and evidently lost some of its own supporters as well.[26] Apparently the LDP—and to a lesser extent the JSP—failed to compete with the NLC for the uncommitted vote. The numbers may also suggest that some LDP supporters abandoned the party's candidates for either the NLC or the DSP. From these limited data, it would appear that, apart from its own backers, the NLC's major source of support was the floating voters who would have

[26] On a national level, the situation was very different. See Passin, Chapter 7 in this volume.

TABLE 2–5

ESTIMATED FLOATING VOTE, BY PARTY, TEN SELECTED NLC-CONTESTED
DISTRICTS, 1976 HOUSE OF REPRESENTATIVES ELECTION
(percent)

	LDP	JSP	KMT	JCP	DSP	NLC	Other	Total
Support rate	30.3	14.3	4.3	4.0	4.9	3.8	38.4[a]	100.0
Percent of vote	27.9	16.7	15.0	10.1	13.9	15.9	0.5[b]	100.0
Difference	− 2.4	+ 2.4	+10.7	+ 6.1	+ 9.0	+12.1	−37.9	± 40.30

[a] The total of those supporting other political groups (0.1 percent), those having no preference (20.4 percent), and those not answering (17.9 percent).
[b] Minor parties and independent candidates.
SOURCE: *Asahi Shinbun*, November 3 and December 7, 1976.

backed the LDP or the JSP if no NLC candidates had run. Of all the parties, the DSP was the least affected by NLC candidacies in these ten districts, followed by the KMT and the JCP.

One dimension of the LDP-NLC relationship can be tapped by analyzing their performances according to urban-rural variations among electoral districts. The NLC's vote percentage exceeded that of the LDP (or of the LDP plus conservative-related independents) by the largest margin in the metropolitan constituencies. This margin was lower in urban, lower yet in semiurban, and lowest in rural districts.

Of the seventeen NLC winners, fourteen finished first in their districts. All five NLC incumbents took the top spot. Twelve NLC winners were standing for election for the first time in 1976; of these, nine finished first. Further, sixteen of the NLC's twenty-five candidates and all but one of its first-place finishers ran in metropolitan or urban districts. The NLC's impact on the number of seats taken by the LDP —which is relatively weak in these areas—was thus minimized, because the LDP endorsed just one candidate in nine of these districts anyway. But outside the cities, in the semiurban and rural districts, NLC candidates, despite their relatively weak drawing power in these areas, cost the LDP some seats. For example, the LDP dropped fifteen seats in semiurban districts compared with 1972. Six of these fifteen were in districts where NLC candidates were running, and one LDP candidate finished in the runner-up position. Since one can assume that many potential LDP votes went to NLC candidates, one can reason that the NLC contributed to the heavy losses suffered by the LDP in these districts in 1976.

Elsewhere it was the JCP, not the LDP, that was the chief victim of the NLC attack. Nine NLC victors displaced Communist incumbents. Even though the JCP's vote percentage in these constituencies dropped only 1.2 points from 1972, the JCP took just three seats, compared with the eleven it had won in the previous election. In five districts the JCP's candidate ended up in the runner-up position.

The NLC's image as a vigorous new party seems to have helped to elect some candidates with little name value or personal appeal. For example, in Kanagawa's First District a completely unknown NLC candidate, who declared his intention to run just forty days before the election, came in first. Four candidates running under the NLC banner in 1976 had run before and lost as conservative independents in 1972. This time only one was defeated, but even his percentage of the vote rose four points over 1972. The three winners were able to raise their vote totals substantially over 1972. One of these, Chūma Kōki, running in Osaka's Sixth District, finished well ahead of the pack with 26.1 percent of the vote, well above his meager 8.5 percent in 1972. While analysts might disagree, Chūma had few doubts himself as to why such a dramatic reversal had taken place in his electoral fortunes: "I am grateful to God, Buddha, and the New Liberal Club," he announced.[27]

The Liberal Democratic Party. The LDP clearly suffered a setback. The party won 249 seats, a postwar low and a far cry from Miki's final preelection promise of 265. Even though twelve conservative-related independents joined the party after the election, the LDP was still left with a precarious five-seat lower-house majority. In terms of its percentage of the vote, moreover, the LDP's showing was its worst ever, as it dropped a full five percentage points (or 10.9 percent) below its 1972 level.

As with the NLC, the nature and meaning of the LDP's performance in 1976 cannot be understood by an analysis of aggregate data alone. Accordingly, Table 2–6 presents the LDP's 1976 election results for comparison with the 1972 results presented in Table 2–2 above, classifying districts according to degree of urbanization and number of Diet seats. These figures suggest the degree of effectiveness of the LDP's defensive endorsement strategy in 1976. Only in the met-

---

[27] *Sankei Shinbun*, December 9, 1976.

TABLE 2–6

Number of Candidates, Losing Candidates, and Percentage of
Vote by Urbanization of District, Liberal Democratic Party,
1976 House of Representatives Election

Number of LDP Candidates per District	Number of Districts	Total LDP Candidates	Vote Percentage[a] (Number of Losers) by District Type[b]				
			Metropolitan	Urban	Semi-urban	Rural	All districts
Three-member districts							
1	10	10	26(0)	19(0)	13(1)	—	22(1)
2	26	52	36(2)	52(1)	54(2)	53(2)	53(7)
3	11	33	—	62(1)	61(5)	68(3)	59(9)
Subtotal	47	95	29(2)	42(2)	53(8)	60(5)	45(17)
Four-member districts							
1	7	7	19(2)	21(0)	—	—	19(2)
2	10	20	37(2)	36(2)	41(0)	50(0)	38(4)
3	20	60	—	46(5)	55(4)	52(5)	52(14)
4	4	16	—	54(2)	57(5)	59(0)	56(7)
Subtotal	41	103	25(4)	40(9)	53(9)	51(5)	41(27)
Five-member districts							
1	3	3	18(0)	—	—	—	18(0)
2	11	22	29(1)	27(2)	30(2)	—	29(5)
3	13	39	—	36(2)	40(7)	—	41(9)
4	13	52	—	52(4)	57(4)	55(4)	55(12)
5	1	5	—	—	68(1)	—	68(1)
Subtotal	41	121	25(1)	42(8)	44(14)	55(4)	40(27)
Total	129[c]	319	36(7)	83(19)	131(31)	70(14)	42(71)

Dash (—): No LDP candidate in this category.
[a] Vote percentages are average figures.
[b] Districts are classified by degree of urbanization according to the system used by the *Asahi Shinbun* (see Table 1–2).
[c] Amami-Ōshima is omitted.
Source: Adapted from Ministry of Home Affairs statistics.

ropolitan districts did the approach clearly pay off. Even with a lower percentage of the vote in these districts than in 1972, the LDP gained one seat. Moreover, the party's urban strategy seemed realistic and successful, inasmuch as its percentage of winning candidates in the

MICHAEL BLAKER

metropolitan and urban districts combined improved over 1972. In the semiurban and rural districts, however, this percentage dipped considerably, as shown in Table 2–7.

The LDP's endorsement of one less candidate in many three-member districts seemed generally effective in cutting potential losses in this type of constituency. Although it ran six fewer candidates in the three-member districts in 1976, the LDP still managed to pick up six more seats than in 1972. Twenty-nine LDP candidates were defeated in these districts in 1972, but only seventeen lost in 1976 (see Tables 2–2 and 2–6).

Monopolization proved a bankrupt strategy for the LDP: in sixteen such attempts in 1976 it worked only twice. Nine of the party's seventeen losses in the three-member districts came from attempts to capture all three seats. Even though the LDP tried this strategy less often in 1976—in sixteen districts as against twenty-eight in the preceding election—its ineffectiveness (a low winning percentage, plus the proven risk that the additional candidates may knock another LDP man out of the running) may mean even fewer attempts at this approach in the next election.

Further, the data in Table 2–6 show that the major LDP losses, in terms of percentage of the vote, were in four-member districts where the party sought to elect three candidates (one-fifth of all LDP losers), in the nonmetropolitan three-member districts, in the semiurban and rural four-member and urban five-member districts where

TABLE 2–7

LIBERAL DEMOCRATIC PARTY CANDIDATES AND WINNERS, 1972 AND 1976
HOUSE OF REPRESENTATIVES ELECTIONS

District Type	1972			1976		
	Endorsed	Won	Percent winning	Endorsed	Won	Percent winning
Metropolitan	40	28	70	36	29	81
Urban	90	69	77	83	64	77
Semiurban	134	110	82	131	100	76
Rural	75	64	85	70	56	80
Total	339	271	80	320	249	78

SOURCE: Calculated from Ministry of Home Affairs statistics.

TABLE 2–8

PERCENTAGE OF VOTE AND SEATS, LIBERAL DEMOCRATIC PARTY, 1972 AND
1976 HOUSE OF REPRESENTATIVES ELECTIONS
(percent; "change" figures in percentage points)

District Type	Vote			Seats		
	1972	1976	Change	1972	1976	Change
Metropolitan	28.9	25.7	−3.2	30.8	29.0	−1.8
Urban	47.1	40.0	−7.1	53.9	47.1	−6.8
Semiurban	54.2	48.9	−5.3	60.4	54.1	−5.3
Rural	60.9	55.7	−5.2	71.1	62.2	−8.9
Total	46.9	41.8	−5.0	55.2	48.7	−6.5

SOURCE: Calculated from Ministry of Home Affairs data and *Asahi Shinbun*, December 7, 1976.

the LDP ran two or three candidates, and in the rural five-member districts where the party fielded four candidates.

This profile suggests that the LDP was perhaps not defensive enough in 1976. In the nonmetropolitan four-member districts in which the LDP ran three candidates, its percentage of the vote declined from an acceptable 57 percent in 1972 to a shaky 52 percent. Had the party run only two instead of three candidates in these marginal four-member districts in 1976, it would have gained seats, even though it would have taken a somewhat lower percentage of the vote. Similarly, in some metropolitan and urban four- and five-member districts where the party endorsed two candidates in 1976, its share of the vote fell beneath the percentage level needed to win two seats. In short, the preferred endorsement strategy, which had worked fairly well in 1972, was less successful in 1976. It was only in the metropolitan constituencies where the LDP, sensing its own weakness and reacting to the threat of the NLC, wisely and effectively ran fewer candidates and minimized its losses. The preferred strategy (two candidates in three-member districts, three in four-member districts, and three or four in five-member districts) was pursued 54 percent of the time, involving 62 percent of all LDP candidates.[28] Unfortunately it generated 61 percent of all LDP losses and failed substantially more often than in 1972.

[28] See Nisihira, Chapter 4 in this volume, for further details.

There are limits to how defensive the LDP can be in candidate selection because of its obligation to endorse all incumbents. Thus, even if the LDP leadership may expect to capture only two seats in a four-member district where the party had previously won three, it has no choice but to endorse all three if they wish to run again.

The impact of the sizable decline of the LDP's vote percentage in 1976 was softened by the fact that the Japanese multimember district electoral system favors the LDP as the strongest party. The LDP has been overrepresented in the Diet, receiving more seats than it would obtain if seats were allocated on a strictly proportional basis. For example, as shown by Table 2–8, in 1972 the LDP garnered 55.2 percent of the seats with 46.8 percent of the vote. And in 1976, even though its percentage of the vote and of seats dropped across the board from 1972 levels, the LDP's 41.8 percent of the vote still gave it 48.7 percent of the seats.

As illustrated in Figure 2–1, the LDP remains heavily dependent on the countryside; in fact, its dependence even rose slightly. Of the party's total vote, 55.4 percent came from semiurban and rural districts in 1972. In 1976 this percentage was 55.9.

The troubling longer-term implication of these figures for the

FIGURE 2–1

DISTRIBUTION OF TOTAL NATIONAL VOTE AND LIBERAL DEMOCRATIC PARTY VOTE, BY DEGREE OF URBANIZATION, 1972 AND 1976 HOUSE OF REPRESENTATIVES ELECTIONS

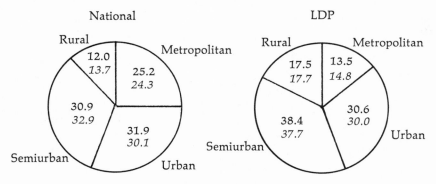

NOTE: Percentages may not add to 100 because of rounding.
SOURCE: Calculated from data from the Ministry of Home Affairs, using the *Asahi Shinbun* classification system. Percentages for 1976 are listed first; italicized figures are percentages for 1972.

LDP is that at a time when the party remains dependent on the less urban districts, there is a shift toward a greater concentration of votes and, through redistricting, of seats in the urban and metropolitan districts. More specifically, while 57.1 percent (up 2.7 percentage points over 1972) of the votes are in the metropolitan and urban districts, only 44.1 percent of the LDP votes (down from 44.8 percent in 1972) came from these districts in 1976.[29] Party strategists have of course long been aware of this trend, but the 1976 lower-house election results reflect their inability to do much about it. Of the twenty newly contested seats in 1976, the LDP won only three, while the NLC picked up seven, including five in Kanagawa prefecture alone. The LDP took just 29 percent of the seats in these redrawn districts, against 33 percent in 1972.

It is significant that fifty-four of the LDP's unsuccessful candidates ended in the runner-up position in their districts, many more than the thirty-seven losers who finished in that spot in the preceding election. At least some of the party's woes in 1976 might be blamed on the loss of many close races, a situation that might easily reverse itself the next time around.

Lockheed. Japanese newspaper post-mortems on the election argued that the voters had reprimanded the LDP at the polls for the Lockheed scandal. But the results do not support such judgments.[30] To begin with, the national impact of the scandal was obscured by Japan's electoral system. Because it resembles a series of local elections, one cannot easily judge how much, if at all, the scandal affected the national LDP vote. Only a fraction of the voting public indicated in surveys that their votes would be decided by Lockheed. One could maintain, although without much conviction, that because the NLC was in some measure the offspring of the scandal and the LDP's failure to achieve party reform, many NLC votes represented an expression of feeling about the incident.

But surely the best index of Japanese reactions to Lockheed is what happened in those districts in which Lockheed-implicated candidates were running. In five of these six constituencies, the "Lockheed candidates" were elected, and the most prominent of the group, Tanaka Kakuei, won decisively in Niigata's Third District with 168,000 votes—60,000 more than the polls had projected and only 14,000 fewer than he had received as an incumbent prime minister in 1972. Of the other four winners, two came out on top and two dropped two

---

[29] See Passin, Chapter 7 in this volume.

[30] See the analysis of this question in Passin, Chapter 7 in this volume.

places from 1972. Even the sole loser, Satō Takayuki in Hokkaido's Third District, barely missed being elected, finishing in the runner-up slot. While Japanese observers pointed to the relatively poorer showing of these Lockheed-associated candidates over their 1972 performances, this, too, is misleading. There was a decline, to be sure, but these candidates actually lost less in percentage terms (3.5 percentage points off their 1972 performances) than the 5 percentage point average LDP national loss in 1976.

LDP factions. For the LDP, which runs more than one candidate in most districts, the competition for party endorsement centers on the factions. The leaders of the major LDP factions have access to the campaign funds needed to endorse more candidates who, if successful, increase the faction's size, its chief's chances of becoming prime minister, and the possibility of faction members being named to a cabinet position. In a sense factional alignments and maneuvers make the LDP a party composed of many parties—a source of weakness in that these divisions seem to inhibit a unified, coordinated national policy. On the other hand, factions are a source of strength in that they encourage policy debate, aid the recruitment of new candidates, and garner a higher percentage of the vote for the party.

Factional rivalries were especially bitter in the 1976 election. Many Japanese observers dubbed the election the *bunretsu senkyo* or "split election," referring to the sharp division in the party between the Miki-Nakasone camp on the one hand and the Fukuda-Ōhira coalition on the other. The final preelection expression of anti-Miki sentiments within the party came when Fukuda resigned as vice–prime minister in November. If the LDP did badly there seemed little doubt that Miki would have to bear the responsibility and that Fukuda would accede to the prime ministership. For his part, as might be expected, Miki sought to promote party solidarity and avoid the negative split-election image.

Nakasone, the one major faction leader allied with Miki, was secretary-general of the party, a position that gave him considerable control over campaign purse strings. He was able to support fourteen new factional candidates for the election, in a bid to become the second largest LDP faction in the lower house. Fukuda, too, was looking beyond the balloting itself to the premiership and backed sixteen new candidates from his faction. Fukuda faction members were the oldest of any in the LDP—most were aged sixty or more. Ōhira was less effective in attracting new faces. His faction made nine new endorsements and half of these, like his faction in general, were former bureaucrats. The faction of discredited Tanaka, headed officially by

Nishimura Eiichi (Ōita Second District), ran few new candidates in 1976—just four compared with fifteen in 1972—in an apparent response to limited funds and the aftershocks of the Tanaka indictment.

During the campaign Fukuda and Ōhira both stumped on behalf of each other's candidates as well as Tanaka faction members in districts where their own members were not running. In a few districts (for example, Hyōgo Fourth, Kōchi, and Ehime Second) where Fukuda and Tanaka faction candidates were locked in battle, it was Ōhira who visited to help out both. Throughout the campaign the "dump Miki" effort was acrimonious and on occasion reached absurd proportions. There were reports, for example, of Miki posters being pasted over with Ōhira's or Fukuda's name or Miki's name being blacked out entirely.[31]

In fifty of the 130 electoral districts there were three or more LDP faction members competing. In only six of these did all the LDP candidates win. In twenty-one constituencies, the LDP lost seats because it ran too many candidates, and in two districts factional battles left a nonfactional candidate as the sole winner.

The Fukuda group was able to retain its top position among the factions in the 1976 election (Table 2–9). Incumbents had the worst winning percentage in LDP history, with forty-nine Diet veterans losing their seats. Of these, the Fukuda faction lost the most—twelve —followed by Tanaka (ten), Ōhira (eight), Miki (six), Nakasone (six), and Shiina (five). Fukuda had run enough new faces largely to offset his incumbent losses, however. Only the Nakasone faction increased in size, as his new candidates did well, although he failed by three seats in his attempt to become the second-ranking faction in the lower house.

Summary and Conclusions

Some Japanese political observers dismissed the 1976 lower-house contest as the *hyō ga yomenai senkyo* or the "unreadable election." This frustrated reaction is natural enough, perhaps, if one is searching for some historic, profound meaning in the outcome or has some ideological ax to grind. For example, it is fruitless to seek to explain the election in terms of a Lockheed-inspired anti-LDP voter backlash. After all, what actually happened was that only one of six Lockheed-associated candidates lost; LDP incumbent losses were roughly the same for all major party factions including that of Miki, Tanaka's

---

[31] *Tokyo Shinbun*, November 6, 1976.

TABLE 2–9

PERFORMANCE OF LIBERAL DEMOCRATIC PARTY FACTIONS, 1976
HOUSE OF REPRESENTATIVES ELECTION

Faction Leader	Preelection Membership	Candidates	Postelection Membership	Change
Fukuda	53	68	48	− 5
Tanaka	46	50	39	− 7
Ōhira	41	49	38	− 3
Miki	34	39	32	− 2
Nakasone	33	48	37	+ 4
Shiina	16	17	11	− 5
Mizuta	11	12	11	0
Funada	8	8	8	0
Ishii	7	4	4	− 3
Nonfaction	16	25	21	+ 5
Total	265	320	249[a]	−16

[a] Twelve conservative-related independents joined the LDP following the election, altering these alignments somewhat: four favored Fukuda, three Tanaka, one Ōhira, two Nakasone, and two nonfaction.
SOURCE: *Tokyo Shinbun*, December 7, 1976; *Asahi Shinbun*, December 7, 1976.

leading party rival on reform and Lockheed issues; the sole faction to register sizable gains in the election was headed by Nakasone, himself a target of widespread Lockheed-related speculation; and Miki was replaced shortly after the election by Fukuda, at best a lukewarm advocate of party reform and active pursuit of the Lockheed culprits. Thus if one were to claim Japanese voters were driven by a wish to "throw the rascals out," it would be hard to judge from the election results themselves precisely who the rascals were. Nor can other indexes such as candidates' career backgrounds, sex, or even party policy positions be causally linked to the outcome. In fact, the single variable that correlates directly with the 1976 results is age, with a significantly lower winning percentage for LDP candidates aged seventy or more.

What conclusions of any consequence can be drawn from the 1976 election experience? One fact is certainly clear: the New Liberal Club recorded a significant and surprising upset. Its impressive showing is attributable to its ability to attract uncommitted urban voters with younger new candidates, to exploit its reformist image, and to reelect all five of its ex-LDP incumbents. The NLC's Cinderella story carried over well into the period after the election, when its popularity tripled; the club won approval from nearly 10 percent of those polled, and forecasters confidently predicted another NLC victory in the 1977 upper-house election. But there the NLC faltered badly, its boom of the previous December turning to bust in July. Just three of the club's thirteen candidates won, and it received a scant 4 percent of the national constituency vote. Worst of all, it failed to achieve the victory so necessary to sustain the momentum and winner's image it had dramatically gained only seven months earlier. In the wake of the Councillors election the NLC was left in disarray, disillusioned, and without a clear sense of direction.

In spite of the NLC's disastrous turnabout in the July balloting, its leaders gamely promised to run sixty to seventy candidates in the next lower-house election and to redouble their efforts to build the club into a national political force. But these ambitions will be difficult to fulfill. The NLC has yet to surmount the imposing obstacles it faced in 1976—a narrow, largely urban base; a frail national organization; no comprehensive, detailed policy platform; and limited financing. Until the NLC can solve these problems, it is likely to remain a minor conservative splinter group, jockeying for modest positional advantage both among the opposition and between the opposition and the LDP. Its scaled-down goal has become that of wielding the deciding vote in the Diet, an objective shared by other small opposition parties and a sizable—if realistic—retreat from the club's original design.

For the LDP, the 1976 election was a distinct defeat. On December 6, party leaders awoke to these gloomy facts: a record LDP loss from 1972 of twenty-two seats, fifteen in pivotal semiurban districts; a five percentage point plunge in popularity, the second highest ever; the unprecedented defeat of three cabinet ministers and forty-nine incumbents; and, on the bottom line, a failure to capture a majority of seats in the lower house for the first time since the party was formed in 1955.

However disheartening the results must have been to LDP leaders, one can interpret the outcome in less catastrophic terms. Indeed, the LDP's losses can be viewed as rather modest, given the unusually bitter intraparty clashes preceding the election, the defection of the Kōno group (with its five otherwise certain LDP victors) from the party, and the ten-month accumulation of much-publicized Lockheed troubles. In short, the LDP could have fared worse. Party leaders could find some comfort, too, in the fact that the LDP seemed to have stemmed the long process of decline in the metropolitan districts.[32] Even though the LDP did not greatly improve upon its 1972 performance in the metropolitan and urban districts, it generally was able to hold its own there through an effective defensive endorsement policy while at the same time continuing to dominate the rural districts.

Even though the LDP performed worst in semiurban districts (thirty candidates lost, and fifteen of twenty-two seats were dropped), the losses may prove a blessing in disguise. First, if the party leadership responds to the 1976 outcome by adopting a cautious, defensive endorsement policy for the next election, naming fewer candidates in certain borderline semiurban constituencies, the LDP could avoid having its contenders defeat each other as happened so often in 1976. Second, the relatively high number of incumbent losers in semiurban districts in 1976 means fewer automatic endorsements for incumbents next time, thus allowing party leaders more flexibility in choosing candidates. Perhaps they will select more of the new, younger candidates who seem so much more palatable to voters in nonrural areas. Finally, the many LDP runners-up in these districts may help to offset future party losses if these losers spend the period before the next election in their districts mobilizing the support needed to rise the extra notch in the rankings to victory. This has been a common pattern in past campaigns.

The LDP's 1976 performance must also be related to that of the opposition parties. Even though the NLC defection hurt the LDP, and NLC candidacies in at least eight districts contributed heavily to LDP defeats in those constituencies, the club is now weaker and poses a far less formidable threat for the next election. More generally, the opposition parties have neither the collective unity nor the individual strength to mount a serious challenge to the LDP. In the three-member and many four-member districts, moreover, the LDP may benefit from a fragmented opposition. Statistics show the LDP's chances of winning actually rise when more opposition party candidates of roughly equal popularity are standing for election in such districts. This is not always true, however, and the key element for the LDP is whether the JSP's popularity will continue to decline. If it does, the Socialists will be unable to field two candidates as frequently as in the past and, inasmuch as the LDP will receive votes from many otherwise JSP backers, the added support could raise some borderline LDP hopefuls to victory.

The LDP has apparently learned from its unhappy 1976 experi-

---

[32] See Nisihira, Chapter 4 in this volume, for amplification of the point that the LDP has bottomed out in the cities.

ence. Following the December election the party proceeded with much caution in Diet affairs, seeking compromises with the opposition on many issues, most notably on the 1977–1978 budget. In a sense the LDP had little choice: it had lost its majority on the Budget Committee and on committees responsible for transportation, education, and local administration (see Table 7–2); and four standing and seven special committees had new opposition party chairmen. Nevertheless, the important fact is that the party has been more conciliatory. Greater LDP flexibility was also evident in its careful preparations for the July Councillors election. Party leaders sought (unsuccessfully, as things turned out) to jettison older incumbents in favor of younger new candidates and to offer fewer candidates for the national constituency competition. Also, the LDP has seemed to moderate its policies somewhat, especially toward support for larger social welfare allocations, which has helped to create a less confrontational and more consensual political atmosphere in Japanese politics than any in recent memory. This growing consensus is likely to work against the opposition by denying it an alternative, politically exploitable set of policy issues.[33]

Despite its serious defeat in the 1976 election and its effective draw in the 1977 Councillors balloting, the LDP continues to confound those predicting its fall from power. While this may happen, it is scarcely an inevitable process, and recent Japanese elections suggest that the LDP will remain in command of the Japanese government for some time to come.

---

[33] See Michael Blaker, "Japan in 1977: An Emerging Consensus," *Asian Survey*, January 1978, pp. 91–102.

3

The Opposition

Gerald L. Curtis

Elections are by definition zero-sum games in which one group of party losses equals another group of party gains. But recent Japanese elections have produced outcomes in which there have been, in a political sense, no winners. In the December 1976 lower-house election the LDP vote declined by 5.1 percentage points from the previous 1972 election, but the combined vote for the four political parties that are referred to as "progressive"—the JSP, the KMT, the DSP, and the JCP—increased by only 0.4 percentage points. Virtually the entire loss in the LDP percentage of the vote could be accounted for by the vote for the New Liberal Club and for conservative independents. Only the KMT among the opposition parties increased its percentage of the vote (from 8.5 percent in 1972 to 10.9 percent in 1976), while the JSP, JCP, and DSP each incurred fractional losses.

The opposition did no better in terms of the number of seats won than in vote percentages. The percentage of total lower-house seats won by endorsed LDP candidates declined from 55.2 percent in 1972 to 48.7 percent in 1976, but the percentage of seats won by the combined opposition increased from 41.5 to only 43.8 percent.

Japan's opposition parties have been strongest in metropolitan areas, but their combined performance in major urban districts in the 1976 election showed no gains. In Tokyo's eleven districts the combined opposition won twenty-four seats, exactly the number it won in 1972, and its share of the vote declined from 64.1 percent in 1972 to 54.3 percent.[1] In Osaka only four seats changed hands among the

---

[1] The JSP popular vote dropped from 19.8 percent in 1972 to 17.2 percent in 1976; the JCP from 19.7 to 15.4 percent; the DSP, running fewer candidates in Tokyo in 1976 than it did in 1972, suffered a decline from 8.0 to 3.5 percent; only the KMT percentage of the popular vote increased from 16.6 to 18.2 percent.

twenty-six at stake. The LDP and KMT won the same number of seats as in 1972. The JSP lost three and the JCP lost one, with the DSP picking up three new seats and the NLC the other one. Overall these four opposition parties lost thirteen seats (twelve JCP and one JSP) among the 100 seats in Japan's twenty-five metropolitan districts and won twelve new ones (seven by the KMT and five by the DSP).[2]

The inability of the opposition to make gains comparable to LDP losses in the 1976 election confirmed a pattern evident in Japanese electoral politics for at least the past decade. Declining support for the LDP has been accompanied by voter criticism of all parties. This has created pressures for party splits and realignments on the left while at the same time impelling the opposition parties to adopt defensive election strategies. Thus, even though more parties ran candidates in 1976 than in any general election since 1955, the competition rate was 1.76 candidates for each seat,[3] the lowest in postwar Japanese elections. The earlier record was set in 1972 when 1.82 candidates ran for each seat.

Japan's opposition parties are themselves something of a subparty system, registering gains and losses at each other's expense while allowing conservative independents and, in 1976, the New Liberal Club to pick up many of the votes lost by the LDP. In the past decade the combined opposition has increased its percentage of Diet seats by 2.7 percentage points (or 6.5 percent) and its share of the popular vote by 2.8 percentage points (or 6.3 percent). In the same period (from the January 1967 election to the December 1976 election) the LDP percentage of seats declined by 8.3 percentage points (or 14.5 percent) and its percentage of the popular vote by 7.0 percentage points (or 14.4 percent).

The following sections review the electoral performance of each of these four parties, their efforts at coordinating candidate endorsement policies, and the major issues they addressed during the campaign. The concluding section discusses the implications of their recent electoral record for the future.

The Japan Socialist Party

The Japan Socialist party's popularity has declined parallel to that of the LDP. In order to avoid a situation in which its candidates defeat each other in the lower-house's multimember districts it now carefully

---

[2] The urbanization index utilized throughout this chapter is the one designed by the *Asahi Shinbun*. (See Table 1–2).

[3] But see Nisihira, Chapter 4 in this volume.

TABLE 3–1

CANDIDATE ENDORSEMENTS AND SUCCESS RATIOS, BY PARTY, HOUSE OF REPRESENTATIVES ELECTIONS, 1958–1976

(number of candidates)

Year	LDP			JSP			KMT			DSP			JCP		
	En-dorsed (A)	Elected (B)	Success ratio (B/A)	En-dorsed (A)	Elected (B)	Success ratio (B/A)	En-dorsed (A)	Elected (B)	Success ratio (B/A)	En-dorsed (A)	Elected (B)	Success ratio (B/A)	En-dorsed (A)	Elected (B)	Success ratio (B/A)
1958	413	287	69.5	246	166	67.5	—	—	—	—	—	—	114	1	0.8
1960	399	296	74.2	186	145	78.0	—	—	—	105	17	16.2	118	3	2.5
1963	359	283	78.8	198	144	72.7	—	—	—	59	23	39.0	118	5	4.2
1967	342	277	81.0	209	140	67.0	32	25	78.1	60	30	50.0	123	5	4.1
1969	328	288	87.9	183	90	49.2	76	47	61.8	68	31	45.6	123	14	11.3
1972	339	271	79.9	161	118	73.3	59	29	49.2	65	19	29.2	122	38	31.1
1976	320	249	77.8	162	123	75.9	84	55	65.5	51	29	56.9	128	17	13.3

Dash (—): Not applicable since the party did not exist.
SOURCE: My calculations from newspaper articles and Ministry of Home Affairs reports.

limits the number of candidates it endorses. Only in 1958 did the JSP run more candidates than the number necessary to secure a Diet majority. Since then, as can be seen in Table 3–1, it has cut back its total number of candidates, particularly in large urban districts where JSP support has dropped most sharply. In 1976 the party ran two candidates in only thirty-one of the nation's 130 districts and three candidates in only one, Hokkaidō's Fifth. The party ran no mutiple candidates in any of the thirty-six districts of the predominantly urban preferences of Chiba, Tokyo, Kanagawa, Aichi, Kyōto, and Osaka. By contrast, in 1963, after the formation of the DSP but before the emergence of the KMT and a strengthened JCP, the JSP ran more than one candidate in seventy-two districts (in five of the districts it ran three candidates) which included virtually all the heavily populated metropolitan constituencies. The performance of the JSP in the 1976 election creates pressures on the party to reduce further the number of its candidates in the next election: in the thirty-one districts where it ran two candidates, both won in only thirteen; in three districts both lost, and in fifteen districts only one of the two candidates was successful. The Socialist party obtained in 1976 the same 24 percent of lower-house seats it had won in 1972, and its percentage of the vote continued its steady decline (from 21.9 percent in 1972 to 20.7 percent in 1976), with major losses incurred in metropolitan and urban districts.

The party made its strongest showing in Hokkaidō, a traditional stronghold. It won ten of the prefecture's twenty-two seats and three of the five contested seats in Hokkaidō's Fifth constituency. The party also did relatively well in semiurban and rural areas and worst in metropolitan areas such as Tokyo, Nagoya, Osaka, and Kobe.

The trend in JSP electoral support has been toward relative improvement in smaller population centers and a weakening in major urban centers. The party has led the opposition in moving out from large cities to make inroads into traditional LDP bases of support in rural areas, but it has relinquished much of its urban support to other opposition parties in the process. In 1976 the JSP won 17 percent of the seats in metropolitan districts (the Kōmeitō won 23 percent and the LDP 29 percent), 23.5 percent of the urban district seats, 28.6 percent of the seats in the semiurban districts, and 23.3 percent of rural district seats. Of the 123 winning JSP candidates in 1976, 53 (43.1 percent) were elected in semiurban districts.[4] Only in the semi-

---

[4] Metropolitan districts accounted for 13.8 percent, urban districts for 20 percent, and rural districts for 17.1 percent.

urban and rural areas did the JSP take over 20 percent of the popular vote and maintain the level of support it received in the 1972 election.[5]

Thirty-nine JSP candidates lost in 1976. In three districts the party ran two candidates and lost both (Aomori First, Shizuoka First, Saga). In fifteen others one of the party's two candidates lost, and in eighteen districts its only candidate was defeated.

Half of the eighteen districts in which the sole JSP candidate lost were metropolitan.[6] As seen in Table 3–2, the party was unable to make any gains in metropolitan districts (it returned one member less than in 1972) despite a loss of twelve seats by the JCP and an increase, through redistricting, of nine seats since 1972 in the number of Diet members elected from these constituences.

Of the fifteen districts where one of the two JSP candidates was defeated, twelve were urban or semiurban. These urban and semiurban constituencies pose the greatest problem for JSP election strategy. They are areas in which the JSP had won two seats in earlier elections but where the KMT and JCP have grown stronger. Now the JSP can either run two candidates at the risk of losing both (as happened in Aomori First and Shizuoka First) or endorse only one candidate and thereby hasten its own decline. The party must have more than one successful candidate in these districts if it is to maintain a significantly greater number of Diet seats than the other opposition parties. Ten of the thirteen districts in which it did manage to elect two candidates in 1976 were urban or semiurban.

The extent to which the JSP has lost its erstwhile position as the major opposition party in urban Japan can be seen in the history of its performance in Tokyo. In 1963 the LDP and JSP split the total of twenty-seven Tokyo Diet seats almost equally between them, the LDP winning thirteen and the JSP twelve, the other two being picked up by the DSP. In the 1967 election the LDP won sixteen, and the JSP thirteen, but there was then a total of thirty-nine seats at stake. The Kōmeitō, in the first lower-house election it contested, won six of Tokyo's seats, the DSP three, and the JCP one. In the 1969 election the JSP suffered a massive nationwide defeat, going from 140 to 90 seats. In Tokyo it was nearly wiped out, winning only two seats. Even though it won seven in 1972, it was unable to recover its former

[5] The JSP obtained 22.5 percent of the vote in semiurban districts (22.8 percent in 1972) and 22.7 percent in rural areas (22.6 percent in 1972). In metropolitan districts its percentage of the vote declined from 19.4 to 17.8 percent and in urban districts from 22.2 to 19.9 percent.

[6] Five were defeated in rural districts, three in urban, and one in semiurban districts.

TABLE 3-2

Party Success in Number of Seats, 1976 House of Representatives Election

District Type	LDP	Conservative Independents	NLC	JSP	KMT	DSP	JCP	Progressive Independents
Metropolitan	29(+1)	3(+1)	7(+7)	17(−1)	23(+7)	9(+5)	10(−12)	2(+1)
Urban	64(−5)	1(0)	7(+7)	32(+1)	18(+8)	10(+4)	3(−8)	1(+1)
Semiurban	100(−10)	6(+1)	2(+2)	53(+3)	12(+9)	9(+1)	3(−1)	0(−2)
Rural	56(−8)	8(+3)	1(+1)	21(+2)	2(+2)	1(0)	1(0)	0(0)
Total	249(−22)	18(+5)	17(+17)	123(+5)	55(+26)	29(+10)	17(−21)	3(±0)

NOTE: Numbers in parentheses indicate change from 1972 election.
SOURCE: *Asahi Shinbun*, December 7, 1976.

position as the leading opposition party because the Communist party won ten seats in that election. The LDP won thirteen, the KMT six, the DSP one, and independents two seats, for a total of thirty-nine. In 1976 the JSP won eight seats in Tokyo, less than a fifth of the total and fewer than the KMT. Moreover, in the decade from 1967 to 1976 the JSP's popular vote in Tokyo declined from 27.1 percent to 17.2 percent.

During the same period the party reduced the number of its candidates to try to maximize the dwindling vote that supported it. In 1963 the JSP ran two or more candidates in all seven Tokyo districts, electing two in four. In 1967, with the number of districts increased to ten, the party ran two candidates in seven but was successful only twice. In 1969 its paired candidates, running in three districts, all lost. In 1972 the party ran two candidates in just two districts: in one both lost; in the other one won and the other was defeated. By 1976 the JSP found itself unable to run two candidates in any Tokyo district, and it won a single seat in only eight of Tokyo's eleven constituencies.

In the 1950s the JSP was *the* opposition party. In the 1958 Diet election it obtained 33 percent of the vote and considerable support from urban and white-collar voters, and its Diet contingent comprised men and women from diverse career backgrounds. Along with labor, farmers' union members, and prewar socialist leaders, the JSP's Diet representatives included former high government officials, business-men, and professional people such as lawyers, doctors, and journalists.

As the JSP's support shrank in the ensuing two decades, unions affiliated with the Sōhyō labor federation steadily increased their hold on the party. That dominance is reflected in the increasingly large number of Sōhyō leaders among the party's Diet candidates, men perceived by the party as able to gain the backing of their own unions', union funds to support their campaigns, and the votes of union workers and their families who might support "one of their own" but not other JSP candidates.

Before 1960 union candidates never accounted for as much as a third of the JSP's successful candidates. In the 1955 election, 22 percent of the party's successful candidates were union based; in the 1959 election, 29 percent were from the unions. In the 1960 election, however, the first after the party's right wing split to form the DSP, the party began to increase its recruitment of candidates from among Sōhyō-affiliated union leaders. In that election, 58 percent of its suc-cessful new candidates were Sōhyō based; in the following election in 1963, 59 percent of new candidates were from Sōhyō. By 1972 fully half of all its candidates, both new and incumbent, were from the unions, and in the 1976 election, 87 of the 162 candidates (53.7 percent) and 67 of the party's 123 winners (54.5 percent) were from the unions.

Most of these winning candidates (48 of 67) were from unions in the public sector, as seen in Table 3–3. Particularly prominent in JSP

TABLE 3–3

Successful Japan Socialist Party (JSP) Sōhyō Candidates, 1976
House of Representatives Election, by Union Affiliation

Union	Number of Candidates Elected
Public Sector	
National Railway Workers (Kokurō)	15
Japan Teachers (Nikkyōso)	14
Japan Postal Workers (Zentei)	5
Telecommunication Industry Workers (Zendentsu)	5
All-Japan Prefectural and Municipal Workers (Jichirō)	3
All-Japan Federation of Municipal Traffic Workers (Toshikō)	2
All-Japan Garrison Forces (Zenchūrō)	2
All-Monopoly Corporation Workers (Zensenbai)	1
All-Agricultural and Forestry Ministry's Workers (Zennōrin)	1
Subtotal	48
Private Sector	
Japanese Federation of Synthetic Chemistry Workers (Gōka Rōren)	5
Japan Coal Miners (Tanrō)	3
National Trade Union of Metal and Engineering Workers (Zenkoku Kinzoku)	2
General Federation of Private Railway Workers (Shitetsu Sōren)	2
All-Japan Express Workers (Zennittsū)	1
Subtotal	13
Others	6[a]
Total	67

[a] The additional six union candidates include one former official in Sōhyō's Tokyo headquarters; three long-term leaders of prefectural Sōhyō chapters in Nagano, Nara, and Shimane; and two candidates supported by the Federation of Electrical Industry Workers (Denki Rōren). Denki Rōren is affiliated with and is the dominant union in the small federation known as Chūritsu Rōren. Both candidates were elected in the Ibaragi Second District and both were leaders of the Hitachi company union.

Source: My calculations from biographical data available in party, newspaper, and Diet publications.

TABLE 3–4

CAREER BACKGROUNDS OF SUCCESSFUL JSP CANDIDATES, 1958 AND 1976
HOUSE OF REPRESENTATIVES ELECTIONS

	1958		1976	
Background	Number	Percent	Number	Percent
Labor union leaders	48	28.9	67	54.5
Professional politicians[a]	38	22.9	16	13.0
Second generation[b]	0	0.0	9	7.3
Farmers' union leaders	22	13.3	12	9.8
Government bureaucrats	9	5.4	4	3.3
Businessmen	14	8.4	2	1.6
Lawyers[c]	13	7.8	2	1.6
Medical doctors	6	3.6	1	0.8
Journalists	6	3.6	1	0.8
Educators[d]	5	3.0	2	1.6
Party headquarters bureaucrats	0	0.0	4	3.3
Others[e]	5	3.0	3	2.4
Total	166	100.0	123	100.0

[a] Taguchi calls this category "socialist movement." "Professional politician" is a broader category that includes longtime local party leaders as well as the small number of leaders of the prewar socialist movement that remain in the Diet.

[b] Second-generation members include four lawyers, two local politicians, one university professor, a local union leader, and a former employee of *Bungei Shunju*, the nation's largest literary monthly. They are all sons of Diet members.

[c] The 1976 figure for lawyers is higher if the four second-generation members who are lawyers are included.

[d] Taguchi is probably including public school as well as university teachers in this category although he does not make this clear in his text. The 1976 figures are for university professors; lower-school teachers are included in the labor-union category since the salient feature in their background is their leadership role in Nikkyōso, the teachers' union.

[e] This category for 1976 includes two former secretaries of Dietmen and a member backed by the Buraku Dōmei, the JSP-affiliated organization of descendants of Japan's ex-untouchables.

SOURCES: Figures for 1958 from Taguchi Fukuji, *Nihon No Kakushin Seiryoku* (Tokyo, 1961), p. 13; figures for candidates elected in 1976 compiled by author on basis of biographical data available in party, newspaper, and Diet publications.

ranks are the Japan Teachers' Union and the National Railway Workers' Union candidates, both, as might be expected, powerful unions in a federation dominated by public sector unions.[7] At the time

[7] Sōhyō had a membership in 1976 of 4,573,000. Workers in public enterprises and in civil service accounted for 61.2 percent of its membership.

TABLE 3–5

Candidates, 1976 House of Representatives Election, by Party and by Age

Age	LDP	JSP	JCP	KMT	DSP	NLC	Independent	Other	Total
20–29	2	0	0	1	0	0	4	2	9
30–39	21	4	17	20	6	7	24	6	105
40–49	49	25	56	40	16	10	44	2	242
50–59	104	82	43	19	11	6	25	1	291
60–69	94	44	11	4	14	2	10	3	182
70 and over	50	7	1	0	4	0	5	3	70
Total	320	162	128	84	51	25	112	17	899

SOURCE: Compiled from Ministry of Home Affairs, newspaper, and party reports.

of the 1976 election the chairman and the secretary-general of Sōhyō headed the Japan Teachers' Union and the National Railway Workers' Union, respectively.

Table 3–4 contrasts the career backgrounds of JSP Diet members elected in 1958, when the party was at the height of its popularity, and in December 1976. The data show that the marked increase in labor union representation has been accompanied by a decline in all other occupational categories. The decline of Diet members with professional backgrounds is particularly conspicuous.[8] Also notable is the significant number of second-generation members, all sons of Dietmen. Their victories parallel a similar trend in the LDP and reflect the extent to which many old-time JSP politicians, like their conservative colleagues, were able to develop local bases of personal support that could be passed on, at least for one or two elections, to their chosen successors.

The average age of JSP Diet members elected in 1976 was 55.6, making the JSP Diet contingent the oldest in average age among the opposition parties. As can be seen in Table 3-5, a considerably higher proportion of JSP candidates were over fifty (82.1 percent of all JSP

---

[8] There is some arbitrariness in any categorization of career backgrounds. Diet members often have multiple career histories. Where a choice had to be made, the aspect of the member's background that seemed most relevant to his eventual recruitment as a candidate was selected. The numbers should therefore be treated as approximations, a sketch of the types of men and two women recruited by the JSP for Diet politics.

TABLE 3–6

New Candidates, Former Diet Members, and Incumbents among JSP Candidates, House of Representative Elections, 1958–1976

Year	Total JSP Candidates	New	Former Member	Incumbent
1958	246	73	17	156
1960	186	48	18	120
1963	198	46	18	134
1967	209	56	21	132
1969	183	38	26	119
1972	161	44	35	82
1976	162	42	17	103

Source: Compiled from Ministry of Home Affairs, newspaper, and party reports.

candidates) than was true for any other party including the LDP. This is because many of the party's candidates had reached top leadership positions in the union movement before entering Diet politics and because two-thirds of its candidates were incumbents or former Diet members, many of whom had been active in the party and the Diet for years. Table 3–6 provides a breakdown of new candidates, former Diet members, and JSP incumbents since 1958. New candidates consistently account for about a quarter of the party's candidates.[9]

Some 60 percent of JSP candidates elected in 1976 were university educated, a lower proportion than for Japan's other parties. Again, this is accounted for by the large number of JSP Diet members with blue-collar and union activist backgrounds.

In their early years socialist and labor parties often have in their leadership ranks a high percentage of union officials who are later replaced by middle-class professionals, intellectuals, and party activists as the party matures and establishes its autonomy. This evolution has been reversed in the case of the JSP. The party in its early years was dominated by intellectuals and party activists and only later became more "representative" of its primary organized support. This evolution reveals a significant loss of autonomy and at least a partial transformation of the party into a body that is disparagingly referred to by Japanese commentators as the "political affairs section of Sōhyō."

Data on JSP Diet members reveal another interesting feature. Of

[9] The only exception was in 1969.

ninety-five candidates elected one or more times, seventy-three (76.8 percent) had clear factional affiliations. But among the twenty-eight candidates elected for the first time in 1976 only ten (35.7 percent) had such ties. There are fewer Diet members associated with intra-party factions today than at any previous time in the party's history. While factional affiliation is of decreasing importance to candidate recruitment, it continues to be of crucial importance to leadership recruitment from among the party's Diet members. Party develop-ments, including the defeat in the 1976 election of the party's three major faction leaders (Eda Saburō, Katsumata Seiichi, and Sasaki Kōzō), have weakened factions without substituting new mechanisms for leadership recruitment.[10] Much of the chaos in the party organi-zation can be traced to the struggle for power that used to be handled among relatively cohesive factional structures.

The Democratic Socialist Party

Democratic Socialists claimed a victory for their small party in 1976 with a gain of ten seats over its 1972 performance. But this increase was no more than a recouping of most of the losses it had incurred in 1972. The DSP had gone into that election with thirty-one seats and came out with nineteen. In 1976 it won twenty-nine seats, a considera-ble improvement over its 1972 performance but slightly worse than 1969 or 1967 when thirty of its candidates were elected.

The DSP ran fewer candidates in 1976 than in any previous elec-tion, less than half the number it fielded in its first campaign of 1960. Almost without exception these candidates ran in districts with large labor unions affiliated with the DSP-supporting Dōmei labor federation. As a result, there are no DSP Diet members in thirty of Japan's forty-seven prefectures. A majority of its successful candidates (nine-teen of the twenty-nine) were elected in districts in and around the major manufacturing centers of Tokyo, Nagoya, and Osaka.

Thirteen of the DSP's fifty-one candidates (25.5 percent) were leaders of labor unions that, with one exception, are affiliated with Dōmei. The exception was Miyata Satae in Fukuoka's Second District. Miyata, former chairman of the Yawata (now Nippon) Steel Company union and head of the Fukuoka Liaison Organization of Private In-dustry Labor Unions, was supported in his election (which he won with the highest vote in the district) by the Sōhyō-affiliated National Federation of Iron and Steel Workers' Unions (Tekkō Rōren), the

---

[10] Other leading JSP politicians defeated in the 1976 election included Vice-Chairmen Akamatsu Isamu and Yamamoto Kōichi.

president of which is Miyata's brother. Tekkō Rōren is the largest private-sector union federation in Sōhyō, and it has been centrally involved in moves to create a new organization of representatives of all private-sector unions that presently are divided in their affiliation among Sōhyō, Dōmei, the smaller Chūritsu Rōren, and the even smaller group called Shinsanbetsu.[11] Tekkō Rōren's support for Miyata was a break with the Sōhyō policy of exclusive support for JSP candidates and, to some extent, reflected the division in Sōhyō between private and public-sector unions.

DSP labor union candidates had a higher rate of success than candidates without comparable union background and backing. Nine of the thirteen union candidates won elections, a success rate of 69 percent compared with a success rate of 52 percent for other DSP candidates. Table 3–7 lists successful DSP labor union candidates and their supporting labor unions.

Dōmei played a key role in the 1976 election in coordinating the campaign effort for the DSP and in obtaining management support for several of the DSP's union-based candidates. Dōmei contributed a total of ¥150 million[12] to the DSP and made each of its member unions responsible for aiding the campaigns of particular candidates.[13] Each candidate was offered the assistance of campaign workers from at least two unions. Member unions that had their own leaders running in the election made separate contributions directly to these individuals.

Management had supported DSP candidates in past elections, particularly in the automobile industry, but in the 1976 general election and in the subsequent upper-house election in mid-1977 management support was more open and enthusiastic than ever before.[14] One reason for such support was summed up in the re-

---

[11] On October 7, 1976, the chairmen of sixteen private-sector labor union federations formed a Policy Promotion Labor Union Conference (Seisaku Suishin Rōso Kaigi). This conference included representatives of all major private-sector unions in the four national "centers" (as Sōhyō and the other national organizations are termed in Japan). The organization is ostensibly limited to consideration of economic issues and, at least for the present, consideration of issues of party support is precluded. Nonetheless, its creation is an important step toward a possible restructuring of Japan's labor union movement and changing formal patterns of union-party relations. The formation of the conference is reported in *Asahi Shinbun*, October 8, 1976.

[12] Approximately $0.5 million at the time.

[13] *Yomiuri Shinbun*, November 11, 1977.

[14] For examples and comment, see *Asahi Shinbun*, October 12 and November 23, 1976; *Yomiuri Shinbun*, November 11 and December 7, 1976; and *Tokyo Shinbun*, November 25, 1976.

TABLE 3–7

Democratic Socialist Party Union-Based Candidates, 1976 House of Representatives Election

Winning Candidate	District	Union
Nishida Hachirō	Shiga	Japan Federation of Textile Workers (Zensendōmei)
Yonezawa Takashi	Miyazaki 1	Zensendōmei
Sasaki Ryōsaku	Hyōgo 5	Federation of Electrical Industry Workers of Japan (Denki Rōren)
Yoshida Yukihisa	Nara	Denrōren
Komiya Takeō	Nagasaki 1	Japan Confederation of Shipbuilding and Engineering Workers (Zōsenjūki Rōren)
Nakamura Masaō	Osaka 2	Japan Railway Workers (Tetsurō)
Ukeda Shinkichi	Yamaguchi 2	New Japan Teachers (Shinkyōso)
Watanabe Takezō	Aichi 4	Federation of Japan Automobile Workers (Jidōsha Rōren [Toyota])
Miyata Satae	Fukuoka 2	National Federation of Iron and Steel Workers (Tekkō Rōren, Sōhyō affiliated)

Source: Compiled from party publications.

marks of an Ishikawajima Harima Heavy Industry plant manager: "More than being a candidate of the DSP he is a colleague who has eaten from the same bowl as we. At a time when the union is giving him its best, its partner, the firm's management, also has to desire the candidate's victory."[15]

Such sentimental factors probably played a role, but more important was the business community's concern to keep the DSP strong enough to make possible a conservative-centered coalition government in the event the LDP were to lose its Diet majority. In the 1974 upper-house election campaign a number of LDP candidates engaged in what was termed a *kigyō gurumi* (enterprise-based) campaign, in which some large corporations attempted to mobilize the entire company to

---

[15] *Asahi Shinbun*, June 10, 1977.

TABLE 3–8

CAREER BACKGROUNDS OF DSP DIET MEMBERS ELECTED IN 1976
ACCORDING TO TIME OF FIRST ELECTION TO THE DIET

Background	Pre-1960	Post-1960	Total
Labor union leaders	2	7	9
Farmers' movement leaders	3	0	3
Government bureaucrats	4	0	4
White-collar workers	1	0	1
Professional politicians	2	3	5
Businessmen	1	1	2
Second generation	0	3	3
Party bureaucrats	0	2	2
Total	13	16	29

NOTE: Twenty-four of the twenty-nine DSP Diet members are college educated (82.8 percent). Five are Tokyo University graduates and five graduates of Kyōto University; eight of the ten national university graduates are from the pre-1960 group. The average age of DSP Diet members is fifty-four. The one businessman among the post-1960 group is the owner of a small company that does subcontract work for Nissan Motor Company.
SOURCE: Compiled from party publications.

support their "representative" candidates.[16] In the national election campaigns of 1976 and 1977 the label of *kigyō gurumi* was pinned on Dōmei labor union leaders running on the DSP ticket.

A listing of the career backgrounds of all successful DSP candidates in the 1976 election suggests that the party draws on a broad constituency for its leadership. But if older members who entered politics through the Socialist party and went to the DSP in the 1960 split are distinguished from Diet members first elected after the split, a different picture emerges, as shown in Table 3–8. In the "new" DSP as in the JSP, labor union leaders occupy a dominant position. They account for nearly half the sixteen candidates elected in 1976 who entered elective politics after 1960. Three are second-generation politicians: two are sons of Diet members (Kanda in Tochigi Second and Nakai in Mie First),[17] and one, Nishimura Shōzō in Osaka Fifth, is the nephew of former DSP chairman Nishimura Eiichi.

[16] See Gerald L. Curtis, "The 1974 Election Campaign: The Political Process," in Michael K. Blaker, ed., *Japan at the Polls: The House of Councillors Election of 1974* (Washington, D.C.: American Enterprise Institute, 1976), pp. 65–70.
[17] Nakai's father was a member of the JSP, and the son first joined the DSP in 1975 after making an unsuccessful race as an independent in the 1972 election.

Former government officials are conspicuous by their absence from the post-1960 party. Politically ambitious bureaucrats have gone where the power lies, and for the past twenty years that has meant the LDP. This situation may change as other parties are perceived as potential participants in government and become the vehicles for the political ambitions of bureaucrats. For the moment, however, the DSP represents a coalition of old time right-wing socialist politicians and Dōmei-affiliated union leaders.

Despite the DSP's recovery from its 1972 defeat, its performance in the 1976 election does not suggest that a major increase in the number of its Diet seats is likely. The party's percentage of the vote nationwide was the lowest of the six lower-house elections it has contested. In its first race in 1960 it obtained 8.8 percent of the vote; in 1969 its vote was 7.7 percent and in 1972 it was 7.0 percent. In the 1976 election it received 107,000 fewer votes than in 1972 and its percentage of the vote declined to 6.3 percent. One cannot make too much of this decline in the party's nationwide aggregate vote because, in an effort to mobilize its financial and human resources to support candidates who stood a credible chance of winning, it ran fewer candidates in the 1976 race than ever before. More significant is the fact that of the twenty-two DSP candidates who lost in 1976, only two (in Nagano Fourth and Hyōgo First) came in as runner-up or *jiten*.[18] There is little chance that many candidates who placed below jiten will be able to obtain the large increases in support necessary to win in the next lower-house election. The DSP may well decide to run more candidates in the next election, and some of these may prove successful, but a marked break with long-term electoral trends would be required for the DSP to obtain many more seats in the next lower-house election than it won in 1976. On the contrary, the party will be hard pressed to fight off the challenge of jiten candidates of other parties in at least the six districts in which DSP candidates came in last among the winning candidates.

---

[18] *Jiten* is a convenient Japanese term that refers to the candidate who places first among the losers, that is, fourth in a three-member district, fifth in a four-member district, or sixth in a five-member district, and who receives a vote equivalent to more than 25 percent of the sum of the total number of valid votes divided by the number of district seats. Under the Japanese election law a jiten candidate automatically obtains a Diet seat should one of the successful candidates in his district vacate his seat within three months of the election.

The DSP candidate in Hyōgo First won in 1967, but failed to win or to be jiten in the three subsequent elections. The candidate in Nagano Fourth won in 1967, was jiten in 1969, won in 1972, and was jiten again in 1976.

The Kōmeitō

By capturing fifty-five seats, the Kōmeitō became the only opposition party since 1955 to join the JSP in having more than the fifty seats necessary to submit budget-related legislation and motions of nonconfidence. The KMT increased its representation in all types of constituencies. In metropolitan districts it gained seven seats over its 1972 performance, winning in twenty-three of twenty-five of these most heavily urbanized constituencies.[19] In the thirty-four urban districts it won eighteen seats, an increase of eight over 1972. Its candidates lost in eight of these districts and the party did not run candidates in another eight. In the forty-six semiurban districts it made significant gains, increasing its representation fourfold with the victories of twelve candidates compared with three in 1972. The KMT ran just six candidates in the twenty-five rural constituencies (which elect ninety Diet members), winning only in two. This was a gain over 1972, but not over 1969.

In contrast to the LDP, JSP, and DSP, all of which ran fewer candidates in 1976 than in the two preceding elections, the KMT ran more candidates in 1976 than ever before. The party first ran candidates for the lower house in the 1967 election, when thirty-two candidates stood for election and twenty-five won their seats. In the next election in 1969 the party put forward seventy-six candidates, forty-seven of whom were successful, nearly doubling its representation in the lower-house. The party declined in the 1972 election—when it endorsed only fifty-nine candidates and won only twenty-nine seats —in part because of a scandal that erupted when the KMT and its supporting religious organization, the Sōka Gakkai, a lay order of the Buddhist Nichiren sect, attempted to block publication of a book critical of the Gakkai. In the aftermath of that election the Sōka Gakkai and the KMT formally separated, the party adopted a new program, and it began a concerted effort to build its organization. By 1976 party leaders felt confident that the KMT could recoup its 1972 losses and ran eighty-four candidates. As a consequence, KMT candidates contested seats in 1976 in at least one district in all but three prefectures,[20] and it won seats in at least one district in each of the twenty-seven prefectures. In the 1969 election the KMT fielded no

---

[19] It was jiten in Tokyo First, and it did not run a candidate in Aichi First.

[20] It did not run candidates in Iwate, Niigata, or Fukushima. The party had intended to run a candidate in Fukushima First but had him withdraw in favor of the DSP candidate in the district as discussed later in this chapter.

candidates in any district in ten prefectures, and its elected candidates came from districts in a total of twenty-two prefectures.

A comparison of the 1969 and 1976 election results, however, reveals that the KMT has been unable to increase its representation beyond the metropolitan districts and the surrounding "bed-town" constituencies. In the semiurban districts it holds only 6.5 percent of the seats and in the rural districts a mere 2.2 percent. In the semi-urban constituencies, the LDP with 100 seats and the JSP with 53 together account for 83 percent of the Diet members elected. In the rural districts the KMT managed to win back only the two seats it had lost in 1972. In total, it won eight more seats in 1976 than it had in 1969. With an increase in the number of lower-house seats from 486 in 1969 to 511 in 1976, the KMT percentage of seats increased modestly from 9.7 percent in 1969 to 10.8 percent in 1976.

With eighty-four candidates running in 1976, the KMT received 6,177,300 votes, roughly a million more than the 5,124,666 votes its seventy-six candidates had taken in 1969. But the percentage of the KMT's vote was precisely the same—10.9 percent—in both elections. Table 3–9 compares the party's share of the 1976 and 1969 vote in those districts where it had won a seat in 1969. In 1976 the KMT vote declined fractionally in just under half these districts, including six of ten Tokyo districts and five of six districts in Osaka.

To qualify the KMT's success in 1976 is not to dismiss its significance. While the DSP never recovered from its early electoral setbacks, the KMT was able not only to make up the losses suffered in 1972 but also to win more seats than in any previous election. It has survived its formal separation from the Sōka Gakkai and occupies an important position in the nation's politics where it is increasingly courted by the LDP, as well as by the JSP and DSP, as a possible legislative ally and eventual coalition partner.

But the party's 1976 performance does not indicate a capacity to attract large numbers of new supporters, nor does it suggest that the party will be able to make major gains in the next election. In the 1972 election KMT candidates were runners-up in twenty-four districts; in 1976 the party won seats in twenty-two of these twenty-four districts.[21] Only eight candidates of the twenty-nine who were defeated in 1976 were runners-up, and four of these lost by more than 10,000 votes to the candidate winning in last place (see Table 3–10). In most districts in which KMT candidates lost, the gap between the KMT candidate and the last place winner was so great that KMT victories

---

[21] It failed to win only in Tanaka Kakuei's Niigata Third District. In Ibaragi First it did not run a candidate in 1976.

TABLE 3-9

COMPARISON OF KŌMEITŌ (KMT) PERCENTAGE OF POPULAR VOTE, 1969
AND 1976 HOUSE OF REPRESENTATIVES ELECTIONS, IN DISTRICTS WHERE
KMT CANDIDATES WON IN 1969

District	1969	1976	Change
Hokkaidō 1	13.9	14.9	+1.0
Hokkaidō 4	12.4	13.5	+1.1
Aomori 1	12.5	13.5	+1.0
Ibaragi 3	14.2	16.0	+1.8
Tochigi 2	10.3	13.7	+3.4
Saitama 1	19.4	23.7	+4.3
Chiba 1	17.6	17.4	−0.2
Chiba 2	11.8	10.0	−1.8
Tokyo 1	16.4	15.9	−0.5
Tokyo 2	19.2	17.1	−2.1
Tokyo 3	15.4	18.5	+3.1
Tokyo 4	15.2	14.0	−1.2
Tokyo 5	19.4	22.8	+3.4
Tokyo 6	19.0	18.9	−0.1
Tokyo 7	15.5	17.8	+2.3
Tokyo 8	16.6	17.4	+0.8
Tokyo 9	22.5	20.2	−2.3
Tokyo 10	23.1	21.5	−1.6
Kanagawa 1	19.5	17.1	−2.4
Kanagawa 2	19.1	16.0	−3.1
Kanagawa 3	14.8	18.7	+3.9
Shizuoka 2	15.0	11.1	−3.9
Kyōto 1	15.8	16.1	+0.3
Kyōto 2	15.9	17.7	+1.8
Osaka 1	26.1	24.6	−1.5
Osaka 2	22.0	21.7	−0.3
Osaka 3	21.1	19.1	−2.0
Osaka 4	20.0	20.8	+0.8
Osaka 5	20.5	19.5	−1.0
Osaka 6	24.0	22.2	−1.8
Nara	11.8	13.9	+2.1
Wakayama 1	20.0	21.5	+1.5
Hyōgo 1	21.3	19.1	−2.2
Hyōgo 2	17.2	15.7	−1.5
Hyōgo 4	14.4	15.0	+0.6
Okayama 1	20.0	16.4	−3.6
Okayama 2	13.0	15.5	+2.5
Hiroshima 3	14.0	15.7	+1.7
Yamaguchi 1	12.9	15.7	+2.8
Tokushima	13.8	12.5	−1.3

Table continued on following page

TABLE 3–9 (continued)

District	1969	1976	Change
Kōchi	13.8	19.5	+5.7
Fukuoka 1	18.0	19.5	−4.6
Fukuoka 2	16.6	16.4	−0.2
Fukuoka 3	14.3	17.8	+3.5
Fukuoka 4	15.9	16.6	+0.7
Nagasaki 1	13.3	12.3	−1.0
Kumamoto 1	13.1	14.8	+1.7

SOURCE: Calculated from publications of the Ministry of Home Affairs.

in the next election are unlikely at best. In many districts in the coming election the KMT may be on the defensive, trying to protect itself against the vigorous efforts of the thirty-seven JCP candidates who lost as jiten in 1976.

The KMT was founded as the political arm of, and has drawn its leadership from, the Sōka Gakkai. Although the party declared its formal independence from the Gakkai at its June 1970 party congress, it continues to be made up almost exclusively of Sōka Gakkai members and to recruit its candidates for public office from among Gakkai activists.[22] But as part of its effort to become what the Japanese call a "national party" (kokumin seitō), as contrasted with a religious or class party, the KMT made a token effort in the 1976 election to reach beyond the Sōka Gakkai membership for its candidates, endorsing one non-Gakkai candidate in the Hyōgo Third District and giving the party's recommendation to a non-Gakkai independent candidate in the Aichi Second District. The regularly endorsed (and successful) candidate, a graduate of Kyōto University and professor of constitutional law at Kōbe Gakuin University (and an adherent of Shinshū Buddhism), was often cited by the party as a symbol of its "new look." The "recommended" candidate, who also won, was the chairman of the Ishikawajima Harima Heavy Industry labor union in Nagoya and an early advocate of cooperation among the KMT, JSP, and DSP.

The Sōka Gakkai first ran candidates for the Diet in the upper-house election of 1956. It elected three candidates then and six in the 1959 upper-house election. In 1962, when it formed the Clean Politics League (Kōmei Seiji Renmei) as its political arm, it won nine seats in

[22] The party claims that about 10 percent of its 120,000 members do not belong to Sōka Gakkai.

TABLE 3–10

COMPARISON OF VOTE FOR LOSING KMT CANDIDATE AND LOWEST PLACED
WINNING CANDIDATE, BY DISTRICT, 1976 LOWER-HOUSE ELECTION

District	Runner-up	KMT	Lowest Winner	KMT Shortfall
KMT candidate was runner-up				
Tokyo 1		45,813	46,117	364
Shizuoka 2		70,569	72,390	1,821
Kanagawa 3		108,182	110,585	2,403
Saitama 5		79,303	86,823	7,520
Gumma 3		45,048	56,454	11,406
Chiba 4		105,225	119,902	14,677
Tochigi 1		49,100	69,824	20,724
Ehime 1		39,317	62,445	23,128
Other party candidate was runner-up				
Kagoshima 1	54,634	49,231	55,152	5,921
Tottori	46,571	40,898	49,594	8,696
Niigata 3	33,333	23,914	37,107	13,193
Hiroshima 2	48,140	42,401	57,371	14,970
Chiba	52,086	36,788	53,269	16,481
Yamanashi	53,565	43,486	61,489	18,003
Saga	51,934	30,679	52,595	21,916
Shiga	57,897	36,901	63,631	26,730
Shimane	49,580	31,493	58,692	27,199
Fukui	49,335	26,329	53,554	27,225
Saitama 4	88,874	64,699	92,595	27,896
Kagawa	58,371	27,412	56,625	31,213
Oita 1	39,718	32,804	69,005	36,201
Miyazaki 1	68,853	32,340	70,611	38,271
Yamagata 2	53,011	21,347	60,199	38,852
Nagano 1	47,934	17,054	65,900	39,846
Ehime 3	58,650	26,780	68,454	41,674
Akita 1	63,493	23,148	65,610	42,462
Toyama 1	28,174	20,994	63,838	42,844
Ishikawa 2	39,799	5,697	48,550	42,853
Ishikawa 1	28,933	20,694	80,545	59,851

SOURCE: My calculations from publications of the Ministry of Home Affairs.

the upper-house contest. Its candidates in these early Diet campaigns
were senior Gakkai leaders. Four of the elected members had had
experience in local elective politics, and their average age was forty-
seven years.

With the formal establishment of the Kōmeitō in 1964, younger

Gakkai leaders were recruited to develop the party organization and to compete in elections. In the 1965 upper-house election, for example, eight of the party's eleven winners were in their thirties, and the average age of all KMT candidates was thirty-seven years. When the KMT contested its first lower-house election in 1967 it relied on young Gakkai leaders with experience in local politics for its candidates. Of the thirty-two candidates put forward in that election, twenty-four had served in prefectural and city assemblies. Candidates in their thirties and early forties predominated, and the average age was forty-one years.

Among the fifty-five KMT candidates elected in 1976, twenty-one came from this "class of '67." Seniority is a key requirement for leadership in the KMT as in other Japanese parties, and this first class of KMT lower-house members has become the core of the party's leadership. Chairman Takeiri, Vice-Chairman Asai, Secretary-General Yano, and Vice–Secretary-General Matsumoto were all elected for the first time in 1967.[23]

Of the forty-seven KMT candidates elected in 1969, twenty-three were running for the first time. They were somewhat younger than the 1967 candidates (their average age was forty) and better educated. Only nine of the twenty-five KMT winners of 1967 had attended college, but sixteen of the twenty-three newly elected candidates in 1969 had university backgrounds. Fourteen of these twenty-three Diet members from the 1969 campaign were among the fifty-five KMT candidates elected in 1976.

Along with the twenty-one incumbents first elected in 1967, the fourteen first elected in 1969, and the one new KMT candidate elected in 1972,[24] there were nineteen new KMT candidates elected in the 1976 election. These candidates were, on the whole, highly educated (thirteen had attended a university, although only one a national university) and, with an average age of forty-five, somewhat older than new KMT winning candidates in the previous three elections. The average age of all fifty-five successful KMT candidates was forty-six. Thus, the image widespread in the 1960s of the KMT as a party led by exceptionally young men without higher education is no longer appropriate. The party recruits its candidates from among the best

[23] The party has another vice-chairman chosen from among its upper-house members and two additional vice–secretaries-general. One is a member of the upper house and the other was elected to the lower house for the first time in the 1969 election.

[24] The twenty-nine candidates who won in that election included twenty-seven incumbents, one former Diet member, and the one new candidate.

educated of its members and predominantly from among men in their forties.

The largest group of KMT Diet members comprises Sōka Gakkai members who had formerly been elected as KMT candidates to local political office (see Table 3–11). Seven of the nineteen newly elected candidates and twenty-one of all fifty-five KMT winning candidates in 1976 had held local elective office.

Writers and editors for party and Gakkai-related newspapers and journals form the second largest group. The nineteen newly elected candidates included the editor of the Gakkai-sponsored monthly intellectual magazine, *Ushio*; the editor of the party newspaper, the *Kōmei Shinbun*; two *Kōmei Shinbun* reporters; and one reporter for the Gakkai's newspaper, the *Seikyō Shinbun*. Twelve candidates elected in 1976 were associated with these Gakkai-KMT publications.

Other KMT Diet members have varied career backgrounds, but the overriding factor is active membership in Sōka Gakkai. The fact that all but one have had this experience reflects the party's strength and its limits. On the one hand, despite the formal proclamations of the "separation of party and religion," it can mobilize for its election campaigns a religious organization with a declared membership of some 7 million families. On the other hand, Sōka Gakkai membership is largely confined to urban areas and is no longer increasing rapidly.

TABLE 3–11

CAREER BACKGROUNDS OF SUCCESSFUL KMT CANDIDATES, 1976
HOUSE OF REPRESENTATIVES ELECTION

Background	Number Elected
Local politicians	21
Party-Gakkai journalists	12
Medical doctors, lawyers	3
Primary- and middle-school teachers	3
White-collar workers	3
Party bureaucrats	2
Businessmen	1
University professors	1
Others, unknown	9
Total	55

SOURCE: My calculations from newspaper reports and party publications.

Consequently, the KMT may be nearing the maximum vote obtainable through Gakkai support. Further, its close identification with the Gakkai also limits its appeal to non-Gakkai voters, particularly now that voters wanting to cast a ballot against the LDP have a variety of self-declared centrist parties from which to choose. The KMT shares with the JCP the dubious distinction of being one of the two parties most disliked by Japanese voters.[25] Whether it can overcome this antipathy and transform itself into the national party it aspires to be remains a question. The 1976 election saw the KMT recover from its 1972 losses and slightly improve its position over that of 1969. But a close reading of the results does not suggest that the party accomplished anything more or is likely to grow rapidly in coming elections.

The Japan Communist Party

The Communist party's share of the national vote in 1976 was almost identical to its 1972 percentage (10.4 percent in 1976 versus 10.5 percent in 1972), but it lost over half its Diet seats, dropping from thirty-eight to seventeen. Its severest losses in the popular vote came in those districts where its candidates were serious contenders; its biggest gains were registered in those areas where its chances of victory were minimal. The JCP gained about 600,000 more votes than in 1972 in semi-urban and rural districts while losing about 300,000 votes in the metropolitan areas, particularly in Tokyo, Kanagawa, Osaka, and Hyōgo.

The JCP vote percentage went down in twenty-four of twenty-five metropolitan districts. Only in Osaka Seventh did the JCP record a gain and even that was insignificant (0.3 percent) and did not win it a seat. In these districts the JCP took just ten seats, whereas it had won twenty-two in 1972; and since the number of metropolitan seats rose from 91 to 100, the party's share dropped from 24 to 10 percent.

The JCP fared slightly better in the thirty-four urban districts, increasing its share of the vote in eighteen while suffering losses in fourteen.[26] Its most impressive gains came in districts where it had no incumbent and was not in serious contention (Niigata First, Gifu

---

[25] See, for example, *Asahi Shinbun*, December 1, 1976; and Karube Kiyoshi, "Nihonjin wa dono yō ni shite shiji seitō o kimeru wa," in Nihonjin Kenkyūkai, ed., *Nihonjin Kenkyū*, Seiji Seitōbetsu Nihonjin Shūdan, no. 2 (Tokyo: Shiseidō, July 1975).

[26] One district showed no change, and in another the party did not run an endorsed candidate but supported an independent.

First, Ishikawa First). In those urban districts where it was an active contender it performed dismally, winning only three seats as against eleven in 1972.

The Communist party added to its 1972 vote in 65 percent of the forty-six semiurban districts (an increase in thirty, a decrease in sixteen) and in 71 percent of the twenty-five rural districts (an increase in seventeen, a decrease in seven, and one district without an official JCP candidate). These rural and semiurban districts elected 275 lower-house members of which the JCP won only four. In the rural and semi-urban areas, where the LDP and JSP are long established and the DSP and KMT run few candidates, the JCP attracted a protest vote that it could not obtain in more politically competitive, highly urbanized districts.

The party's defeat was not confined to metropolitan areas but was nationwide. It lost seats won in 1972 in Akita First, Miyagi First, Shizuoka First, and Fukuoka Second as well as seven seats in Tokyo, five in Kanagawa, and three in Osaka. In Tokyo, JCP gains of the previous decade were lost as its vote retreated below its 1969 level (16.2 percent in 1969, 19.7 percent in 1972, 15.4 percent in 1976), and it won two fewer seats than eight years before (six seats in 1969, four in 1976). Its winning candidates were from ten prefectures.

The seventeen successful JCP candidates in 1976 included six lawyers, five public school teachers who were local leaders of the "antimainstream" (that is, the Communist party) faction of the Japan Teachers' Union, two medical doctors, one former newspaper reporter, and three longtime party activists and professional politicians.

Conspicuous by their absence from this list are labor union leaders. In contrast with France or Italy where Communist party elements dominate the major labor union federations, the JCP exerts only limited influence. The major labor federation, Sōhyō, supports the JSP and the other major federation, Dōmei, backs the DSP. No major labor federation is aligned with the Communist party. Before the "red purge" of 1950 and the subsequent reorganization of the labor movement, the JCP dominated organized labor, but it has never been able to reassert that influence. It controls just five relatively small labor union federations in Sōhyō.[27] The modest influence it does exert in the labor movement comes from its control of some local branches of

[27] These are the Federation of National Government Employees (Kokka Rōren), All-Japan Workers' Union (Zennichijirō), National Federation of Automobile Transport Workers' Unions (Zenjiku), Federation of Construction Industry Workers' Unions (Zenkensetsu), and the National Federation of Paper Pulp Industry Workers' Unions (Kamipan Rōren).

Sōhyō-affiliated unions—such as the Japan Teachers' Union and the National Railway Workers' Union—that on the national level support the JSP.[28]

The two groups among the JCP Diet members that provide the party's main links with organized labor are Japan Teachers' Union activists and the party's considerable group of lawyers. Almost all the lawyers are labor law specialists who serve as advisers to Sōhyō and who have figured importantly in major labor disputes. Shibata Mutsuo, the JCP candidate elected in Chiba's First District, won fame as a lawyer for one of the defendants in the Matsukawa incident;[29] the party's Dietman from Aichi's Sixth District has been a key figure in many pollution-related cases in the Nagoya area; and the successful candidate in Osaka's First District is a top labor lawyer in western Japan.

Two other points about JCP candidates merit attention. First, it is the only party to run a significant number of women. Twelve of the twenty-five women hopefuls in the 1976 election were from the JCP.[30] Second, the party lent its support to two nonparty candidates who ran as independents under the banner of "united progressives" (Kakushin Kyōdō). Both were successful and, though elected as independents, they vote in the Diet with the Communist party. Recommending Kakushin Kyōdō independent candidates is a tactic first introduced by the JCP in 1972 in order to bring to Diet elections something of the mood of the united progressive campaigns in local urban politics. But, as described in the following section, truly united action by opposition parties, particularly united action with the Communists, did not materialize in the 1976 campaign.

---

[28] Estimates of JCP strength in the organized labor movement are based on the percentage of delegates to Sōhyō conventions who vote for a motion demanding the "freedom of party support." This is a catch phrase for ending Sōhyō support of the JSP and is regularly submitted by Communist labor leaders. Voting on this motion at the 1976 convention suggest that the JCP is able to control somewhat under a third of Sōhyō convention delegates. This figure has remained constant for the past decade.

[29] On the Matsukawa incident see Chalmers Johnson, *Conspiracy at Matsukawa* (Berkeley: University of California Press, 1972). Shibata was the lawyer for the defense of Ōta Shōji.

[30] The LDP ran four women, the JSP three, and the DSP three. There was one minor-party woman candidate and two independents. The KMT and NLC ran no women. Six women were elected, including two from the JCP. One woman was elected on the LDP ticket, two from the JSP, and one independent (one of the two united progressive candidates supported by the JCP). (See Table 5–14.)

Opposition Party Cooperation

Beginning with the 1971 upper-house election, opposition parties have attempted to coordinate their endorsements of candidates so as to minimize competition among them in selected constituencies and maximize the chances of defeating LDP candidates. The history of these cooperative efforts has been dismal. The opposition parties have been unable to repeat in any of the subsequent four national elections the successes achieved in the 1971 upper-house race when eight Socialist candidates in single-member local constituencies were elected with the support of the KMT and the DSP. The general disintegration of opposition party cooperation was most recently evident in the 1977 upper-house election when the JSP failed to gain KMT and DSP backing for the eight candidates first elected in 1971. All were defeated.

Cooperation is a recurrent theme in the rhetoric of all the opposition parties. Each has its own formula for maximizing the anti-LDP vote and its own vision of the makeup of an anti-LDP coalition government. But the rhetoric barely conceals the fact that each is trying to advance its own position relative to the other opposition parties in anticipation of the bargaining that will take place if the LDP loses its Diet majority.

One contentious issue on electoral cooperation has been whether to include the Communist party. The DSP and KMT adamantly oppose such cooperation while the JSP adheres formally to a policy of cooperating with all opposition parties, including the Communists. The Democratic Socialist party has staked out a position far on the right of the opposition, strong anti-Communism being one feature of its ideological core. The party chairman at the time of the 1976 election, Kasuga Ikkō, constantly attacked the JCP during the campaign and demanded that the Socialist party decide whether it was pro-Communist or anti-Communist.

Animosities between Kōmeitō and JCP also are bitter, reflecting their struggle for the urban protest vote and for the position as the second largest opposition party in the Diet. In 1972, when the KMT dropped eighteen seats and the JCP gained twenty-four, there were eleven districts in which the JCP won and the KMT came in as runner-up.[31] In 1976, when the KMT gained twenty-six seats and the JCP lost twenty-one, the reverse occurred: new or former KMT candi-

---

[31] Hokkaidō 1, Chiba 1, Tokyo 1, 3, 5, and 8, Kanagawa 2, Kyōto 1 and 2, Kōchi, Fukuoka 4.

dates won in eleven constituencies where JCP candidates lost.[32] Moreover, in seven of these districts the winning KMT candidate had lost to the JCP in 1972.

In 1975, Eda Saburō, the leader of the JSP right wing, together with the secretaries-general of the KMT and the DSP formed the Society to Think about a New Japan (Atarashi Nihon O Kangaeru Kai). Ostensibly established to study policy, the group was widely regarded as a significant step toward an alliance of the DSP, KMT, and the Eda wing of the JSP. But Eda was unable to obtain much support from within his own party. After his defeat in the lower-house election, he was ousted from the party vice-chairmanship at the February 1977 party congress. Shortly thereafter he abandoned the JSP completely to form a new party, the Socialist Citizens League. Eda's sudden death on the eve of the 1977 House of Councillors election deprived his fledgling party of its one nationally known and popular leader and left the Socialist party leadership awash in a debilitating power struggle.

Such animosities among the opposition left scant room for electoral cooperation. The cooperation that did materialize was minimal, came late in the campaign, and had little impact on the outcome. There were instances in the 1976 campaign of KMT-DSP and KMT-JSP cooperation, but none involving the JCP. In all cases, cooperation followed a formula that Japanese call "give and take," borrowing the words from English—that is, another party's candidate was supported in one district in return for support of one's own candidate elsewhere. In no case did a party withdraw a candidate with a reasonable chance of winning to support another party's candidate. Rather, a party would merely recommend another's candidate in a district where it did not plan to run its own candidate anyway. In one instance discussed below, a candidate not expected to win was withdrawn in favor of a stronger candidate from another opposition party.

The most extensive cooperation was between the KMT and the DSP. Cooperative agreements were negotiated at the district or prefectural level, and local parties, Dōmei unions, and Sōka Gakkai organizations entered them with varying degrees of enthusiasm. The KMT supported DSP candidates in six districts.[33] For its part the DSP lent its official support for KMT candidates in five districts,[34] and local

---

[32] Hokkaidō 1, Miyagi 1, Tokyo 3, 5, 8, and 11, Kanagawa 2, and 4, Shizuoka 1, Kyōto 1, and Fukuoka 4.

[33] Kanagawa 5, Shizuoka 3, Hyōgo 5, Fukushima 1 and 2, Nagano 4.

[34] Aomori 1, Shizuoka 1, Wakayama 1, Kanagawa 3, Nagano 1.

DSP and Dōmei organizations gave KMT candidates informal support in five other constituencies.[35]

The most interesting and significant case of cooperation was the DSP-KMT barter arrangement in the Fukushima First and Aomori First districts. The KMT, despite the dismay and the protests of its Fukushima prefectural branch, withdrew its candidate in Fukushima's First District and supported the DSP candidate there. In return the KMT won DSP support for the KMT candidate in Aomori. Actually, cooperation was between the KMT and the Dōmei-affiliated Tōhoku Electric Power Company union. The DSP candidate in Fukushima was the former prefectural head of the union, and in supporting him the KMT exacted a promise that union leaders would actively support the KMT candidate in Aomori.[36] In the end the KMT had the best of the bargain: the DSP candidate was defeated in Fukushima while the KMT not only picked up a new seat in Aomori but established a new relationship with a powerful labor union.

The DSP won seats in three of the six districts where it received KMT support. The KMT was successful in three of the five districts where KMT support was official and in three of the other five districts where that support was less formal. Fukushima First was the only district in which a party withdrew a candidate for purposes of electoral cooperation.

For months prior to the election the KMT and the JSP held inconclusive negotiations over election cooperation. Finally, a week before the election, KMT Chairman Takeiri and JSP Chairman Narita signed two agreements, one on election cooperation and another on election policy.[37] The two parties had worked together earlier in upper-house elections, but the first effort at coordination in a lower-house campaign was in 1976.

The agreements were vaguely worded, characterizing the election as a crucial step in the process of ousting the "structurally corrupt" LDP government. They called for a shift in economic policy from support for big business to an increase in social welfare, the establishment of a progressive coalition government committed to the maintenance of the spirit of Japan's peace constitution, and in foreign policy the abolition of the U.S.-Japan Mutual Security Treaty through diplomatic negotiations. The agreements did not bind the parties to electoral cooperation in specific districts but simply stated they would

[35] Ibaragi 3, Gumma 3, Saitama 2, Gifu 1, Hiroshima 2.
[36] *Mainichi Shinbun*, November 9, 1977.
[37] *Yomiuri Shinbun*, November 29, 1976.

encourage cooperation and leave implementation to local party officials.

The JSP finally agreed to support only one KMT candidate—in the Gifu First District—and that support proved a disaster to the Socialists. In this five-member district the JSP had elected two members in the 1969 election but only one in 1972, party Vice-Chairman Yamamoto Kōichi; the other four seats were taken by the LDP. Given the party's 1972 experience, the JSP leadership viewed the election of two candidates in Gifu First in 1976 as hopeless and decided to run only the incumbent Yamamoto. Although convinced that it lacked the votes to elect two candidates, the JSP nonetheless felt that it could comfortably elect Yamamoto and channel the "surplus" JSP votes to the KMT candidate, thereby possibly unseating one of the LDP incumbents. Despite some initial opposition to this strategy from local JSP and labor union leaders, agreement was finally reached late in the campaign to provide support for the KMT candidate in exchange for KMT support for Socialist candidates in other districts.[38] Formal KMT support for JSP candidates materialized in two districts (Wakayama Second and Miyazaki Second) and less formal support in five others (Yamagata Second, Akita Second, Aichi Fourth, Ehime Second, and Ōita Second). Nine JSP candidates were running in these seven districts.

In Gifu First the election produced a surprisingly easy victory for the new KMT candidate, who won the most votes in the district, and for the four LDP incumbents. The JSP had totally misread the voters' mood and, by encouraging some of its own backers to support the KMT candidate, had given away the votes needed to elect its own candidate. Thus Yamamoto joined several other high-ranking Socialist leaders in electoral defeat.

Eight of the nine JSP candidates running with KMT formal or informal backing won, but it is unlikely that the outcome would have differed even without KMT support. The KMT had not planned to run candidates in any of these districts. In five of these seven districts the JSP received virtually the same share of the vote as in 1972.[39] The only significant increases in the JSP vote were in Akita Second and

[38] JSP-KMT negotiations on cooperation in Gifu received almost daily press coverage. Some of the more important articles are *Sankei Shinbun*, October 3, 1976; *Mainichi Shinbun*, October 15, November 2, and November 9, 1976; *Asahi Shinbun*, November 17, 1976.

[39] These were: Yamagata 2, +1.5 percentage points; Aichi 4, −0.2 percentage points; Wakayama 2, −1.8 percentage points; Ehime 3, +0.6 percentage points; and Miyazaki 2, −1.8 percentage points.

Ōita Second,[40] but in neither case does the KMT seem to have been a significant factor in the increase.

For the DSP, too, the results of the electoral cooperation were ambiguous. Although the DSP share of the vote increased significantly in two of the six districts where its candidates were supported by the KMT (Shizuoka Third and Kanagawa Fifth),[41] in other districts the decline in its vote was just as significant.[42]

The KMT's vote percentage rose in districts where it had DSP or JSP support, but the increase was not much higher than in districts without cooperation.[43] Nonetheless, the KMT appears to have benefited most by the cooperation that did occur. Its victories in Aomori First and Gifu First seem attributable to the support, respectively, of the DSP and the JSP. This evidence of the acceptability of the KMT to the established opposition parties enhanced its image as a national rather than a narrowly based religious party, and it succeeded in supplanting the JSP as the bridge among the non-Communist opposition parties. Personal enmities, rivalry between Sōhyō and Dōmei, deep policy differences, and other factors made JSP-DSP cooperation impossible in 1976. The Kōmeitō emerged as the only party able to deal with the DSP on the one hand and the JSP on the other. This, and the generally successful performance of the KMT relative to the other opposition parties, has encouraged its leadership to believe that the party can become the nucleus for a future coalition government, or at least the pivotal actor in any bargaining for a coalition.

But the significance of opposition party cooperation in 1976, and even more so in the 1977 upper-house election, lies in the parties' lack of enthusiasm for it. Now that the LDP's loss of a Diet majority is a distinct possibility, relations among the opposition parties are even more competitive. At the same time, internal strains within the parties, particularly the JSP, have worsened. No opposition party expects to become a majority party, but each is endeavoring to add to its own numbers at the expense of other opposition parties in anticipation of bargaining for a coalition in the event that the LDP loses its majority. In the fluid political situation from the end of 1976 to the summer of 1977, there were few incentives to coordinate candidate endorsement policies and cooperate in defeating the LDP.

[40] In Akita 2 the JSP vote rose by 7.1 percentage points and in Ōita 2 by 7.4 percentage points.
[41] An increase from 17.7 to 23.2 percent in Shizuoka 3 and from 12.6 to 22.3 percent in Kanagawa 5.
[42] In Hyōgo 5, for example, it went down from 30.5 to 23.4 percent.
[43] The party registered a 2.7 percentage point gain in cooperation districts over 1972 as compared with 2.4 points nationally.

Campaign Issues

During the two decades of LDP dominance, Japan's opposition parties' primary function was that of protest—to criticize the LDP, the government, and the system that denied them governmental power. Behind the scenes the Socialists, Democratic Socialists, and Kōmeitō often have worked out compromises with the LDP to secure benefits for their respective party constituencies (and have been roundly criticized by the Communists for doing so). But in public they maintained the appearances of an adamant opposition making demands for basic, structural change.

Recently, however, they have tried to demonstrate their moderation and pragmatism in order to convince the voters that their participation in government would bring beneficial, incremental reform, not immediate, radical change. But election campaigns are a form of political theater, and in their campaigns these parties still feel somewhat compelled to play out their traditional protest role.

In the 1976 election attacks on the party in power, though offering little in the way of policy alternatives, were reinforced by the Lockheed scandal. Lockheed and the deeper questions it raised about political corruption were treated by the opposition as the paramount issue of the campaign. Each vied with the other in expressing outrage at the LDP's "money politics" and called for prohibition of political contributions by business firms. Beyond that, however, the opposition parties offered little in the way of specific proposals for political reform. The main theme in the opposition's campaign was that corrupt politics were caused by one-party rule and the LDP's ties with big business. A transfer of power from the LDP, it was argued, would in itself purge the political system of the LDP's "structural corruption."

The possible loss of an LDP Diet majority itself was treated as a campaign issue. This was particularly true in the 1977 House of Councillors election, which the opposition parties hoped—without success, as it turned out—would bring about a "reversal of the conservatives and the progressives." The JSP's campaign slogan in this later race was "Make the JSP big and strong—that is the road to the transfer of power."[44] The other opposition parties made similar appeals, the spirit of which was most succinctly captured by a Kōmeitō slogan: "Political Change!"[45]

Despite such calls, the opposition parties were criticized by political commentators and, as would be expected, by LDP politicians for

[44] "Shakaitō o tsuyoku ōkiku—seiken kōtai e no michi desu."
[45] "Seiji Tenkan!"

having become accustomed to, and even comfortable in, a role of opposing for opposition's sake and for lacking the "will" to assume the responsibilities of government. The Socialists bore the brunt of this criticism, and a much discussed JSP campaign poster for the 1977 upper-house election revealed the party's sensitivity. Showing a striking young girl in the dress and makeup of a performer of traditional Japanese dance, the poster announced: "It's our turn. We will do it. The Japan Socialist Party."[46] Each opposition party sought to convince the voters of its readiness to "do it" by emphasizing its commitment to moderation and reform and by retreating from, or deferring to the future, policy proposals that might appear extreme. This effort to blur the line that had previously separated the conservative and progressive camps was symbolized by opposition party positions on *anpo*, the U.S.-Japan Mutual Security Treaty.

The abrogation of the security treaty remains the officially stated goal of the KMT, JSP, and JCP. The DSP until 1975 maintained a policy known as "*anpo* without bases," the objective being to maintain security ties with the United States but to revise the treaty itself so as to remove American troops from Japanese soil. But in its 1975 congress, the DSP adopted a position of support for the treaty almost identical to that of the LDP. During the 1976 campaign, DSP Chairman Kasuga demanded JSP acceptance of the treaty as a condition for cooperation between the two parties.[47]

The Kōmeitō's position has swung in the past few years from a demand for immediate abrogation of the treaty to tacit acceptance of it. In the party's first platform in 1964 it urged abrogation but took a more moderate position than the JSP or the JCP by cautioning against "immediate" abrogation. In 1967 its position was that the treaty relationship should be dissolved gradually over ten to twenty years. For a short time following its defeat in the 1972 lower-house election, the KMT tried to forge a close alliance with the JSP and, at its 1973 congress, fell into line with the JSP stand on the treaty by adopting a policy plank calling for "immediate" abrogation. The KMT was not long, however, in retreating from this position. In 1975 it adopted its current position in favor of abrogation "through diplomatic negotiations," meaning, in effect, termination of the treaty at some

---

[46] "Deban desu. Yarimasu. Nihon Shakaitō."

[47] In a press conference in Niigata on November 30, for example, Kasuga declared the DSP's minimum conditions for cooperation with the JSP to be a JSP commitment to retain the security treaty and reject electoral cooperation with the Communists. See *Asahi Shinbun*, December 1, 1976.

future time so long as it would not harm U.S.-Japan relations or compromise Japanese security.

The "vision" published in 1976 by the Society to Think about a New Japan (organized, as mentioned earlier, to bring together KMT, DSP, and right-wing JSP leaders) included a statement on the treaty that most closely describes the KMT and right-wing JSP position: "to make diplomatic efforts to create an environment in which military alliances will be unnecessary so that the security treaty can be dissolved."[48] By putting the emphasis on creating a peaceful environment before abolishing the treaty, this formulation completely reversed the view long held by the Japanese left that the treaty itself is a source of international tension and its abrogation an essential step in creating a peaceful international environment.

For many years the Socialist party has demanded the treaty's immediate abrogation. This position is still confirmed at each year's party congress. In reality, however, the party has moved decidedly to the right on the issue. Leaders now say that "immediate" does not mean as soon as a Socialist-led government comes to power but as soon as unspecified conditions are realized that would ensure continued close ties with the United States. On December 1, the start of the last week of the 1976 campaign, Chairman Narita stated that if the Socialist party came to power, the security treaty "would be dissolved through a process of diplomatic negotiations."[49] This statement received front-page coverage in the press because its use of the KMT phraseology suggested a marked departure from the JSP's earlier position.

In its official ideology, the Communist party claims that Japan is a semicolony of the United States and the security treaty the mechanism for America's subjugation of Japan. Central to the party's nationalistic appeal is the demand that Japan recover its full independence and autonomy by abrogating the treaty. Until the 1976 campaign the JCP had been calling for the establishment of a "democratic coalition government" that would assign priority to abolishing the treaty. But following a mid-November statement by JSP Chairman Narita indicating his party's support for a broadly based coalition government, including conservatives who might defect from the LDP,[50] JCP Chairman Miyamoto issued a call for the formation of a transi-

---

[48] Atarashi Nihon o Kangaeru Kai, "Ashita no Nihon no tame ni" (mimeo, 1976), p. 12.

[49] *Asahi Shinbun*, December 2, 1976.

[50] Made at a press conference in Tokushima on November 16, 1976, and reported on the front pages of all major newspapers the following day.

tional coalition government including non-LDP conservatives as the first step toward the democratic coalition government advocated in the party program. After Narita's *anpo* statement, Miyamoto quickly announced that, if a broadly based coalition were formed, the JCP would support the shelving of the treaty issue. The JCP shows no sign of revising its basic treaty position, but the fact that it saw a tactical advantage in making its policy on *anpo* somewhat more ambiguous indicates that it felt a strong antitreaty stance had become something of a political liability.

On Japan's domestic economy, the opposition parties, with varying degrees of specificity, recommended tax reform, a stronger antimonopoly law, greater government intervention to control price increases, and increased government expenditures for social welfare. The Kōmeitō, in particular, stressed the importance of expanding social welfare programs and published a 581-page five-year social welfare plan in October.[51] The document is particularly notable for its advocacy of high economic growth policies as the only way to produce the revenue necessary to expand the government's welfare programs. Previously, the Kōmeitō and other opposition parties had criticized the government's high growth policies and had joined the chorus in favor of "stable economic growth." Despite this rhetoric, none of the opposition parties was prepared to propose during the campaign a radical reordering of government budgetary priorities, at least for the short run. Their solution to what they viewed as inadequate social services was to make the economic pie larger, thereby avoiding the political costs of holding back expenditures for some programs to achieve increases elsewhere or of increasing taxes to pay for new programs. This approach, similar to the one pursued by the LDP for over twenty years and evident in the proposals of all the opposition parties, led the KMT in its five-year plan to project a 7.2 percent average annual growth rate for the 1975–1980 period, 1.2 percentage points higher than the official government target.

The opposition parties have retained their long-term goals, but, with the decline of the LDP's Diet position, they increasingly emphasize moderate short-term objectives in their appeals for electoral support. The results of the lower- and upper-house elections in 1976 and 1977 do not offer evidence, however, that their efforts to occupy the political center have brought greatly increased popularity. Support for both the JSP and the JCP has continued to erode; the KMT has

---

[51] Kōmeitō Sōgō Seisaku Kenkyū Iinkai, *Fukushi Shakai Tōtaru Puranu* (Tokyo, 1966). The plan applied to the 1975–1980 period.

remained unable to expand its appeal far beyond Sōka Gakkai membership; and the DSP has not drawn significantly new support. The move to the center by Japan's political opposition does increase the number of potential coalition partners for the LDP—or for a group of LDP members assuming a new party label—should the erosion of LDP support result in a loss of its Diet majority. But should the LDP be able to reverse the trend of declining support, there is no guarantee that some of the parties in the opposition camp would not return to an emphasis on what has been traditionally a more radical policy line. Intraparty differences over the political benefits to be gained from centrist policies already are evident in the internal factional conflict in the JSP and in the reports of apparent discontent among some JCP members with their party's policy line.

Thanks partly to the Lockheed scandal, the Japanese opposition was able to avoid coming to grips with difficult policy questions in the 1976 campaign. They appealed mostly to voter discontent with the political behavior of Japan's ruling party rather than to dissatisfaction with its policies. It should not be particularly surprising that the 1976 and 1977 elections did not focus clearly on issues, because Japan's opposition parties still have not completely transformed themselves from protest parties into active contenders for government power. Nor is this likely to occur until and unless the LDP governmental monopoly is broken.

A parallel decline in electoral support for the LDP and JSP, and an increase in the number of political parties, none of which has hopes of becoming a majority party, are central features of present Japanese party politics. Formerly the system was ideologically polarized, and the LDP exercised exclusive control over the government with the JSP playing the major role in aggregating public opposition to the ruling party. Now Japan seems headed toward a multiparty system in which ideological differences among parties are less sharply defined and no one party has unchallengeable authority or dominates the opposition.

In retrospect it is evident that the "one-and-a-half" party system of the late 1950s began to give way almost immediately under the pressures of rapid social and economic change. Greater affluence and the growth of middle-class values weakened the appeal of class parties, while urbanization, the spread of higher education, and other social changes undercut the strength of traditional networks of social relationships so crucial to the LDP's techniques of mobilizing support. In turn, these social changes prompted the creation of new parties and encouraged the established opposition parties to eschew ideological confrontation in favor of more pragmatic policy lines. In 1959 a right-wing faction of the JSP split away to form the Democratic Socialist party, advocating a more moderate program of reform than was being offered by the JSP. Five years later the Kōmeitō entered national elective politics with the support of the Sōka Gakkai and an appeal aimed at the dissatisfied lower-middle-class urban dweller. In the early 1970s the Japan Communist party reemerged as a significant electoral force with a new reformist and pragmatic line. In 1976 the first serious split occurred in the conservative camp when six Diet members left the LDP to form the New Liberal Club and to offer the voters a conservative alternative. In the spring of 1977 the leader of the JSP right wing, Eda Saburō, left the party to form the Socialist Citizens League and to create an alliance between advocates of a British Labour party type of social democracy and leaders of nonparty-affiliated citizen movements. In September of the same year, three more JSP members, led by upper-house member Den Hideo, the only politician in Japanese electoral history to win the top vote in the national constituency in two elections, left the party because of its inability or unwillingness to control its extreme left. The Den group and the Socialist Citizens League, led by Eda Saburō's son, merged in March 1978 to form the Social Democratic League (Shakai Minshu Rengō).

No opposition party is demonstrating an ability to win substantially increased support. Despite the steady and, so far, irreversible decline in LDP support, each of them views its own future with apprehension. The JSP is locked in an intense power struggle and has lost some of its most popular members through defections. Public support is declining, and the party expects to suffer further reversals at the polls and in all probability will do so.

The Kōmeitō, despite its recouping of earlier losses, remains a party largely limited to urban Sōka Gakkai support and is unlikely to increase substantially its Diet representation. Rumors current in the Japanese press that the Kōmeitō hopes eventually to merge into a new centrist party are symptomatic of KMT leaders' worries about their inability to expand their support much beyond the Sōka Gakkai membership.

The DSP vote does not grow, and it has been forced to restrict its candidates to districts with strong Dōmei-affiliated unions that provide it with financial and organizational backing. As a result of a concerted party effort, the DSP has won some backing from big business concerned about the increasingly precarious position of the LDP and from the small and medium-sized business sector. With this support the DSP may be able to increase modestly the number of its candidates in coming elections and gain a few additional seats. But it appears destined to remain a small party whose viability will depend on the extent to which it can cast a crucial swing vote in Diet bargaining over legislation and, possibly, over the composition of a coalition government.

The Communist party had so many runner-up candidates in the 1976 election that it might recover some of the seats it lost in that election. But its support is likely to continue to be restricted to active supporters who constitute no more than 5 percent of the electorate, and to another 5 percent or so of the voting public that turns to it as the means for lodging a protest vote.

Japan's opposition parties are, for the most part, seeking to attract broad public support, particularly among the large number of urban voters who support no party.[52] In their efforts to broaden their bases of support, they are trying to advocate policies that will not alienate any significant sector but will gain broad public backing. This, of course, contributed to the lack of focus on issues in the opposition parties' campaigns in 1976 and 1977 and to their preoccupation with attacking LDP behavior rather than government policy.

Furthermore, the speed with which Japan's opposition parties have shifted toward the political center and away from ideological confrontation has outpaced their ability to give real substance to their alternatives to government policy. As a consequence, the Japanese voter faces more parties but few clear policy choices. Over the long run, the continuation of a trend toward centrism is likely to result in the development of more coherent platforms by the Japanese opposition parties and the emergence of a more competitive party system. Dramatic and adverse changes in Japan's economic situation or in its international position could, of course, undercut the present trend toward political centrism. But provided Japan continues to enjoy a relatively stable and favorable environment, the trends evident in 1976 and 1977 are likely to result in a multiparty system characterized by a relative absence of ideological confrontation and a relative effectiveness in articulating the concerns and representing the interests of the Japanese voting public.

---

[52] Public opinion polls in late 1976 indicated that more than a quarter of the voting public supported no political party. The percentage of nonparty supporters was particularly high among young voters. In a nationwide *Yomiuri* poll published on November 2, 1976, for example, 28.6 percent of the respondents supported no party; the percentage for voters in their twenties was 43.4 percent. See discussion in Passin, Chapter 7 in this volume.

4
Historical Statistics

Nisihira Sigeki

In this chapter, election results for the nation as a whole will be analyzed in terms of political parties, electoral districts, and administrative districts. Some comparisons will be made with Western European countries in order to elucidate the distinctive characteristics of Japanese elections.

Although there have been thirteen general elections in the postwar period, only the seven since 1958 will be examined here, because it was in the 1958 election that the two leading parties, the LDP and the JSP, first took their present form.[1] Since 1958 a total of six political parties have held seats in the House of Representatives. Minor parties took one seat in 1958 and one in 1960; in 1972, two minor parties won one seat apiece. But the total voting percentage of minor parties has never reached as much as 1 percent.

Changes in National Election Results

In 1958 the LDP obtained 57.8 percent of the popular vote; in 1976, 41.8 percent, a decline of more than a quarter (see Table 4–1). The decrease in vote is linear. Since 1967 the LDP has failed to win a majority of votes in the lower-house elections.

At the same time, the LDP's seat percentage has been dropping at almost the same pace. In both 1960 and 1969 this trend took a slight upturn, so that the decline in seats won between 1958 and 1976 was held to 13 percentage points. In 1972, when the LDP dropped to 55 percent of the seats, it felt itself in crisis. In the 1974 upper-house election, the LDP won only 48 percent of the seats, and in the 1976

---

[1] The LDP was established in 1955 but entered its first election in 1958. The JSP was united in 1958, but in 1960 the right wing split off to form the present DSP.

TABLE 4–1

VOTE AND SEAT PERCENTAGES WON, BY PARTY, IN HOUSE OF REPRESENTATIVES ELECTIONS, 1958–1976

Party		1958	1960	1963	1967	1969	1972	1976
LDP	Votes	57.8	57.6	54.7	48.8	47.6	46.9	41.8
	Seats	61.5	63.4	60.6	57.0	59.2	55.2	48.7
JSP	Votes	32.9	27.6	29.0	27.9	21.4	21.9	20.7
	Seats	35.5	31.0	30.8	28.8	18.5	24.0	24.1
KMT	Votes	—	—	—	5.4	10.9	8.5	10.9
	Seats	—	—	—	5.1	9.7	5.9	10.8
JCP	Votes	2.6	2.9	4.0	4.8	6.8	10.5	10.4
	Seats	0.2	0.6	1.1	1.0	2.9	7.7	3.3
DSP	Votes	—	8.8	7.4	7.4	7.7	7.0	6.3
	Seats	—	3.7	4.9	6.2	6.4	3.9	5.7
NLC	Votes	—	—	—	—	—	—	4.2
	Seats	—	—	—	—	—	—	3.3

Dash (—): Not applicable.

NOTE: Percentages do not add to 100 because table excludes small other parties and independents.

SOURCE: Calculated from publications of the Ministry of Home Affairs.

lower-house election, about the same share, 48.7 percent. But because in both cases several independents joined up after the elections, the LDP was able to retain its slight majority in both houses of the Diet. As a result of the 1976 elections, "conservatives" still hold about 54 percent of the seats, if the seventeen seats of the New Liberal Club are included, plus the independent conservatives who joined the LDP immediately after the elections and the conservatives who continued to remain independent.

Paradoxically, when the opposition is more active, the LDP gains, because the other parties compete with each other for the available pool of opposition votes. As long as the opposition is divided and fighting among itself, a plurality is sufficient for the LDP to win a seat. Moreover, the present allocation of constituencies favors the LDP; its share of seats is consistently six points or more higher than its voting percentage among the electorate.

The JSP also usually wins a higher share of seats than its voting percentage warrants (except in 1969), although not as much as in the case of the LDP. The difference results from the large number of so-called bubble candidates, that is, minor-party or independent candidates, who tend to draw some of the opposition votes away from the JSP. In 1958 the JSP won one out of every three votes. After 1960, however, when the right wing split off to form a separate party, the JSP has consistently run below 30 percent of the votes. In 1969 it declined sharply toward the 20 percent level, and since then the JSP share has been just over 20 percent.

The JSP seat share has followed the same pattern. When the left and right wings were reunited in fall 1957, the JSP had a clear minimum goal: one-third of the seats in the House of Representatives. This was to prevent the LDP from amending the Constitution; since amendment requires a two-thirds majority, a one-third-plus-one seat share would stop it. The other opposition parties had too few seats to count upon for this purpose (the JCP, two; the Farmer-Worker party, four), so the JSP felt it needed single-handed veto control. Since 1960, however, the JSP has not been able to win one-third of the seats, and in 1969 it dropped to a decisively lower level, 18.5 percent. In the two elections since then (1972 and 1976), the JSP has been unable to break the one-quarter barrier. In 1976 the JSP won 123 seats, an increase of five; but its percentage remained about the same, 24 percent, because the total number of seats in the House of Representatives had been increased by twenty over the 1972 election. The JSP's voting percentage had also declined by 1.2 percentage points. All in all, the JSP position is not a hopeful one, but because the LDP has declined even more rapidly, the possibility of an opposition coalition centering around the JSP has remained alive.

The JSP was established in 1945 but split into a right and a left wing in the early 1950s over the ratification of the San Francisco Peace Treaty and the U.S.-Japan Mutual Security Treaty. In October 1955 the two wings reunited. However, when the JSP decided to oppose the continuation of the U.S.-Japan security pact in 1959, forty sitting members left the party and established the DSP in January of 1960.

The DSP aroused high expectations in the mass media that it would break free of the JSP mold of a "class party" and become a "people's party." In the November 1960 election DSP candidates ran for the Diet in 105 (out of the then 118) electoral districts, but only 17 of them were successful. Since that time, the DSP has increased its share of seats, but at a painfully slow and uneven rate. In 1969, as may be seen in Table 4–1, it became the fourth-ranking party, and in 1972 it dropped to the fifth position—below the JCP. In 1976 it returned to the fourth position, with a strong increase in seats, but its seat share, 5.7 percent, is below that of 1967 and 1969.

The DSP does not run candidates in all electoral districts. Except for 1960, it has run one candidate in each of between fifty and sixty-nine districts (see Table 4–2). Therefore, changes in its national voting percentage do not mean much. On the average, it runs at about 7 percent. If only the districts where it runs candidates are counted, its voting share is about 14 percent, which is slightly less than that of the Kōmeitō.

The Kōmeitō, although it was established by the Sōka Gakkai, is now nominally independent. Nevertheless, all Kōmeitō candidates are considered to be members of the Sōka Gakkai.[2] By 1969, with a total of 47 seats (9.7 percent) in the House of Representatives, the Kōmeitō became the third-ranking party. It ran into some difficulties, however, and in the 1972 elections it was displaced as the third party by the JCP. A dramatic recovery in 1976 virtually doubled the number of its seats, and the Kōmeitō returned triumphantly to an even stronger third position than before with 10.8 percent of the seats.

Since the Kōmeitō, like the DSP, does not run candidates in all electoral districts, the nationwide changes in the voting percentage do not lend themselves to extensive speculation. However, in the eighty-four electoral districts the Kōmeitō contested, its average voting percentage is 14.8, higher than the JCP's. In the past four elections the Kōmeitō has won one out of every seven votes in the electoral districts it contested.

By contrast, the JCP contests virtually every district; not that it expects realistically to win, but it likes to test out its strength and to use the elections as an opportunity for propaganda and public relations. In the thirteen general elections since the end of World War II, the highest voting percentages obtained by the JCP were 10.5 in 1972, 10.4 in 1976, and 9.8 in 1949. One may conclude that under optimal conditions, one voter out of ten is responsive to the JCP appeal .

In terms of seats, the JCP's best performances were 1972, when it won thirty-eight seats, or 7.7 percent, and 1949, when it won thirty-five seats, or 7.5 percent of the total. In 1976, however, it dropped to seventeen seats, or 3.3 percent. In 1972 the JCP ranked third after the LDP and the JSP, but in 1976 it fell into a tie for fifth place with the newly formed NLC.

The New Liberal Club made its first appearance in the July 1976

---

[2] In the 1976 House of Representatives election, one independent ran with Kōmeitō support. After the election, he did not join the party, but, together with its members, formed an in-House group called the Kokumin Kaigi (National Conference).

TABLE 4–2

THE FOUR MINOR PARTIES IN HOUSE OF REPRESENTATIVES ELECTIONS, 1960–1976

	1960	1963	1967	1969	1972	1976
Number of electoral districts	118	118	123	123	124	130
DSP						
Candidates	105	59	60	68	65	51
Percent of votes won nationally	8.8	7.4	7.4	7.7	7.0	6.3
Percent of votes won in districts contested	9.8	12.7	13.3	12.4	11.5	13.6
Seats won	17	23	30	31	19	29
Percent of seats won	3.7	4.9	6.2	6.3	3.8	5.7
KMT						
Candidates	—	—	32	76	59	84
Percent of votes won nationally	—	—	5.4	10.9	8.5	10.9
Percent of votes won in districts contested	—	—	14.8	15.2	14.3	14.8
Seats won	—	—	25	4.7	29.3	55
Percent of seats won	—	—	5.1	9.7	5.9	10.8
JCP						
Candidates	118	118	123	123	122[a]	128[a]
Percent of votes won nationally	2.9	4.0	4.8	6.8	10.5	10.4
Percent of votes won in districts contested	2.9	4.0	4.8	6.8	10.6	10.6
Seats won	3	5	5	14	38	17
Percent of seats won	0.6	1.1	1.0	2.9	7.7	3.3
NLC						
Candidates	—	—	—	—	—	25
Percent of votes won nationally	—	—	—	—	—	4.2

Table continued on following page

TABLE 4–2 (continued)

	1960	1963	1967	1969	1972	1976
Percent of votes won in districts contested	—	—	—	—	—	18.5
Seats won	—	—	—	—	—	17
Percent of seats won	—	—	—	—	—	3.3

Dash (—): Not applicable.
[a] Two candidates in Kyōto First District.
SOURCE: Calculated from publications of the Ministry of Home Affairs.

elections. It ran twenty-five candidates in the lower-house elections, and seventeen were elected. Its share of the national vote is a mere 4.2 percent, but in the twenty-five electoral districts it contested its share was a hefty 18.5 percent. This brings it close to the JSP's 20.7 percent nationwide figure. Although the NLC regards itself as an opposition party, unlike the four other opposition parties it has declared itself conservative. If the votes of the NLC are added to those of the LDP, the total of 46 percent is almost the same as the 46.9 percent the LDP won in the 1972 elections.

The Councillors elections show just about the same trends.[3] This justifies the conclusion that, in the national aggregate, the Japanese people's political preferences have been shifting away from both the government party, the LDP, and from what has been since the end of World War II the principal opposition party, the JSP. However, this is only at the national level. To understand what is happening, we have to look at the electoral districts in detail.

Party Voting Percentages by Electoral Districts

The competitiveness of an election can be measured by the "competition rate," that is, the number of candidates divided by the number of seats being contested. In the first postwar election in 1946, the competition rate reached 5.9, but this was unusual. In 1947 it fell to 3.4, and by 1963 it dropped to 1.9. Since then (except for a slight upturn in 1969), it has continued to decrease at a slow rate, reaching 1.7 in 1976. If candidates who failed to obtain the legally designated minimum number of votes are eliminated, however, the competition

---

[3] See Passin, Chapter 5 in this volume.

TABLE 4-3

PERCENTAGE DIFFERENCE BETWEEN LOWEST WINNERS AND RUNNERS-UP BY
ELECTORAL DISTRICTS, HOUSE OF REPRESENTATIVES ELECTIONS, 1963–1976

	Percentage Point Difference between Lowest Winners and Runners-up (number of electoral districts)					Percent of Districts with 0.0–0.9 Differ-	Total Number of
Year	0.0–0.9	1.0–1.9	2.0–2.9	3.0–4.9	5	ence	Districtsᵃ
1976	53	25	15	13	23	41	129
1972	45	33	13	8	24	37	123
1969	26	34	21	26	15	21	122
1967	23	43	21	16	19	19	122
1963	37	36	11	10	22	32	116

ᵃ Excluding Amami-Ōshima.
SOURCE: Calculated from publications of the Ministry of Home Affairs.

rate works out at a flat 1.5 in all seven elections since 1958. In effect, therefore, there has been no change in the competitiveness of election campaigns, at least as measured by the competition rate.

However, a comparison of the difference between those elected with the lowest number of votes and those defeated with the highest number of votes (see Table 4–3) shows that the trend is increasingly for the last seat to be won by a small number of votes. In 1976 the last seat in 41 percent of all electoral districts was decided by a difference of less than 1 percent. In other words, while elections seem to be becoming less competitive if only the competition rate is considered, in fact more electoral districts are becoming competitive, largely because the Kōmeitō and the JCP are contesting more vigorously.

Table 4–4 shows the number of electoral districts in which the parties gained varying percentages of the votes. The LDP ranges from a low of 13 percent (Kanagawa Fifth) to a high of 77.8 percent (Ishikawa Second). Of the ten districts where the LDP won less than 20 percent of the vote, the NLC had cut into its vote in nine and an independent conservative in the tenth. Conservatives, therefore, constituted 20 percent or more of the voters in all districts. In 110 districts, that is, 85 percent of the total of 130, the LDP ranked first in votes, and in forty-nine districts (more than one-third), the LDP took more than half the votes. In other words, although the LDP vote is decreasing election by election, it still remains the strongest party.

TABLE 4–4

ELECTORAL DISTRICTS BY PERCENTAGE OF VOTES WON BY EACH PARTY,
1976 HOUSE OF REPRESENTATIVES ELECTION
(number of districts)

Percent of Votes Won	LDP	JSP	DSP	KMT	JCP	NLC
70–79	3	—	—	—	—	—
60–69	22	—	—	—	—	—
50–59	24	—	—	—	—	—
40–49	31	3	—	—	—	—
30–39	22	9	—	—	—	2
20–29	18	53	10	9	5	11
10–19	10	62	58	29	57	5
0–9	0	2	16	13	65	7
Total	130	129	84	51	127	25
Number of districts in which the party ran no candidates	0	1	46	79	3	105
Number of districts in which the party won the largest number of votes[a]	110	5	1	2	1	10

Dash (—): Not applicable.
[a] One district was topped by an independent.
SOURCE: Calculated from publications of the Ministry of Home Affairs.

The Socialist party ran candidates in 129 districts,[4] but it surpassed the LDP in only eleven. Even in these eleven districts, however,
it ranked first only in five, second in the remainder. Its lowest percentage was 8.3 (Tokyo Eighth), its highest 46.2 (Ibaragi Second). In only
twelve districts did it run higher than 30 percent. The JSP wins no
more than 10–29 percent of votes in 115 districts (nearly 90 percent).
Therefore, although the JSP is the second-ranking party, there are few
districts where it can compete on equal terms with the LDP.

The Kōmeitō and the DSP have never reached 30 percent, the
JCP only in 1972 when it won 30 percent in the Kyōto First District.
In 1976 the smaller opposition parties ranked first in the following
districts: Kōmeitō in Osaka First (24.6 percent); DSP in Aiichi First

[4] All except the one-member Amami-Ōshima Island district.

(26.5 percent) and Aiichi Sixth (22.2 percent); and the JCP in Kyōto First (24.4 percent). Generally, their share is between 10 and 19 percent in most districts. Because the JCP runs in all districts, it wins less than 10 percent of the votes in about half. Therefore, it is difficult to see it reaching the second position. In most districts its main battle is for the third-ranking spot.

The NLC, in its first contest, 1976, ran twenty-five candidates, coming in first in ten districts and winning more than 20 percent of the votes in half of these. Whether this showing will continue into the future cannot be known at this time.

In summary, then, the LDP is still the strongest party in almost every district, the JSP second in most districts, and the Kōmeitō, the DSP, and the JCP compete for the third position.

Voting Rates by Degree of Urbanization

Table 4–5 shows party support in five categories of urbanization for the 1969, 1972, and 1976 general elections. For example, the LDP took 31 percent of the votes in metropolitan districts in 1969, but decreased to 30 percent in 1972 and 26 percent in 1976.[5] The LDP's voting percentage has declined in each category, reflecting its national decline. Nevertheless, the LDP wins the largest number of supporters in all categories.

The JSP vote has not varied much among the different categories in the past three elections. That is, its voting percentage is about the same in all elections. The JSP won more than 20 percent in the intermediate, semirural, and rural districts, and a little less in the metropolitan and urban. But the differences among these five types are very small. Compared with the LDP's 56 percent in rural and 26 percent in metropolitan districts, a difference of 30 points, there are only 4 percentage points between the JSP's 23 percent in semirural areas and its 19 percent in metropolitan areas.

Therefore the JSP can no longer be characterized as a party supported by organized labor in the urban areas, that is, a "class party." It is now beginning to show characteristics of the kind of "national party" that its mainstream professes to oppose. Since the Kōmeitō and JCP are fighting aggressively in the same metropolitan areas, the comtition among the three parties there is likely to become even more intense.

---

[5] The *Asahi Shinbun* classification system yields the same results: 30.2 percent in 1972 and 25.7 percent in 1976.

TABLE 4–5

PERCENTAGE OF TOTAL VOTE, BY PARTY AND DEGREE OF URBANIZATION,
IN 1969, 1972, AND 1976 ELECTIONS, HOUSE OF REPRESENTATIVES
(percent)

Party	Year	Degree of Urbanization					All Constitu-encies
		Metro-politan	Urban	Inter-mediate	Semi-rural	Rural	
LDP	1969	31	47	51	55	61	47.6
	1972	30	49	52	59	61	46.9
	1976	26	45	49	50	56	41.8
JSP	1969	19	18	20	23	21	21.4
	1972	21	20	23	23	20	21.9
	1976	19	18	23	23	21	20.7
KMT	1969	19	12	10	6	3	10.9
	1972	16	8	6	3	4	8.5
	1976	18	11	9	6	3	10.9
JCP	1969	13	5	3	4	4	6.8
	1972	18	10	6	7	4	10.5
	1976	15	11	8	7	6	10.4
DSP	1969	14	11	9	5	2	7.7
	1972	11	9	6	4	1	7.0
	1976	9	7	6	3	1	6.3
Number of constituencies		14	26	36	20	34	130

NOTE: Degree of urbanization is based upon the proportion of the labor force engaged in the primary industrial sector (agriculture, forestry, fishery): metropolitan, 0–9 percent; urban, 10–19 percent; intermediate, 20–29 percent; semirural, 30–39 percent; rural, 40 percent and over (see also Table 1–3).
SOURCE: Calculated from census data and publications of the Ministry of Home Affairs.

The Kōmeitō puts up scarcely any candidates in the rural and semirural districts. Nevertheless, its support trend shows a consistent pattern, which can be represented by a V shape. While it declined in almost all districts in 1972, in 1976 it came back to virtually the same level it had attained in 1969. As Table 4–6 shows, both the Kōmeitō and JCP concentrated on metropolitan, urban, and intermediate areas, and since they are fighting for the same constituencies, the competition is bound to be fierce.

TABLE 4–6

DISTRIBUTION OF PARTY VOTE, BY DEGREE OF URBANIZATION, 1976
HOUSE OF REPRESENTATIVES ELECTION
(percent)

Party	Metro-politan	Urban	Inter-mediate	Semi-rural	Rural	Total Party Vote
LDP	19.6	18.2	32.4	19.8	10.0	100.0
JSP	29.0	14.6	30.6	18.3	7.5	100.0
KMT	51.1	16.9	21.6	8.7	1.7	100.0
JCP	47.2	16.5	21.0	11.3	4.0	100.0
DSP	44.0	19.7	26.7	8.7	0.9	100.0
NLC	62.1	12.8	18.4	3.9	2.8	100.0
National vote	31.7	16.9	27.5	16.6	7.4	100.0

NOTE: Degree of urbanization is same as in Table 4–5.
SOURCE: Calculated from publications of the Ministry of Home Affairs.

When considering the urban characteristics of the electoral districts, it is usual to use categories based upon the proportion of the labor force in primary industry. However, this results in an odd situation in which "rural" voters number only 7.4 percent but metropolitan voters 31.7 percent of the total. This is not a representative distribution. Another index, designed to represent the degree of urbanization by population density, is calculated on the basis of the proportion of people inhabiting what the census calls DIDs, that is, densely inhabited districts in each electoral district.[6] Districts with a high DID ratio are "densely populated" and correspond to metropolitan and urban districts; districts with a low DID ratio are "underpopulated."

Tables 4–7 and 4–8 show party support in the six types of electoral district, divided on the basis of DID ratio. The JSP's vote structure resembles the national vote structure very closely. This means that it does not have particularly strong or particularly weak constituencies but that it draws its votes fairly uniformly from all types of constituencies. It is clear from the same table that the LDP is strong in low-density districts and weak in high-density districts. Both the

[6] The Bureau of Statistics of the Prime Minister's Office defines a densely inhabited district as an area composed of a group of contiguous enumeration districts, each of which has a population density of 4,000 inhabitants or more per square kilometer and whose total population exceeded 5,000 as of October 1, 1970.

TABLE 4–7

DISTRIBUTION OF PARTY VOTE, BY DEGREE OF POPULATION DENSITY,
1976 HOUSE OF REPRESENTATIVES ELECTION
(percent)

Party	High	Mid-High	Inter-mediate	Mid-Low	Low	Total Party Vote
LDP	9.0	8.0	15.3	37.7	29.0	100.0
JSP	11.1	13.1	13.7	39.4	22.7	100.0
KMT	23.4	21.6	15.5	29.9	9.6	100.0
JCP	21.5	18.9	16.7	29.7	13.2	100.0
DSP	19.6	19.0	14.7	36.1	10.6	100.0
NLC	16.3	26.5	17.3	31.0	8.9	100.0
National vote	14.1	13.0	12.8	38.1	21.9	100.0

NOTE: Degree of population density is based on the proportion of densely inhabited districts (DIDs) per electoral constituency (see text, note 6): high, 90–100 percent; mid-high, 70–89 percent; intermediate, 50–69 percent; mid-low, 30–49 percent; low, 0–29 percent.

SOURCE: Calculated from census data and publications of the Ministry of Home Affairs.

TABLE 4–8

PARTY SHARE OF TOTAL VOTE IN EACH CATEGORY OF POPULATION
DENSITY, 1976 HOUSE OF REPRESENTATIVES ELECTION
(percent)

Party	High	Mid-High	Inter-mediate	Mid-Low	Low
LDP	26.7	25.5	35.9	47.0	55.5
JSP	16.3	20.8	22.0	21.3	21.5
KMT	18.1	18.1	13.2	8.6	4.9
JCP	15.8	15.1	13.5	8.1	6.3
DSP	8.7	9.1	7.2	5.9	3.0
NLC	4.8	8.5	5.6	3.4	1.7
Other[a]	9.6	2.9	2.6	5.7	7.1
Total	100.0	100.0	100.0	100.0	100.0

NOTE: The degree of population density is based on the proportion of densely inhabited districts per electoral constituency (see text, note 6, and Table 4–7).

[a] Other parties and independents.

SOURCE: Calculated from census data and publications of the Ministry of Home Affairs.

JCP and the Kōmeitō have their base in the high-density districts with a DID ratio of 90–100 percent, and the NLC was strong in districts with a DID ratio of 70–85 percent.

Japan's rapid industrial growth since the late 1950s has been accompanied by a decline in primary industries and an increase in the secondary and tertiary sectors. But these structural changes did not occur uniformly throughout the country. Between 1960 and 1975 the percentage of primary industries declined in all prefectures, and in most of them the decline was as much as 25 percent. In the same fifteen-year period,[7] the vote-share of the four opposition parties rose in the majority of prefectures, but it fell in seven out of the forty-six.[8] When the primary-industry ratio falls below the 10 percent mark, the share of the four reform parties rises rapidly. Conversely, in 1960 in prefectures where one-third or more of the inhabitants were engaged in primary industries, the reform parties did not do too well. In other words, the greater the decline in the primary sector, the greater the change in voting patterns.

Distribution of Seats by Size of Constituency

As already noted, the House of Representatives is elected through a multimember or "medium" constituency system, in which each district elects between three and five members.[9] The main problem of this type of system is that if a party runs more than one candidate per district, very often its candidates end up fighting each other for the available pool of party votes. Before the conservative unification of 1958, the main competition was among the candidates of the different conservative parties. Today, it is between the candidates of the LDP, including the independents who run without official party endorsement but join the LDP later if they are elected. The term for this internecine competition is *tomo-daore*, or "going down together." On a number of occasions the JSP has run additional candidates in districts where its vote had increased in the preceding election, only to have all of them lose.[10] Today this medium-constituency system is one of the causes of the JSP's difficulty in increasing its votes. And re-

---

[7] Actually, sixteen years, but the census data for 1976, by electoral district, are not available at the time of this writing.

[8] Gumma, Niigata, Ishikawa, Fukui, Nagano, Ehime, and Ōita. Okinawa is excluded because in 1960 it was still under American occupation and thus not able to vote in a national Japanese election.

[9] Except for Amami-Ōshima, as noted in Chapter 1.

[10] See Curtis, Chapter 3 in this volume, for examples.

TABLE 4-9

NUMBER OF SEATS WON PER PARTY, BY SIZE OF CONSTITUENCY, IN FIVE HOUSE OF REPRESENTATIVES ELECTIONS, 1963–1976

Size of Constituency	LDP	JSP	KMT	JCP	DSP	NLC	Other	Total
Number of winners								
Three seats	385	160	27	12	31	7	26	648
Four seats	445	210	43	27	36	5	22	788
Five seats	536	245	86	40	65	5	23	1,000
Total	1,366	615	156	79	132	17	71	2,436
Percent of winners								
Three seats	59.4	24.7	4.2	1.9	4.8	1.0	4.0	100.0
Four seats	56.5	26.6	5.5	3.4	4.6	0.6	2.8	100.0
Five seats	53.6	24.5	8.6	4.0	6.5	0.5	2.3	100.0
All categories	56.1	25.3	6.4	3.2	5.4	0.7	2.9	100.0
Percent of party seats								
Three seats	28.2	26.0	17.3	15.2	23.5	41.2	36.6	26.7[a]
Four seats	32.6	34.2	27.6	34.2	27.3	25.4	31.0	32.3[a]
Five seats	39.2	39.8	55.1	50.6	49.2	25.4	32.4	41.0[a]
Total	100.0	100.0	100.0	100.0	100.0	100.0	100.0	100.0

NOTE: The figures represent the totals for the five elections pooled. Amami-Ōshima is excluded.

[a] Share of each category in total seats won.

cently, in the urbanized districts, it is the opposition parties that have been experiencing the same *tomo-daore* phenomenon—knocking each other out.

Table 4–9 shows the relation between the number of seats in the district and the number of winners by party. In the five elections between 1963 and 1976, there has been a total of 2,436 winners. Over half (56.1 percent) were from the LDP, and about one-quarter (25.3 percent) were from the JSP. The Kōmeitō did not exist in 1963, but it accounts for 156 (6.4 percent), while the DSP won 132 (5.4 percent) and the JCP 79 (3.2 percent). However, in three-member districts the LDP won 59.4 percent of the seats, in four-member districts 56.5 percent, in five-member districts 53.6 percent; the smaller the district, the larger its share of seats. Nevertheless, it took a majority even in five-member districts. The JSP gained 25 percent of the seats in the three- and five-member districts, with a fractionally better showing in the four-member districts. The Kōmeitō and the DSP were more successful in five-member districts than in three- or four-member districts, and the JCP was quite clearly unsuccessful in three-member districts. In its one lower-house election to date, the NLC gained only seventeen seats, so that little can be said about its vote-drawing characteristics.

From a different viewpoint, these statistics reveal that more than one-fourth of the seats come from three-member districts, about one-third from four-member districts, and 41 percent from five-member districts. However, Kōmeitō, JCP, and DSP won about half or more of their seats in five-member districts, while the LDP and the JSP won only 40 percent of theirs in the same districts. It is obvious that the smaller political parties do better in districts with a larger number of seats.[11]

In the 1967 and 1976 elections a reapportionment of seats was effected by dividing some of the urban districts. This indeed reduced the population per seat, but it also reduced the number of seats per constituency in the reapportioned and new districts. For the smaller parties, whose main base is the large cities, the reapportionment turned out to be unfavorable, another demonstration that the small constituencies favor the larger parties.

In the medium-constituency system, a strong party can put forward more than one candidate with some chance of success. Table

---

[11] The same phenomenon may be seen in the upper-house elections as well, despite differences in the size of districts. See Herbert Passin, "The House of Councillors: Promise and Achievement," in Michael K. Blaker, *Japan at the Polls: The House of Councillors Election of 1974* (Washington, D.C.: American Enterprise Institute, 1976).

TABLE 4–10

Seats Won by Size of District, LDP and JSP, in Five House of Representatives Elections, 1963–1976

District Size	Number of Districts Where Party Won:						Total Districts	Total Seats Contested	Seats Won		Average per district
	0 seats	1 seat	2 seats	3 seats	4 seats	5 seats			Number	Percent	
LDP											
Three seats	4	56	139	17	—	—	216	648	385	59.4	1.8
Four seats	2	28	85	81	1	—	197	788	445	56.5	2.3
Five seats	0	22	64	73	38	3	200	1,000	536	53.6	2.7
Total	6	106	288	171	39	3	613	2,436	1,366	56.1	2.2
JSP											
Three seats	60	152	4	0	—	—	216	648	160	24.7	0.7
Four seats	21	142	34	0	0	—	197	788	210	26.8	1.1
Five seats	25	108	64	3	0	0	200	1,000	248	24.6	1.2
Total	106	402	102	3	0	0	613	2,436	618	25.4	1.0

Dash (—): Not applicable.

Note: The figures represent the totals for the five elections pooled. Amami-Ōshima is excluded.

Source: Calculated from publications of the Ministry of Home Affairs.

4–10 shows how the two leading parties have fared in this regard. As for the smaller parties, the JCP has run two candidates in a single district (Kyōto First) only twice, in 1972 and 1976: both were successful in 1972, but in 1976 only one of the two was elected. None of the other small parties has ever put up more than one candidate per district.

In the past five elections, the LDP has had candidates in all districts, yielding a total of 613 electoral districts in which it competed. It failed to gain even a single seat in only six cases: three in 1976 (two four-seat districts and one three-seat district), and three in 1972 (all in three-seat districts). In most of these six districts, successful independent candidates later joined the LDP. On the other hand, the LDP has won all seats in three-seat districts in seventeen contests, once in four-seat districts, and three times in five-seat districts. In most cases, it manages to get two out of three seats in three-seat districts, two to three in four-seat districts, and two to three in five-seat districts.

The JSP has also run candidates in all electoral districts during the past five elections. Of the total of 216 three-seat district contests, the JSP failed to elect a single member in sixty, or twenty-eight percent. In the four-seat contests, it struck out in 11 percent, and in the five-seat contests, in 12.5 percent. The JSP has never taken all the seats in a district, and it has taken over half of them no more than seven times in the last five elections.

On average, the LDP has maintained a success rate of 1.8 seats per three-seat district, 2.3 seats per four-seat district, and 2.7 seats per five-seat district over the past five elections (see Table 4–10).

Table 4–11 shows the relation between the degree of urbanization and the number of seats won for the past three elections. Of the 1,488 members elected during this period, 350 (23.5 percent) were from metropolitan districts, 225 (15.1 percent) from urban areas, 380 (25.6 percent) from intermediate areas, 347 (23.3 percent) from semirural areas, and 186 (12.5 percent) from rural areas. However, only 14.2 percent of the LDP's 808 seats came from the urban districts, less than the average of 23.5 percent for all parties. On the other hand, 15.3 percent of the LDP's seats came from the rural areas, substantially higher than the national average of 12.5 percent. It is clear that the LDP tends to represent rural districts.

The JSP tends to be slightly stronger in the intermediate and semirural districts while the JCP with 71 percent, the Kōmeitō with 53 percent, and the DSP with 43 percent, find their main strength in

TABLE 4–11

DISTRIBUTION OF PARTY SEATS WON, BY DEGREE OF URBANIZATION, IN THE
1969, 1972, AND 1976 HOUSE OF REPRESENTATIVES ELECTIONS
(percent)

Party	Metro-politan	Urban	Inter-mediate	Semi-rural	Rural	Total Percent	Total Seats
LDP	14.2	15.2	27.8	27.5	15.3	100.0	808
JSP	18.7	14.2	30.5	25.1	11.5	100.0	337
KMT	53.4	19.1	15.3	9.9	2.3	100.0	137
JCP	71.0	10.1	7.3	7.3	4.3	100.0	69
DSP	43.0	20.3	22.8	12.7	1.2	100.0	75
NLC	64.7	23.5	5.9	5.9	0.0	100.0	17
All parties	23.5	15.1	25.6	23.3	12.5	100.0	1,443[a]
Total seats (number)	350	225	380	347	186		1,448[a]

NOTE: Degree of urbanization is based upon proportion of labor force in primary industry.

[a] Since independents and minor parties are excluded, this analysis is based upon 1,443 seats; there were, however, 1,488 members elected in all.

SOURCE: Calculated from census data and publications of the Ministry of Home Affairs.

the cities. Consequently, these three parties, for the most part, represent the views of the urban electorate.

Table 4–12 looks at the same data, but from a different angle, to show the proportion of seats elected in each type of constituency by party. In the past three elections, 186 Diet members have come from rural districts, and of this number two-thirds (66.7 percent) were LDP candidates. Although the LDP share goes down in semirural, intermediate, and urban districts, it is still a clear majority in these four types. In the metropolitan districts, where the LDP is relatively weak, it falls to no more than one-third (32.9 percent) but nevertheless still holds a plurality.

The JSP took about 20 percent of the seats in each of the five types of district. It is possible to say that it has a slightly greater strength in intermediate and semirural areas, but the JSP is distinctive in being neither particularly strong nor particularly weak in any type of area; its strength varies little among the five categories.

The other four parties have each taken one or two seats in rural districts during the last three elections, but these should be regarded

TABLE 4–12

PARTY SHARE OF ALL SEATS WON, BY DEGREE OF URBANIZATION, IN THE
1969, 1972, AND 1976 HOUSE OF REPRESENTATIVES ELECTIONS
(percent)

Party	Metro-politan	Urban	Inter-mediate	Semi-rural	Rural	Party Share of Total Percent	Number
LDP	32.9	54.7	59.0	64.0	66.7	54.3	808
JSP	17.7	20.9	26.6	23.9	20.5	22.6	337
KMT	20.0	11.1	5.3	3.8	1.6	9.2	137
JCP	14.0	3.1	1.3	1.4	0.0	5.0	75
DSP	9.7	7.1	4.7	2.9	0.5	4.5	69
NLC	3.1	1.8	0.2	0.0	0.0	1.1	17
Total[a]	97.4	98.7	97.1	96.0	89.3	96.7	1,443
All parties	23.5	15.1	25.6	23.3	12.5	100.0	1,443
Total seats (number)	350	225	380	347	186		1,488

NOTE: Degree of urbanization is based on the proportion of labor force in primary industry.

[a] In these three elections, a total of 1,488 members were elected. For this table, only 1,443 have been analyzed (independents, minor parties, and others have been excluded from tabulation). The percentages therefore do not add up to 100.

SOURCE: Calculated from census data and publications of the Ministry of Home Affairs.

as exceptions. Successful rural candidates from the four smaller parties win on their personal reputations, not because of their party, as in the case of the JCP's Tsukawa Takeichi of the Aomori Second District, a medical doctor who has been reelected three times. The overwhelming majority of small party victories are in metropolitan areas. Nevertheless, it was the LDP that won the largest number of seats in the metropolitan areas, the Kōmeitō taking second place in 1969 and 1976, and the JCP in 1972. The JSP came in third in the cities in 1972 and 1976 and fourth in 1969.

Tables 4–13 and 4–14 show the relation between population density and seats, which parallels that found in Tables 4–11 and 4–12. The LDP is strong in underpopulated districts, while the JSP draws its strength evenly from all types of district. The JCP tends to represent the high-density areas, and this is true of the Kōmeitō as well. The DSP seats mostly represent intermediate types.

TABLE 4–13

DISTRIBUTION OF PARTY SEATS WON, BY DEGREE OF POPULATION DENSITY,
IN THE 1969, 1972, AND 1976 HOUSE OF REPRESENTATIVES ELECTIONS
(percent)

Party	High	Mid-High	Inter-mediate	Mid-Low	Low	Total Seats Percent	Total Seats Number
LDP	7.7	4.7	7.4	41.0	39.2	100.0	808
JSP	7.5	8.5	10.3	42.3	31.4	100.0	337
KMT	29.8	18.3	14.5	26.7	10.7	100.0	137
JCP	44.9	21.7	13.0	10.2	10.2	100.0	75
DSP	22.8	11.3	17.7	35.5	12.7	100.0	69
NLC	23.5	23.5	23.5	23.5	6.0	100.0	17
All parties	12.5	7.9	9.6	38.0	32.0	100.0	1,443[a]
Total seats (number)	186	118	143	565	476		1,448[a]

NOTE: Population density is based on proportion of DIDs (see Table 4–7).

[a] In all, 1,488 seats were elected; this table excludes independents, minor parties, and others and analyzes only 1,443.

SOURCE: Calculated from census data and publications of the Ministry of Home Affairs.

Table 4–14 demonstrates that the LDP share falls sharply as the DID ratio increases. In high DID districts (90 percent or more), the JSP takes fourth place, after the Kōmeitō and the JCP, while in all other districts it gains about one-quarter of the seats. The JCP is strong in the high-density areas, following closely behind the Kōmeitō. The DSP and NLC have less than a 10 percent share in any district type.

Vote Share by Size of Municipality

Table 4–15 indicates the relation between the size of municipality and the distribution of the vote among the parties.[12] For the last four

---

[12] These data are not easy to come by. Although in European countries ballots are counted in the polling place, this is not the case in Japan. In 1972, for example, the ballots from the 48,338 polling places throughout the country were delivered over to 3,527 counting stations. In these, the ballots are mixed together and counted, so that once this has been done it is impossible to estimate the distribution of the vote in each polling place. Generally, the cities, towns, and villages are the smallest units for which detailed data are available. And even these data usually become available only in limited quantities one or two years after the elections, when the local data are delivered to the winning candidate by the House of Representatives Secretariat.

TABLE 4–14

PARTY SHARE OF ALL SEATS WON, BY DEGREE OF POPULATION DENSITY,
IN THE 1969, 1972, AND 1976 HOUSE OF REPRESENTATIVES ELECTIONS
(percent)

Party	High	Mid-High	Inter-mediate	Mid-Low	Low	Party Share of Total Percent	Number
LDP	33.3	32.2	42.0	58.9	66.6	54.3	808
JSP	13.4	23.7	23.8	24.8	21.9	22.6	337
KMT	21.0	20.4	13.3	6.2	2.9	9.2	137
JCP	16.7	12.7	6.3	1.2	1.4	5.0	75
DSP	9.7	7.6	9.8	5.0	2.1	4.5	69
NLC	2.1	3.4	2.8	0.7	0.3	1.1	17
Total[a]	96.2	100.0	98.0	96.8	95.2	96.7	1,443
All parties	12.5	7.9	9.6	38.0	32.0	100.0	1,443
Total seats (number)	186	118	143	565	476		1,488

NOTE: Population density is based on proportion of DIDs (see Table 4–7).

[a] This table excludes independents, minor parties, and others from the 1,488 total seats elected and analyzes only 1,443. Percentages therefore do not add up to 100.

SOURCE: Calculated from census data and publications of the Ministry of Home Affairs.

elections, all municipalities are divided into six categories on the basis of the size of the population under their administrative jurisdiction.[13] In the case of the LDP, it is quite clear that the larger the population, the smaller the vote share. However, in municipalities of under 50,000 population, the LDP still wins a majority. But in the six major cities, it took only one-quarter of the votes in 1976, representing a drop of seven to eight percentage points during the nine years from 1967 to 1976.

In the case of the JSP, size of municipality seems to have little effect on its performance, except that in the six major cities it was about five percentage points below its showing in other areas. The JSP was most successful in towns with a population at the 100,000–200,000 level. But, regardless of population size, its vote share fell drastically between 1967 and 1969, registering a drop of as high as eight points in the second- and third-ranking cities (population over

[13] I use the term "municipality" for the Japanese shichōson, "city, town, and village," which is too cumbersome for constant repetition.

TABLE 4–15

PARTY SHARE OF TOTAL SEATS IN EACH CATEGORY OF MUNICIPALITY, FOR 1967, 1969, 1972, AND 1976 HOUSE OF REPRESENTATIVES ELECTIONS
(percent)

Party	Election Year	Six Major Cities	More than 200,000[a]	100–200,000	50–100,000	Less than 50,000	Towns and Villages
LDP	1967	30	45	46	52	57	58
	1969	31	41	43	49	54	58
	1972	28	40	44	50	54	59
	1976	25	37	37	43	51	53
JSP	1967	25	31	32	29	29	26
	1969	17	23	24	23	32	21
	1972	19	23	25	23	22	21
	1976	16	22	23	22	22	20
KMT	1967	14	7	5	4	2	1
	1969	20	14	11	10	7	7
	1972	17	11	8	7	5	4
	1976	18	13	12	10	7	6
JCP	1967	10	5	4	4	3	3
	1969	15	7	7	6	4	4
	1972	20	13	11	9	7	5
	1976	16	12	11	10	7	7
DSP	1967	15	8	9	6	5	4
	1969	14	9	10	7	6	4
	1972	11	8	8	6	5	4
	1976	10	7	7	6	5	4
NLC	1967	—	—	—	—	—	—
	1969	—	—	—	—	—	—
	1972	—	—	—	—	—	—
	1976	7	4	5	4	2	3

Dash (—): Not applicable.

NOTE: Size of municipality depends on population size of administrative district and official definition of municipal entity. Towns and villages are administrative entities usually, but not always, with less than 10,000 population.

[a] Excludes the six major cities in the preceding column.

SOURCE: Data for 1967 and 1969 from House of Representatives Secretariat; 1972 and 1976 data are based on materials of the local Election Commission or on the local editions of *Mainichi Shinbun*.

100,000, but excluding the six largest cities), and it was unable to recover this ground in either the 1972 or 1976 elections.

As the other analyses have shown, the JSP is characterized by a relatively even diffusion of support, regardless of type of electoral district. It is not weak in rural areas and strong in the cities, as is usually thought. Nevertheless, except in the metropolitan centers, the JSP clearly remains the second-ranking party in the country, even though it wins no more than 20 percent of the vote. In the six major cities it no longer holds second place. In 1969, it fell into third place and has remained there since.

While in most elections the JCP runs candidates in every district, the Kōmeitō, the DSP, and the NLC do not. Therefore comparisons have to be made carefully. All three do best in the large cities, although the DSP share has been tending to drop there. The JCP vote share has gone up in localities with a population of less than 200,000, but reached little more than 10 percent. At the same time, however, it has turned down slightly from its high point in cities over 200,000, and in the six major metropolitan areas its share went down by four points between 1972 and 1976, a full 20 percent. The Kōmeitō recorded its largest proportion of votes in 1969 in all categories, dropped down in 1972, but was unable to recover fully in 1976. While the NLC took around 5 percent of the votes in all localities over 100,000 inhabitants, in smaller localities its share did not exceed 2 percent. One obvious reason is that since the NLC ran very few candidates in the smaller districts, electors who might have favored them had no chance to give them their votes.

The same data may be viewed as the percentage of each party's total vote that is derived from the six municipality sizes, as in Table 4–16, which indicates whether the party's principal base is urban or rural. In the case of the LDP, for example, in the 1967 election 39 percent of its vote came from rural areas, which is more than the 33 percent rural share in the electorate. This phenomenon is not limited to the 1967 election: the same pattern can be seen in every election. The LDP is also strong in the small towns. Its strength, clearly, is in the countryside and the small cities.

However, the structure of the JSP's vote, broken down by population type, comes very close to the structure of the national electorate in every election. This reinforces my view that the JSP does not represent a particular type of constituency, whether rural or metropolitan, but rather that it collects votes in about the same degree from all over the country.

By contrast, the remaining four parties have made the metro-

TABLE 4–16

DISTRIBUTION OF PARTY VOTE, BY SIZE OF MUNICIPALITY, FOR 1967, 1969, 1972, AND 1976 HOUSE OF REPRESENTATIVES ELECTIONS
(percent)

| Election Year and Party | Six Major Cities | Population of Cities | | | | Towns and Vil-lages | Total |
		More than 200,000[a]	100– 200,000	50– 100,000	Less than 50,000		
1967							
National	16.7	16.8	11.2	11.4	10.5	33.4	100.0
LDP	10.2	15.4	10.5	12.1	12.5	39.3	100.0
JSP	15.2	18.5	13.1	11.9	10.8	30.5	100.0
KMT	44.4	22.9	10.0	8.1	3.8	10.8	100.0
JCP	34.8	18.6	10.4	10.5	7.1	18.6	100.0
DSP	32.9	19.1	13.2	9.0	6.9	18.9	100.0
1969							
National	15.4	16.4	12.6	12.2	11.2	32.2	100.0
LDP	9.8	14.0	11.4	12.6	12.8	39.4	100.0
JSP	12.4	17.3	14.4	12.8	11.8	31.3	100.0
KMT	27.6	20.8	12.3	11.5	7.3	20.5	100.0
JCP	33.8	18.1	13.4	10.0	6.9	17.8	100.0
DSP	27.3	19.7	16.2	10.7	8.9	17.2	100.0
1972							
National	15.2	22.9	9.9	11.9	12.0	28.1	100.0
LDP	9.2	19.5	9.4	12.6	13.9	35.4	100.0
JSP	13.2	24.3	11.2	12.5	12.3	26.5	100.0
KMT	29.7	28.9	9.5	10.0	7.6	14.3	100.0
JCP	28.5	27.9	10.3	10.6	8.3	14.4	100.0
DSP	23.5	27.2	11.8	10.3	8.8	18.4	100.0
1976							
National	15.3	22.9	12.1	12.6	9.1	28.0	100.0
LDP	9.2	20.5	10.6	13.0	11.1	35.6	100.0
JSP	11.9	24.6	13.1	13.1	9.7	27.6	100.0
KMT	25.4	27.5	13.4	11.5	5.7	16.5	100.0
JCP	23.3	27.4	13.2	11.9	6.5	17.7	100.0
DSP	25.0	24.8	13.7	11.0	6.9	18.6	100.0
NLC	26.8	23.9	15.2	13.2	3.2	17.7	100.0

NOTE: Size of municipality depends on population size of administrative district and official definition of municipal entity. Towns and villages are administrative entities usually, but not always, with less than 10,000 population.

[a] Excludes the six major cities in the preceding column.

SOURCE: Same as Table 4–15.

politan areas their principal base. In the 1976 election, though the six major cities accounted for 15 percent of the electorate, each of the four smaller parties won over 20 percent of its votes there. Conversely, although rural voters made up 28 percent of the voting population (1976), these same parties won less than 20 percent of their total votes there.

In other words, while the LDP tends strongly to represent the residents of rural and small urban communities, the Kōmeitō, DSP, JCP, and NLC reflect the views of big-city residents. The JSP has no such inclination: it is supported at a uniform rate throughout all types of electoral districts. But it is still the LDP that represents the largest number of people, even in the big cities.

Characteristics of the Parties

The NLC became a minor sensation when it was formed as the result of its public opinion poll showings. But since no other Diet members followed the example of the original six and left the LDP, they found it hard to produce twenty-five candidates for the December 1976 lower-house elections.[14] Of the twenty-five candidates, five had already held seats and were reelected. Four who had tried but failed in previous elections—one four times, another twice, and two once— were elected for the first time. The remaining candidates were standing for the first time, and half of them won election. Of the seventeen successful candidates, fourteen came in at the top of their districts, and three took second place. If the club had been able to find more good candidates, it should have been able to win more seats.

Since the NLC was running for the first time, whose votes did they manage to steal in order to make their showing? Given that voting is by secret ballot and that there is great discrepancy between what people say in response to public opinion polls and how they actually vote when they enter the voting booth, no exact data are available for analyzing individual voting behavior. The change can be observed only macroscopically by comparing the votes won by the NLC with those lost by the other parties.[15]

The most striking example is the NLC leader, Kōno Yōhei. Kōno won 37 percent of the votes in his district, Kanagawa Fifth. These may be presumed to have come from several sources: first, from the 17

[14] If at least twenty-five candidates are not run, a party is treated as a "minor party" by the Central Election Administration Commission and the Ministry of Home Affairs.
[15] For a slightly different analysis, see Blaker, Chapter 2 in this volume.

percent that Kōno himself won as an LDP candidate in 1972; second, from normally LDP voters who this time did not vote for the LDP candidate; and the remainder from the 13 percent the Kōmeitō gave up by not putting up a candidate for reelection.[16] Except for Kōno, the increase in votes for the four other sitting members who formed the nucleus of the club was not very great, and they won primarily on the basis of their own strength in the previous election plus some accretion of support from independent conservatives.

The next four had lost in the previous election (only one of them had stood as an official LDP candidate; the other three had run as independents). All except one garnered more than twice the votes they had in the previous election. It would not be amiss to assume that all of them benefited from the fact that the DSP did not run candidates in their districts this time.

The same may be said of the eight who ran for the first time; their victories owed much to the DSP's not running a candidate in their districts. This does not mean that the DSP and NLC had an electoral agreement. According to opinion polls, however, NLC supporters and DSP supporters resemble each other in their political views. It is as though in a number of districts the DSP and the NLC did not fight each other. Nevertheless, six of the eight new members clearly won most of their support from the votes of the LDP in the previous election. It would therefore seem that most of the NLC voters were conservative. However, since the JCP vote declined in Tokyo, Yokohama, Osaka, and Kyōto, one can conclude that many of the so-called floating votes that formerly went to the JCP this time switched to the NLC.[17]

In any event, while the election was undoubtedly a great success for the NLC, it still remains the sixth-ranking party, and its activities in the Diet will inevitably be restricted. The NLC is likely to find it difficult to capture the floating vote and make large advances next time. Unless the LDP splits or there is a major regrouping on the political scene, the NLC will not be able to become a major political factor, even if it were to retain the casting vote.

As already noted, the DSP was formed in January 1960 by a group of Diet members in their forties who had broken away from

---

[16] These estimates can be only approximate because of the change in districting between 1972 and 1976. In 1972 Kōno ran in the Kanagawa Third District, which had 838,000 votes and returned five seats. In 1976 Kōno ran from the newly districted Kanagawa Fifth, which had only 435,000 votes and returned only three seats.

[17] See the analysis in Passin, Chapter 7 in this volume.

the JSP. But in the election in November that same year, only thirteen of them were reelected. However, these same members won enough votes in the previous election in 1957 so that they should in no sense be described as weak. Nevertheless, the DSP never again reached the forty-seat level it had when it first broke away from the JSP. The main reason was that most of the party's effective candidates won on the basis of their personal popularity rather than because of public support for the party itself. As evidence of this, in the six elections since its formation, the DSP has had successful candidates in fifty-one electoral districts; yet in the 1976 election, it failed to put up candidates in thirteen of these. Despite the fact that in seven of these districts DSP candidates had taken 10 percent or more of the votes in previous elections, it was unable to find suitable successors when the incumbent member had died, become too old, or retired.

The DSP's prospects, therefore, are not bright. Nevertheless, it will continue on its course of gaining a district here and losing one there. Its chances for becoming the first- or second-ranking party are nonexistent. But it might form part of a new governmental coalition or, in the general reorganization going on, it might make a fresh start as part of a new party.

One possibility might be the formation of a middle-of-the-road party centered on the Kōmeitō and the DSP. But at the moment the two parties together hold less than ninety seats, far less than is needed to make them the second-ranking party in the Diet. There are also problems about how much participation would be forthcoming from the conservative wing of the JSP, which would be essential to making a go of it.

The DSP is rather like its Italian namesake, the Social Democratic party (PSDI), in both the character of its political support and its history. But, whereas the PSDI has given its country a president, no such post of honor has ever gone to the DSP.

As already noted, both the Kōmeitō and the JCP are strong in the big cities. The Kōmeitō made a big jump in the 1969 elections, but fell back in 1972 and was overtaken by the JCP; the JCP in its turn suffered a reversal in 1976 (see Table 4–1). This suggests that despite the considerable ideological differences between the two parties, one part of the electorate oscillates between them. However, a look at each of the eighty-four electoral districts where both parties put forward candidates in 1976 indicates that in thirty-three both parties gained, while in thirty-nine the Kōmeitō gained but the JCP declined. This cannot be interpreted to mean that the reversals take place only in the peripheral areas and that in the major urban areas votes merely alternate between the two parties. In the past three elections either the Kōmeitō or the JCP has gained at least one seat in sixty-four electoral districts. The Kōmeitō was dominant in twenty-six, the JCP in seven, and they competed against each other in the remaining thirty-one districts.

While the Kōmeitō certainly bases its strength on the Sōka Gakkai members, many nonmembers must also be voting for it. Why this should be so is not clear. Neither the Sōka Gakkai nor the Kōmeitō is popular. In opinion polls, for example, when people are asked "What party do you dislike?" or "What party would you not support or not vote for?" the Kōmeitō, along with the JCP, stands out strongly. Clearly, some further inquiry is necessary on this question.[18]

The JCP continued to grow at high speed after the election of 1969 and, although in 1976 it won 380,000 more votes than in 1972, the actual percentage declined by 0.1 percent. However, with its total of 5,878,000 votes, the JCP became the second largest communist party in the free world, ranking next to the Italian party's 12 million (in an election held six months prior to the Japanese election), although in percentage of votes polled it was below the French party. In the 1976 election, the JCP's vote percentage declined in thirty-eight out of forty-three high-density districts, but it increased in low-density districts. The party has some way to go, however, before it can recover the seats it lost in the cities or raise its rural support to a level that will bring it Diet seats.

The JCP leadership no doubt has given thought to the success of the Italian Communist party as compared with the failure of the German party during the Weimar Republic. Formally the party hopes to participate in a coalition government made up of opposition parties. But it probably realizes that this would be difficult unless it reaches the level of fifty to seventy seats and therefore thinks in terms of cooperation with such a government from a position outside the cabinet. Its faltering performance in the 1976 election comes all the more as a shock in view of the fact that the party had deliberately tried to behave inoffensively and to present an image of sweet reasonableness and moderation in order not to frighten off independent voters. This should teach the new parties now springing up on all sides that capturing the floating vote is no simple matter.

In 1976 the JSP dropped off 1.2 percentage points below its 1972 showing, about the same 21 percent it won in 1969. The JSP draws relatively evenly from all over the country, but when it makes a

---

[18] On this point, see Curtis, Chapter 3, note 25, in this volume.

serious effort to grow, the medium-constituency system creates problems for it. In a district where the JSP has enough votes to win more than one seat, but not enough for two, running two candidates often makes both lose. If, say, 100 votes are needed to elect one member, and the party in fact has the support of 150 voters, putting up two candidates means they may divide the pool and end up with only 75 votes apiece; both therefore lose. This is an underlying factor in the party's poor electoral showing. In addition, the Kōmeitō and the JCP have been taking away the votes of dissatisfied JSP supporters. And as more and more of its candidates come from the trade unions, the party becomes increasingly rigid.[19]

These trends are likely to continue for the time being. Therefore, so long as the LDP does not split up, there is not much likelihood of the JSP's becoming the largest party. Even if the LDP were to break up—unless this split is close to 50-50, and not 60-40 or 70-30, as such things usually go—the JSP would still be unlikely to become the leading party. But if the LDP were to lose its Diet majority, despite the accretion of votes from the successful independent conservatives who usually join the party after the election, then the JSP would have a chance to form a government in coalition with other opposition parties. This would not mean that the JSP itself would be any stronger but only that the parties to the left and right of it would have become strong enough to create a situation that might put a JSP prime minister into office. Even were such a coalition established, there is not much likelihood that it would be strong.

No matter how the situation is analyzed, the LDP appears to be on the wane. The emergence of a second conservative party, the NLC, in 1976 seems significant. While the NLC is still small and in its present form does not present much of a threat to the LDP, it represents an appeal to the conscience of the conservative party and to its supporters. By disrupting the party, it may very well stimulate a realignment and reorganization of the conservative forces.

A Comparison with the Political Parties of Europe

To further clarify the position of the political parties in Japan, their election results may be compared with those of political parties in Germany, France, Great Britain, and Italy. Table 4–17 shows the vote distribution for recent elections in Japan and four European countries. The Japanese LDP (1976) received about the same popular support as

---

[19] See Curtis, Chapter 3 in this volume, including Tables 3–3 and 3–4.

TABLE 4-17

VOTE AND SEAT SHARES OF MAIN PARTIES IN JAPAN AND EUROPE, 1976

(percent)

Japan

Rank Order of Party	Party	Votes	Seats
1	LDP	41.8	48.7
2	JSP	20.7	24.1
3	KMT	10.9	10.8
4	JCP	10.4	3.3
5	DSP	6.3	5.7
6	NLC	4.2	3.3

West Germany

Rank Order of Party	Party	Votes	Seats
1	Christian Democratic Union Christian Social Union (CDU/CSU)	48.6	49.0
2	Socialist party (SPD)	42.6	43.1
3	Free Democratic party (FDP)	7.9	7.9

England

Rank Order of Party	Party	Votes	Seats
1	Labour	39.3	50.2
2	Conservative	35.8	43.6
3	Liberal	18.3	4.1

Italy

Rank Order of Party	Party	Votes	Seats
1	Christian Democratic party (DC)	38.7	41.6
2	Communist party (PCI)	34.4	36.2
3	Socialist party (PSI)	9.6	9.0
4	Italian Social Movement	6.1	5.0
5	Social Democratic party (PSDI)	3.4	2.4
6	Republican party (PRI)	3.1	2.2

France

Rank Order of Party	Party	Votes	Seats[a]
1	Union of Democrats for the Republic (UDR)	23.9	36.6
2	Communist party (PCF)	21.6	15.4
3	Socialist party (PS)	19.2	21.6
4	Social Reform Movement (MRS)	12.1	5.9
5	Independent Republicans (RI)	7.0	11.4
6	Democratic Center (CD)	3.7	6.8

[a] Note that the rank order of the French parties is different in terms of seats from their order in terms of votes: PS is second, PCF third, RI fourth, and MRS fifth.

SOURCE: Calculated from various publications of the individual governments.

the German Christian Democratic Union and Christian Social Union (CDU/CSU) in 1976, and its popularity compares favorably with that of the leading European parties. The German CDU/CSU and Socialist party (SPD), the British Labour and Conservative parties, the Italian Christian Democratic (DC) and Communist (PCI) parties, and the Japanese LDP are all leading parties that receive between one-third and one-half of their nation's votes. Second-place parties, with support at about the 20 percent level of the electorate, are the three French parties—the Union of Democrats for the Republic (UDR), Communist (PCF), and Socialist (PS) parties—the Liberal party of England, and the Japanese JSP. In other words, among socialist parties, the SPD of Germany and the Labour party of Great Britain are both top-ranking parties, while the Socialist parties of Japan and France are in second place. The Italian Socialist party is a third-place party, with about 10 percent of the vote. Other third-place parties in the 10 percent class are the German Free Democratic party (FDP), the Italian Socialist party (PSI), and the Japanese Kōmeitō and JCP. Among communist parties, the Italian is first rank, the French second, and the Japanese third. Parties in the fourth rank, that is, with less than 10 percent of the vote, include the DSP of Japan, the Social Democratic party (PSDI) of Italy, the Independent Republicans of France, and the right-wing Italian party, Italian Social Movement (MSI), all of which are at the 5 percent level.

Table 4–17 shows the seat share of each of the parties at the time of the last election. The LDP along with the British Labour party and the German CDU/CSU took about 50 percent of the seats. If parties holding from one-third to one-half of the seats are also considered in the top rank, the British Conservative party, the SPD, DC, UDR, and PCI would be included. The Japanese LDP has a far greater number of seats in relation to its second party than do the ruling parties in any of the other four countries, and for this reason it should have greater stability. The Socialist party of Japan, like that of France, holds a little over 20 percent of the seats and is in the second rank.

The Kōmeitō strength is similar to that of Germany's FDP, and therefore it is not unrealistic for it to think in terms of an influential role in the establishment of a coalition government. As for the JCP, its share of seats is of a very different order from that of its Italian and French counterparts.

In other words, while the LDP continues to weaken, it remains relatively strong compared with the leading Western European parties. Or, to put it another way, it has the same problems as the other lead-

111

ing parties. Furthermore, in England and Germany the second-ranking parties are right on their tails in number of seats. In fact, in Germany, it is the third-ranking party that has the deciding vote on what the governing coalition will be. In countries with a multiparty system, the ruling parties are not socialist, as is the case in England and Germany, but conservative. In France and Italy the UDR and the DC have wielded power for a long time and, rather like the Liberal Democratic party of Japan, their ebbing is a slow process. The three conservative ruling parties are also similar in having members whose views range widely from the right to the left.

In degree of multipolarization of parties, Japan resembles Italy rather than France, although the difference in size between the first and second parties is much larger in the case of Japan, and the LDP still has considerable potential for wielding power. But the travails of the LDP come not so much from outside, from the rising threat of the other political parties, as from its own internal problems.

PART TWO
The 1977 House of Councillors Election

5

The House of Councillors

Herbert Passin

Hardly had the dust settled on the lower-house elections when Japan started moving into gear for the upper-house, or House of Councillors, election, scheduled for July 1977, a bare seven months later.

A Note on the Upper House

The House of Councillors is modeled to some extent, but not entirely, on the U.S. Senate.[1] (The House of Representatives is essentially similar to the U.S. House of Representatives.) The councillors have a six-year term, and half the members are elected every three years. This stands in marked contrast to the representatives, who have a maximum of four years but in practice an average of two and one-third years since the end of World War II. In 1976 there was an exception to this average when the Diet ran to full term because intra-LDP factional maneuvering made it impossible to settle on an earlier dissolution date. The timing of lower-house elections cannot be predicted, because it depends on the political situation and the balance of power—not only among parties, but among LDP factions—at any given time. But the timing of the upper-house elections is definite: midsummer, every third year. Since the establishment of the House of Councillors in 1947, there have been eleven triennial elections.

Although it is customary to refer to the Councillors as the "upper house," it is, in fact, constitutionally inferior in its powers. The House of Representatives holds the decisive controls—budget, treaty ratification, election of the prime minister—and therewith the power. An

---

[1] For a detailed account, see Herbert Passin, "The House of Councillors: Promise and Achievement," in Michael K. Blaker, ed., *Japan at the Polls: The House of Councillors Election of 1974* (Washington, D.C.: American Enterprise Institute, 1976).

ambitious politician runs for the lower house, not the upper. If a councillor develops serious political intentions, he will stand for a lower-house seat at the earliest opportunity.

The House of Councillors was intended originally to provide a different kind of representation from that of the lower house. It was expected to be broader in outlook, more national in its assessment of problems, less tied to narrow local constituencies and interests, more independent of parties, in effect, somewhat above the daily clash of petty politics. Whether this happy condition can ever be said to have prevailed, by 1955 it was clearly on the way out. Independent members declined from a high of 111, or 44 percent of all seats, to a mere handful. Today the councillors are as politicized as the representatives despite occasional brave attempts to maintain some of the trappings of independence, and the composition of the upper house is a close duplicate of the lower house.

The principal feature that requires attention is the constituency system, which for the House of Councillors is made up of two types: local and national. The local constituencies are prefecturewide, and they elect between one and four members each (see Table 5–1). They are essentially similar to the lower-house constituencies, except that

TABLE 5–1

DEGREE OF REPRESENTATIVENESS, BY SIZE OF CONSTITUENCY, 1977 HOUSE OF COUNCILLORS ELECTION

Constituency	Number of Constitu- encies	Number of Seats Elected[a]	Percent of Seats Elected	Percent of Qualified Voters	Percent of Votes Cast
Local					
One seat	26	26	34.2	27.7	29.1
Two seats	15	30	39.5	36.1	36.3
Three seats	4	12	15.8	20.9	19.7
Four seats	2	8	10.5	15.3	14.9
Subtotal, local	47	76	100.0	100.0	100.0
National	1	50	—	100.0	100.0

[a] This is the number elected in each triennium; the total number of members is double in every category.

SOURCE: Nisihira Sigeki, ed., *Naigai Senkyo Data—Mainichi Nenkan Bessatsu* (Tokyo: Mainichi Shinbunsha, 1978), pp. 10–14.

they are larger in size and fewer in number (47 to the Representatives' 130). They elect 152 members in all, or 76 in each triennial election.

The national constituency, however, is unique. Each triennium fifty members are elected at large (there are a hundred national seats in all). Each voter casts one vote for his national choice, and the top fifty win. The national constituency election is, in effect, a kind of national popularity contest, and winning requires a fundamentally different strategy and organization from winning in the local constituencies. There are therefore two upper-house elections, and the voter casts two ballots, one for his local choice and one for his national choice.

The Political Environment

After the 1976 lower-house election had ended inconclusively, the question remained: Would the LDP hold its bare majority or would it lose it? Would the apparent trend toward a reversal of power be strengthened or stemmed? The public was waiting for the other shoe to drop.

Apart from this, no major issue surfaced. The international issues confronting the country were such that they tended to unify the parties against the outside world rather than divide them. Japan was still recovering from the battering it had taken from the Soviets over the North Pacific fisheries. During the hundred days of tense negotiations in the spring, bitterness mounted over the tough and uncompromising Soviet position on the 200-mile fishing zone, fishing quotas, and the northern territories. This was compounded by the Soviet habit of increasing or decreasing the arrest of Japanese fishing vessels to underline their arguments. All parties, including the Socialists, and even the Communists—if somewhat reluctantly—supported the national position against the Soviets; to do otherwise would have seriously harmed their election prospects. In the same way, the North Korean declaration of its 200-mile fishing zone, the disturbing rise of the yen in world markets against the dollar, and the stalling of the treaty negotiations with China over the "hegemony" clause, found the parties in agreement, even if tacit, on international issues.

U.S.-Japan relations were, on the whole, on a reasonably even keel, although problems were by no means absent. The United States had also declared its 200-mile fishing zone, but it was much friendlier about quotas than were the Soviets. The principal issue, other than the trade imbalance, was the conflict over the reprocessing of nuclear materials. Although the issue was temporarily resolved by a two-year agreement permitting reprocessing to continue in Japan, the negotiations left the Japanese public with an increasingly somber view of its international position.

Nor did domestic issues lend themselves to clear-cut disagreements. The continuing stagflation, the lagging recovery from recession, the unemployment (even if small by the standards of the other advanced industrial nations), and the lingering underemployment that many people feared might threaten the lifetime employment system were serious problems, to be sure, and the parties approached them with slightly different nuances—advocating more or less investment in public works, more or less taxation relief, more or less social security, more or less public bond financing. But the differences were neither significant enough nor dramatic enough to play an important role in the elections. And with regard to foreign, principally U.S., pressure for increased import liberalization and export restraint, all parties were in essential agreement on resisting them.

The campaign was not without issues, but those that surfaced were not the main problems facing the nation. Lockheed lingered on, but did not stir the excitement it did during the lower-house elections. Was the NLC showing in the lower-house elections only a flash in the pan or a portent of things to come? Would the NLC simply take votes away from the LDP, or would it compete with the opposition parties for the protest vote, the undecided, and the nonpoliticals? What would happen to the tiny splinter groups appearing on all sides: the Socialist Citizens League, the Progressive Freedom League, the Women's party (there was even an Ainu Liberation League[2])?

The Elections

On election day, only 68.5 percent of the voters turned up at the polling booths, which means that 31.5 percent did not vote. This represents a decline from the 73.5 percent who voted the previous December in the lower-house elections and a decline from the relatively high level of the preceding upper-house election of three years before, when 73.2 percent of the electorate voted. But the turnout was about average for all upper-house elections. In general, the rural areas, as usual, produced higher voting rates than the urban. The

---

[2] The Ainu are a small group of indigenous inhabitants of the Japanese archipelago, rather like the American Indians. Today they number about 17,000, almost all living on the northernmost of the main islands, Hokkaidō.

range was from a high of 85.2 percent in rural Shimane prefecture to a low of 60.7 percent in urban Kanagawa prefecture (the capital city is Yokohama). More women than men voted. Not only are there more women than men voters—51.1 percent to 47.9 percent—but their voting rate has been consistently higher since 1968, when the female voting rate overtook the male for the first time.

The voters had to choose 76 of the 218 candidates for local-constituency seats, a slight drop from the 237 candidates in the preceding triennium, and 50 of the 102 candidates for the national seats as against 112 previously.

The elections held virtually no surprises (see Table 5–2). The results were essentially the same as three years earlier, and they did little more than confirm the trend already visible in the previous upper-house election, and then again seven months earlier in the December lower-house election (see Table 1–3). The LDP's slow decline continued, although the party managed to hold on, even if by the finger-nails, to its seat share. The major surprise was the weakening of the JCP and the failure of the NLC to live up to the promise of its lower-house performance.

The LDP did relatively better, as it usually does, in the local districts than in the national constituency, taking 59.3 percent of the seats at stake in the local and only 36.0 percent in the national. Since its local vote share was only 39.5 percent, the seat share was over-represented by twenty percentage points, or 50 percent; its national seat share, however, was just about the same as its vote percentage.

The NLC did reasonably well in votes, comparing favorably with its lower-house showing. In seats, however, its showing was disappointing—only one in the national and two in the local constituency; its total of five seats[3] constitutes 2.0 percent of the Councillors as against its seventeen seats, or 3.3 percent in the lower house.

The JSP dropped eleven seats in local constituencies and one in the national constituency compared with the election six years earlier, suffering a decline in its popular vote share. In 1971 the JSP had won eight rural district seats with the help of the KMT and DSP, but in 1977 the KMT and DSP withdrew their support of these eight JSP candidates and all were defeated. Compared with the 1974 upper-house election the JSP decline was not significant, but since upper-house Dietmen serve six-year terms, the crucial comparison is with the 1971 election results. From that point of view the JSP defeat was little short of disastrous. As a result, both party chairman Narita

---

[3] Counting one holdover and one independent who joined the NLC after the election.

TABLE 5-2

PARTY PERFORMANCE, HOUSE OF COUNCILLORS ELECTIONS, 1971–1977

		1971			1974			1977		
		Percent of vote	Seats won Number	Percent	Percent of vote	Seats won Number	Percent	Percent of vote	Seats won Number	Percent
LDP	National	44.5	21	42.0	44.3	17	34.6	35.8	18	36.0
	Local	44.0	42	55.3	39.5	43	56.5	39.5	45	59.3
JSP	National	21.3	11	22.0	15.2	10	20.0	17.4	10	20.0
	Local	31.0	28	36.9	26.0	18	23.7	25.9	17	22.4
KMT	National	14.1	8	16.0	12.1	9	18.0	14.2	9	18.0
	Local	3.4	2	2.6	12.6	5	6.2	6.2	5	6.6
JCP	National	8.0	5	10.0	9.4	6	12.0	8.4	3	6.0
	Local	12.0	1	1.3	12.0	5	6.7	9.9	2	2.6
DSP	National	6.1	4	8.0	5.9	4	8.0	6.7	4	8.0
	Local	4.7	2	2.6	4.4	1	1.3	4.5	2	2.6
NLC	National	—	—	—	—	—	—	3.9	1	2.0
	Local	—	—	—	—	—	—	5.7	2	2.6
SCL	National	—	—	—	—	—	—	2.8	1	(2.0)
	Local	—	—	—	—	—	—	1.2	0	(0)
PFL	National	—	—	—	—	—	—	2.7	1	(2.0)
	Local	—	—	—	—	—	—	0.9	0	(0)
Other	National	0.1	0	0	0.1	0	0	0.7	0	(0)
	Local	0.6	0	0	0.6	1	1.3	1.4	1	(2.0)
Independents	National	5.9	1	2.0	13.0	4	8.0	7.4	3	(6.0)
	Local	4.3	1	1.3	4.9	3	3.9	4.8	2	(2.6)

Dash (—): Not applicable.
SOURCE: Calculated from Nisihira, ed., *Naigai Senkyo Data.*

and secretary-general Ishibashi resigned in December 1977. Asukata Ichiō, then mayor of Yokohama, was elected chairman.

The Kōmeitō claimed a modest victory, as it won fourteen seats (nine in the national constituency, five in local districts) compared with ten in 1971. But the party's share of the national constituency vote was virtually the same as 1971 (14.2 percent in 1977; 14.1 percent in 1971), and it won the same number of seats as in 1974. The swings in the party's vote in the local constituencies—3.4 percent in 1971, to 12.6 percent in 1974, to 6.2 percent in 1977—reflect changing party endorsement strategy rather than swings in popular support. In 1971 the KMT ran just two candidates in the local constituencies; in 1974 it put forward thirty-six candidates; and in 1977 it endorsed only six candidates. Consequently, the party's performance in the national constituency is a more meaningful index of its national strength. In the districts it contested, however, it did as well as it did in the national constituency (see Table 5–3).

TABLE 5–3

PARTY SHARE OF NATIONAL VOTE AND OF VOTE IN CONTESTED DISTRICTS, 1974 AND 1977 HOUSE OF COUNCILLORS ELECTIONS, LOCAL CONSTITUENCIES
(percent)

| | 1977 | | 1974 | |
	Contested districts[a]	National vote[b]	Contested districts[a]	National vote[b]
LDP	42.7	39.5	39.5	39.5
JSP	26.1	25.9	26.4	26.0
KMT	17.9	6.2	11.8	12.6
JCP	10.2	9.9	12.8	12.0
DSP	14.2	4.5	11.8	4.4
NCL	14.5	5.7	—	—
SCL	3.9	1.2	—	—
PFL	3.7	0.9	—	—
WP	0.4	0.4	—	—

Dash (—): Not applicable.
[a] Since these figures are party shares in *contested* districts only, they do not add up to 100 percent. Other parties and independents are excluded.
[b] The share of the total national vote includes both contested and uncontested districts.
SOURCE: Calculated from Nisihira, ed., *Naigai Senkyo Data*.

The Communist party's percentage of the 1977 national constituency vote was the same as in 1971 (8.4 percent in 1977; 8.0 percent in 1971) but it was lower than in 1974 (9.4 percent) and, more important, it was insufficient to elect as many candidates as were successful in 1971. Only three of seven JCP candidates were elected in the national constituency in 1977 compared with five in 1971. Six candidates had been elected in 1974.

The DSP performance was almost exactly the same as in the 1971 election both in its percentage of the vote and the number of candidates elected.

Together, these four opposition parties lost nine seats from 1971, and their combined vote declined from 49.5 to 46.6 percent. The upper-house election, in short, presented the same pattern of intraparty competition and failure to benefit at the expense of the LDP as did the preceding election.

The parties did not all contest every district. The LDP, the JSP, and the JCP ran candidates in almost all, but not so the others. The KMT, for example, contested only six districts, the DSP seven, and the NLC nine. In the districts actually contested, all the parties did better than their national performance. The smaller parties had chosen districts more favorable to themselves in which to run (Tables 5–3). While the LDP and the JSP continue to rank first and second in local constituencies, as they do nationally, the KMT comes third in the districts it contested, and both the DSP and the NLC outperform the JCP in contested districts.[4]

As usual, the LDP took the lion's share of seats in the single-member constituencies, which are heavily rural, just as it did in 1974 (see Table 5–4). The two-member districts were split between the LDP and the JSP, although the LDP increased its lead slightly. The three-member districts came out about the same as before, and the LDP improved its position slightly in the four-member districts. The reason is that in 1974 the right-wing groups within the LDP, the Seirankai, had run a candidate in one of the two four-member districts, Hokkaidō, as an independent, taking just enough votes away from the LDP to defeat both its candidates. This time, the Seirankai did not run separately, and the LDP took two seats. It is clear that the present system gives the LDP inordinate advantages in the one- and two-member districts (see Tables 5–4 and 5–5). The JSP has a serious disadvantage in the one-member seats, taking only two seats, or 7.7 per-

---

[4] In the eleven districts where the JCP had reasonable chances, however, its vote share rises to about the same level as the DSP and NLC, but it does not reach the KMT level.

TABLE 5–4 *

WINNING SEATS, BY PARTY AND SIZE OF CONSTITUENCY, 1974 AND 1977
HOUSE OF COUNCILLORS ELECTIONS, LOCAL CONSTITUENCIES
(number)

Party	Year	Total Seats	One-Member	Two-Member	Three-Member	Four-Member
LDP	1977	45	23	15	4	3
	1974	43	24	14	4	1
JSP	1977	17	2	11	2	2
	1974	18	0	13	2	3
KMT	1977	5	0	0	4	1
	1974	5	0	0	3	2
JCP	1977	2	0	1	1	0
	1974	5	0	1	2	2
DSP	1977	2	0	0	1	1
	1974	1	0	0	1	0
NLC	1977	2	0	1	0	1
SCL	1977	0	0	0	0	0
PFL	1977	0	0	0	0	0
Other	1977	1	1	0	0	0
	1974	1	0	1	0	0
Independ-	1977	2	0	2	0	0
ents	1974	3	2	1	0	0
Total		76	26	30	12	8

SOURCE: Calculated from Nisihira, ed., *Naigai Senkyo Data.*

cent of the total, with 36.2 percent of the votes; in the larger districts, however, the JSP consistently takes a larger share of the seats than its vote share. In terms of purely proportional representation, the smaller parties do better in the larger districts.

The LDP remains essentially a rural-based party, drawing the majority of its seats and the largest part of its votes from the rural areas (see Tables 5–6 to 5–9). But so does the JSP. It is, if anything, even more strongly dependent on the rural areas for votes than is the LDP (47.2 to 42.2 percent). But the LDP takes the majority of rural votes and seats (Table 5–9). The other parties depend primarily on the metropolitan and urban areas for their support, and even though the JCP won 34.9 percent of its vote in rural areas (Table 5–7), these are not effective votes. As in the lower-house election, the votes that bring seats for the smaller opposition parties, including the communists, come from the cities.

TABLE 5–5

DEGREE OF REPRESENTATIVENESS, BY PARTY AND SIZE OF CONSTITUENCY, 1977 HOUSE OF COUNCILLORS ELECTION, LOCAL CONSTITUENCIES

Party	One-Member			Two-Member			Three-Member			Four-Member		
	Percent of vote	Seats Number	Seats Percent	Percent of vote	Seats Number	Seats Percent	Percent of vote	Seats Number	Seats Percent	Percent of vote	Seats Number	Seats Percent
LDP	49.7	23	88.5	41.3	15	50.0	30.0	4	33.3	29.7	3	37.5
JSP	36.2	2	7.7	28.1	11	36.7	14.3	2	16.7	16.7	2	25.0
KMT	0.0	0	0.0	0.0	0	0.0	20.0	4	33.3	15.1	1	12.5
JCP	7.3	0	0.0	9.5	1	3.3	12.9	1	3.3	10.3	0	0.0
DSP	0.0	0	0.0	3.2	0	0.0	10.7	1	3.4	8.2	1	12.5
NLC	2.8	0	0.0	2.3	1	3.3	10.0	0	0.0	11.6	1	12.5
SCL	0.3	0	0.0	1.5	0	0.0	0.9	0	0.0	2.6	0	0.0
PFL	0.0	0	0.0	0.5	0	0.0	0.4	0	0.0	4.3	0	0.0
Other	3.7	1	3.8	0.5	0	0.0	0.5	0	0.0	0.8	0	0.0
Independents	0.0	0	0.0	13.0	2	6.7	0.3	0	0.0	0.7	0	0.0
Total	100.0	26	100.0	100.0	30	100.0	100.0	12	100.0	100.0	8	100.0
Share of electorate[a]	27.7			36.1			20.9			15.3			10.5

[a] All qualified voters, not merely those who actually cast a ballot. See Table 5–1.

SOURCE: Calculated from Nisihira, ed., *Naigai Senkyo Data.*

TABLE 5-6

Winning Seats, by Party and Degree of Urbanization, 1974 and 1977, House of Councillors Elections, Local Constituencies

(number)

Party	Total		Metropolitan		Urban		Intermediate		Semirural		Rural	
	1977	1974	1977	1974	1977	1974	1977	1974	1977	1974	1977	1974
LDP	45	43	4	5	7	5	11	10	9	11	14	12
JSP	17	18	2	2	5	7	1	1	4	4	5	4
KMT	5	5	3	3	2	2	0	0	0	0	0	0
JCP	2	5	2	4	0	1	0	0	0	0	0	0
DSP	2	1	1	0	1	1	0	0	0	0	0	0
NCL	2	—	1	—	1	—	0	0	0	0	0	0
Others	1	1	0	0	0	0	0	0	1	0	0	1
Independents	2	3	1	0	0	0	0	1	1	0	1	2
Total	76	76	14	14	16	16	12	12	15	15	19	19

Dash (—): Not applicable.

NOTE: For definition of degree of urbanization, see Table 1–3.

SOURCE: Calculated from Nisihira, ed., *Naigai Senkyo Data.*

TABLE 5–7

Percentage of Party Votes (1977) and Seats Won (1977, 1974), by Degree of Urbanization, House of Councillors Elections, Local Constituencies

Party		Metropolitan 1977	Metropolitan 1974	Urban 1977	Urban 1974	Intermediate 1977	Intermediate 1974	Semi-rural 1977	Semi-rural 1974	Rural 1977	Rural 1974	Total
LDP	Votes	14.5		22.5		20.7		18.8		23.4		100.0
	Seats	8.9	9.3	15.6	11.6	24.4	25.6	20.0	20.9	31.1	32.6	100.0
JSP	Votes	14.6		20.1		17.1		21.4		25.8		100.0
	Seats	11.8	11.1	29.4	38.9	5.9	5.6	23.5	22.2	29.4	22.2	100.0
KMT	Votes	63.0		37.0		0.0		0.0		0.0		100.0
	Seats	60.0	60.0	40.0	40.0	0.0	—	0.0	—	0.0	—	100.0
JCP	Votes	15.3		34.1		15.7		14.8		20.1		100.0
	Seats	0.0	80.0	0.0	20.0	0.0	—	0.0	—	0.0	—	100.0
DSP	Votes	41.4		50.1		0.0		0.0		8.5		100.0
	Seats	50.0	0.0	50.0	100.0	0.0	—	0.0	—	0.0	—	100.0
NLC	Votes	26.3		46.1		8.9		9.2		9.5		100.0
	Seats	50.0	—	50.0	—	0.0	—	0.0	—	0.0	—	100.0

						Total
SCL Votes	54.9	37.9	4.6	0.0	2.6	100.0
Seats	0.0	0.0	0.0	0.0	0.0	—
PFL Votes	72.7	27.3	0.0	0.0	0.0	100.0
Seats	0.0	0.0	0.0	0.0	0.0	—
Other Votes	21.3	2.8	32.3	43.6	0.0	100.0
Seats	0.0	0.0	33.3	66.7	0.0	100.0
Independents Votes	68.8	7.7	7.7	11.0	4.8	100.0
Seats	50.0	0.0	0.0	50.0	0.0	100.0
Share of electorate[a]	29.9	24.1	14.6	14.6	16.8	100.0

Dash (—): Not applicable.

NOTE: For definition of degree of urbanization, see Table 1–3.

[a] All qualified voters, not merely those who actually cast a ballot.

SOURCE: Calculated from Nisihira, ed., *Naigai Senkyo Data*.

This analysis is reconfirmed by Table 5–10. The nine largest prefectures cast 47.3 percent of the national vote. The NLC, JCP, and KMT won a disproportionately large share of their votes in these heavily urban areas; the LDP won a disproportionately small percentage; and the JSP and DSP shares were roughly proportionate.

No significant changes presented themselves with regard to the candidates. Although there were slightly fewer candidates than previously, as was the case in the lower-house election, no particular pattern was evident. Incumbents did somewhat better than the preceding time, but such a fluctuation is normal. New candidates did not do as well in the upper-house election as they did in the lower-house election (see Tables 5–11 and 5–12), but it would be a mistake to read too much into this because different kinds of electoral districts require different strategies.

While, on the whole, the established parties nominated much the same kinds of candidate as always—bureaucrats, politicians, businessmen, and trade unionists—this time, the so-called *tarento* (literally, "talents"), or media celebrities, did not do as well as usual. Although the top national winner was Socialist Den Hideo, a former TV news-

---

TABLE 5–8

PARTY SHARE OF VOTES WON, BY DEGREE OF URBANIZATION, AND OF SEATS, HOUSE OF COUNCILLORS 1977 ELECTION, NATIONAL CONSTITUENCY
(percent)

Party	Metropolitan	Urban	Intermediate	Semirural	Rural	Total	Share of Seats
LDP	24.5	36.3	42.2	43.9	40.6	35.8	36.0
JSP	14.8	17.6	17.1	20.6	18.9	17.4	20.0
KMT	16.5	14.6	14.3	12.5	11.2	14.2	18.0
JCP	11.5	8.3	7.2	4.7	7.7	8.4	6.0
DSP	7.1	6.5	6.5	6.2	6.8	6.7	8.0
NCL	5.9	3.9	2.6	2.0	3.4	3.9	2.0
Other	9.7	5.5	4.5	5.4	4.1	6.2	4.0
Independents	10.0	7.3	5.6	4.7	7.3	7.4	6.0
Total	100.0	100.0	100.0	100.0	100.0	100.0	100.0
National	29.9	24.1	14.6	14.6	16.8	100.0	100.0

NOTE: For definition of degree of urbanization, see Table 1–3.
SOURCE: Calculated from Nisihira, ed., *Naigai Senkyo Data*.

caster, this was his second term, and he had already established himself as a serious political figure, not simply as a tarento. Three other tarento won at the same time, including the redoubtable vaudevillian Yokoyama Nokku (Knock), who came in thirty-sixth on the national list, the PFL's sole winner. But the glamour had worn off them this time, and many voters seemed to feel that Japan's international problems were too serious to allow frivolous and politically inexperienced Dietmen. It is probably too early to proclaim the final demise of the tarento candidate as a permanent feature of Japan's upper-house elections, but they are not likely to continue getting by solely on the basis of their well-known faces and media popularity, as they did in the past. Women candidates did about as well (or as badly) as before, five elected in the national constituency and three in the local, for a total of eight in all—exactly the same number as previously (see Table 5–13).

Among local constituencies there was, on a nationwide basis, an average of 1,030,549 qualified voters per elected councillor (if only those who actually cast a ballot are counted, the ratio is 1:705,821).[5] But the representation varied from a low of 1:423,014 in rural Tottori prefecture to a high of 1:2,226,927 in urban Kanagawa, a high-low ratio of 5.26 times. In other words, a candidate needed 5.26 times more votes to win in Tottori than in Kanagawa, and the Kanagawa voters were underrepresented by that same ratio. The highest winner in Kanagawa, independent Kōno Kenzō, received 1,086,512 votes, and the highest (and only) winner in Tottori, Socialist Hirota Kōichi (a first-time winner and secretary-general of the prefecture's General Council of Trade Unions), received 159,866 votes, a difference of 6.8 times.[6] But the highest number of votes received in the local constituency election—1,245,118 votes won by Hara Bumpei (LDP, Tokyo)—was 7:79 times the lowest number received by a winner—Hirota's 159,866.

In contrast to the halcyon days of the House of Councillors—the first years after World War II when the House came close to exhibiting the independence its founders wanted of it—the plight of the independents this time was sad (see Table 5–2). Only six were elected in all (including one classified under "other"), three in the national (two of them TV personalities), and three in the local constituency. Three joined the LDP immediately after their election, one joined the NLC, and two remained as independents. One of these latter two was Kōno

---

[5] For the national constituency, 1:1,566,434 in the qualified electorate; 1:1,072,693 among those who actually cast a ballot.

[6] Kōno's vote represented 41.3 percent of his prefecture's; Hirota's, 47.8 percent.

TABLE 5-9

Party Share of Votes and Seats Won, by Degree of Urbanization, 1974 and 1977 House of Councillors Elections, Local Constituencies

(percent)

Party		Metropolitan		Urban		Intermediate		Semirural		Rural		Total	
		Percent votes	Percent seats	Percent votes	Percent seats	Percent votes	Percent seats	Percent votes	Percent seats	Percent votes	Percent seats	Percent votes	Percent seats
LDP	1977	20.8	28.6	37.7	43.8	54.6	91.7	47.7	60.0	50.5	73.7	39.5	59.3
	1974	34.3	35.7	41.9	31.3	50.9	83.4	52.5	73.3	51.2	63.2	39.5	56.6
JSP	1977	13.7	14.3	23.1	31.3	29.6	8.3	35.7	26.6	36.5	26.3	25.9	22.4
	1974	12.0	14.3	16.7	43.8	14.0	8.3	17.2	26.7	17.4	21.1	26.0	23.7
KMT	1977	14.1	21.5	9.7	12.5	0.0	0.0	0.0	0.0	0.0	0.0	6.2	6.6
	1974	14.5	21.4	12.5	12.5	11.5	0.0	10.6	0.0	9.4	0.0	12.6	6.6
JCP	1977	14.4	14.3	10.2	0.0	7.4	0.0	6.7	0.0	7.8	0.0	9.9	2.6
	1974	13.8	28.6	9.5	6.2	7.6	0.0	5.5	0.0	7.0	0.0	12.0	6.6
DSP	1977	10.0	7.1	6.3	6.2	0.0	0.0	0.0	0.0	1.4	0.0	4.5	2.6
	1974	6.2	0.0	5.8	6.2	6.4	0.0	5.6	0.0	5.6	0.0	4.4	1.3

NCL	1977	9.2	7.1	8.4	6.2	2.5	0.0	2.5	0.0	2.3	0.0	5.7	2.6
	1974	—	—	—	—	—	—	—	—	—	—	—	—
SCL	1977	2.3	0.0	1.9	0.0	0.3	0.0	0.0	0.0	0.2	0.0	1.2	0.0
	1974	—	—	—	—	—	—	—	—	—	—	—	—
PFL	1977	2.4	0.0	1.1	0.0	0.0	0.0	0.0	0.0	0.0	0.0	0.9	0.0
	1974	—	—	—	—	—	—	—	—	—	—	—	—
Other	1977	1.1	0.0	0.0	0.0	3.1	0.0	4.0	6.7	0.0	0.0	1.4	1.3
	1974	—	—	—	—	—	—	—	—	—	—	0.6	1.3
Independents	1977	12.0	7.1	1.6	0.0	2.5	0.0	3.4	6.7	1.3	0.0	4.8	2.6
	1974	19.2[a]	0.0[a]	13.6[a]	0.0[a]	9.6[a]	8.3[a]	8.6[a]	0.0[a]	9.4[a]	15.7[a]	4.9	3.9
Total		100.0	100.0	100.0	100.0	100.0	100.0	100.0	100.0	100.0	100.0	100.0	100.0
National		29.9	18.4	24.1	21.1	14.6	15.8	14.6	19.7	16.8	25.0	100.0	100.0

[a] 1974 percentage for other parties and independents combined.
SOURCE: Calculated from Nisihira, ed., *Naigai Senkyo Data.*

TABLE 5–10

SHARE OF PARTY VOTES AND SEATS IN THE NINE LARGEST PREFECTURES, 1977 HOUSE OF COUNCILLORS ELECTION, LOCAL CONSTITUENCIES

Party	Share of Party Vote from the Nine Largest Prefectures[a]	Share of Seats
National	47.3	34.2
LDP	38.9	20.0
JSP	49.1	35.3
KMT	52.2	100.0
JCP	56.4	50.0
DSP	47.1	100.0
NLC	62.9	100.0

[a] Tokyo, 9.8 percent; Osaka, 6.7 percent; Hokkaidō, 5.2 percent; Kanagawa, 5.2 percent; Aichi, 5.0 percent; Hyōgo, 4.3 percent; Saitama, 4.0 percent; Fukuoka, 3.8 percent; Chiba, 3.3 percent.

SOURCE: Calculated from Nisihira, ed., *Naigai Senkyo Data*.

TABLE 5–11

WINNERS BY CANDIDACY STATUS, 1969, 1972, AND 1976 HOUSE OF REPRESENTATIVES ELECTIONS

Election Year		New (1)	Former (2)	Total of (1) and (2) (3)	Incumbent (4)	Total (5)
1969	Percent	19.3	6.2	25.5	74.5	100.0
	Number	94	30	124	362	484
1972	Percent	19.0	7.3	26.3	73.7	100.0
	Number	93	36	129	362	491
1976	Percent	24.3	9.2	33.5	66.5	100.0
	Number	124	47	171	340	511

NOTE: "New" means a first candidacy; "former" means that the candidate had been elected in the past but was not a sitting member at the time of the election; "incumbent" means a sitting member.

SOURCE: Calculated from Nishira, ed., *Naigai Senkyo Data*, p. 11.

TABLE 5–12

WINNERS BY CANDIDACY STATUS, 1974 AND 1977 HOUSE OF COUNCILLORS ELECTIONS

		New (1)	Former (2)	Total of (1) and (2) (3)	Incum-bent (4)	Total (5)
National constituency						
1974	Percent	51.8	1.9	53.7	46.3	100.0
	Number	28	1	29	25	54[a]
1977	Percent	46.0	4.0	50.0	50.0	100.0
	Number	23	2	25	25	50
Local constituencies						
1974	Percent	56.6	2.6	59.2	40.8	100.0
	Number	43	2	45	31	76
1977	Percent	46.1	0.0	46.1	53.9	100.0
	Number	35	0	35	41	76

[a] Four vacant seats left over from the previous term were contested in this election.
SOURCE: Calculated from Nisihira, ed., *Naigai Senkyo Data*, p. 16.

Kenzō, uncle of the NLC leader Kōno Yōhei and former speaker of the House of Councillors for two terms (1971–1974, 1974–1977). During his first term as speaker, Kōno tried to restore some elements of independence to the upper house. The speaker, he contended, should be nonpartisan, and in accord with his conviction he resigned from the LDP. In 1977 he ran as an independent and won handsomely in his home Kanagawa prefecture, taking 41.3 percent of the votes, but he was defeated for the speakership by the LDP's candidate, party regular Yasui Ken.

The Results

If the Councillors election did not bring nearer the solution of the main national problems, what did it show about some of the other problems on the voters' minds? For the main question, whether the LDP would be dislodged from office, the answer was no. The LDP lost a large number of votes (see Table 5–14), but the outcome of the election, in terms of vote share, was about the same as the previous time.

TABLE 5-13
WOMEN CANDIDATES AND WINNERS

| | House of Representatives, 1976 | | | House of Councillors, 1977 | | | | |
| | Candidates | Winners | Party | National constituency | | Local constituencies | | Membership[a] |
Party				Candidates	Winners	Candidates	Winners	
LDP	4	1	LDP	3	3	1	0	6
JSP	3	2	JSP	3	1	3	0	2
KMT	0	0	KMT	0	0	1	1	2
DSP	3	2	JCP	1	1	6	2	5
JCP	12	0	DSP	0	0	1	0	0
Other	1	0	PFL	1	0	2	0	0
Independents	1	1	WP	7	0	1	0	0
Total	25	6	Total	15(9)[b]	5(5)[b]	15(9)[b]	3(3)[b]	15

[a] Including holdovers and newly elected members.
[b] Figures in parentheses are for 1974.

SOURCE: Calculated from Nisihira, ed., *Naigai Senkyo Data.*

TABLE 5–14

Votes Obtained, by Party, 1974 and 1977 House of Councillors Elections, National Constituency

Party	Actual Votes Obtained[a]		Change, 1977 − 1974
	1977	1974	
LDP	18,160,060	23,332,773	− 5,172,713
JSP	8,805,617	7,990,456	+ 815,161
KMT	7,174,458	6,360,419	+ 814,039
JCP	4,260,049	4,931,649	− 671,600
DSP	3,387,540	3,114,895	+ 272,645

[a] Only for parties that ran both in 1974 and in 1977.
SOURCE: Calculated from Nisihira, ed., *Naigai Senkyo Data*.

Although this left the LDP somewhat uncomfortable, it was by no means a disaster. The combined opposition—including the conservative NLC—won a tiny majority, but there was nothing it could do with it. The LDP was clearly the overwhelmingly dominant force. The prospects for an all-opposition leadership were nil, and short of this the LDP inevitably remained in the saddle—a somewhat uncomfortable one, to be sure, but firm nonetheless. The ambiguity of the outcome was reflected in newspaper headlines: "The LDP Neatly Avoids Reversal," "A Difference of Four but the House Is Drawn," and a hopeful editorial comment: "But Still the Political Situation Has Changed."[7]

The situation is even clearer if the NLC is excluded from the opposition count, as it properly should be since it would not conceivably join the opposition in a serious way. The true opposition, that is, the "centrists" (DSP, KMT) and the "progressives" (JSP, JCP), remained well below the LDP (as of January 1978, 111–123). The LDP's candidate, Yasui Ken, was elected speaker by a huge majority (215–29) and the JSP's Katō Kan vice-speaker by an even larger majority (236–7). Both promptly resigned from their parties in order to serve as nonpartisan house leaders, thus following the tradition established by the previous speaker, Kōno Kenzō.

The NLC star did not continue shooting straight up. The promise of its spectacular takeoff in the lower-house elections was not ful-

[7] *Asahi Shinbun*, July 11 and 12, 1978.

filled, and the NLC made no improvement in its position. Nevertheless, to put a more optimistic interpretation on it, the NLC did reasonably well in the districts it contested, and it may be said to have confirmed its existence and established a modest foothold from which to operate in the future. The hopes aroused in the breasts of such liberal conservatives as world-famous economic planner Ōkita Saburō, who had been sufficiently optimistic to run as a New Liberal in the national constituency, were dashed. Ōkita, economist, engineer, intellectual, and the brightest jewel in the NLC's crown, limped home fifty-ninth in the field of 102, well out of the running. While the NLC drained votes from the LDP, particularly in the national constituency, it clearly drew votes from the opposition as well, particularly in the local districts.

The new groups produced no clear signs of a hopeful future. The Women's party seems definitely to be out. The PFL, if it can really mobilize the new left and the elements disaffected with established politics, may find a place for itself in the pluralist spectrum of Japan's politics; but in this election, it neither did so nor showed any promise of doing so. One candidate alone, celebrity Yokoyama Nokku, accounted for 54.9 percent of its total national vote. The one possible exception among the new groups was the SCL. Eda Satsuki, its leader, came in second in the national list. Although Eda was undoubtedly the beneficiary of his deceased father's public support and of some sentimental sympathy voting, his showing was a satisfactory one for a new political figure. The rest of his slate, however, did not do well. The adhesion of Den Hideo, another of the most popular winners in the national constituency, and two of his followers offers promise to the SCL. Nevertheless, it is too early to speculate on their prospects.

Representativeness and Reform

Perhaps the principal result of the election was some puzzlement about the raison d'être for an upper-house that seems to do little more than duplicate the lower house and a growing public feeling that at the very least some reforms are in order.

Proposals for such reform have not been lacking. When Kōno Kenzō became speaker of the House in 1971 he called upon all the parties for reform proposals and established an informal committee to advise him. The proposals concern two aspects of the House: its operations and its representativeness. For at least fifteen years now, the councillors have failed to evince any independence or even distinctiveness of function. The question thus arises, Why have an upper house at all? If all it can do is duplicate the work of the lower house at high cost, then perhaps it should be abolished. However, none of the literally hundreds of proposals that have come pouring in have as yet been sufficiently persuasive to overcome party calculations of advantage and disadvantage.

It is clear that when an urban seat, say in Kanagawa prefecture, represents 5.26 times as many voters as does a rural seat, the present distribution of seats cannot be characterized as properly representative. The ratio of seats to qualified voters is 1:5.6; if only those who actually cast a ballot are considered, the disproportion is 1:3.95. One-member districts, which are mainly rural, win 34.2 percent of the seats with 27.7 percent of the votes, but four-member districts, which are urban, win only 10.5 percent of the seats for their 15.3 percent of the electorate, an underrepresentation of 31.4 percent (see Table 5–5). The same distinction can be seen when districts are classified by degree of urbanization (Table 5–15). Rural districts are overrepresented by 48.8 percent, metropolitan districts underrepresented by 38.5 percent. The nine largest prefectures in the country account for 47.3 percent of the electorate but only 34.2 percent of the seats, an underrepresentation of 27.7 percent (see Table 5–10).

On the whole, the larger parties benefit from the constituency system: the smaller the constituency, the greater the disadvantage. In

TABLE 5–15

DEGREE OF REPRESENTATIVENESS, BY DEGREE OF URBANIZATION, 1977
HOUSE OF COUNCILLORS ELECTION, LOCAL CONSTITUENCIES
(percent)

Constituency	Qualified Voters	Valid Votes	Seats
Metropolitan	29.9	27.6	18.4
Urban	24.1	23.6	21.1
Intermediate	14.6	15.0	15.8
Semirural	14.6	15.5	19.7
Rural	16.8	18.3	25.0
Total percent	100.0	100.0	100.0
Total number	78,320,000	51,795,000[a]	76

[a] The actual number who voted was slightly higher, 53,642,412, but in every election some invalid ballots are cast.
SOURCE: Calculated from Nisihira, ed., *Naigai Senkyo Data*.

the single-member districts, the LDP wins 49.7 percent of the votes but an overwhelming 88.5 percent of the seats; the JSP's 36.2 percent of the votes brings it only 7.7 percent of the seats (see Table 5–5). But in the national constituency the LDP consistently takes a smaller share of seats relative to its votes (see Table 5–2). In the same way, the LDP is highly overrepresented in the rural districts and only slightly so in the metropolitan (see Table 5–9).

While these rates of unrepresentativeness are extreme by the standards of the U.S. House of Representatives, they are not so by the standards of other legislative bodies. In the British Parliament, for example, the rate of disproportion is on the order of 10–1, in the U.S. Senate 62–1. But whatever the relevant comparison may be, there is considerable discontent in some quarters. Chiba prefecture, which is rapidly urbanizing and becoming a bedroom town for Tokyo, has several times filed suit in court against the government of Japan, demanding rectification of the imbalance. The courts have ruled that the question is a political one for the Diet itself to decide. So far the Diet has not been able to come up with an acceptable proposal. It seems likely, therefore, that the House of Councillors will continue for some time longer in roughly its present shape.

PART THREE
Overview

6

Financing Politics

Katō Hirohisa

Japanese political history has no shortage of financial scandals. The prewar Siemens incident and the postwar Shōwa Denkō, shipbuilding, Black Mist, and Lockheed affairs have become famous.[1] But political scandals of this kind occur frequently, even though on a small scale.

The majority of them, if the opposition is to be believed, arise from favor seeking by big business and huge political contributions and bribes. Very often "political merchants," as they are called, are active behind the scenes. When a scandal is exposed, the government may be brought down, but if a powerful politician manages to be cleared by the courts, it is not at all unusual for him to make a come-

---

[1] In 1914 several naval officers and high officials were involved in a bribery scandal with the German firm Siemens.

In 1947–1948 Shōwa Denkō, a major manufacturer of electrical machinery, spent tens of millions of yen trying to secure favors from the Japanese government and U.S. Occupation officials. The scandal eventually touched not only civil servants and politicians, but high-ranking officials and leading political figures, including cabinet ministers and Prime Minister Ashida himself. Although Ashida was found innocent, his conservative-socialist coalition government fell.

The shipbuilding scandal involved bribery and illegal campaign contributions that led to the fall of the Yoshida cabinet in 1954. Satō Eisaku, later prime minister for eight years, was the highest personage involved; he was at that time secretary-general of the Liberal party (one of the forerunners of the present LDP). Prime Minister Yoshida, using his "right of command," ordered the justice minister not to arrest Satō. The minister resigned, and the ensuing flap ended in the resignation of the cabinet.

In 1966 a series of scandals, collectively known as the Black Mist, unfolded. These included the national forest subsidy cases, the Kyōwa Sugar Company case, political contributions, pork-barreling by the minister of transportation, and several others. One leading politician withdrew from politics, and the transportation minister resigned his post.

back.[2] A number of politicians have even been elected despite convictions, arrests, or indictments.[3]

In the public view, the scandals that surface are only the tip of the iceberg. There is a deeply rooted general belief that "money controls politics" and that "politics needs money." The politician knows that it takes a lot of money to win an election, and he feels little moral compunction about favors and bribes. The voter, for his part, takes the corrupt relation between big business and politics so much for granted that he has not even tried to do anything about it. However, the recent series of scandals—the House of Councillors election in July 1974, Prime Minister Tanaka's resignation in November of the same year, and the surfacing of the Lockheed scandal in February 1976—has brought public thinking on the question of money and politics to a decisive turning point.

In the summer of 1972, it is widely believed, Tanaka spent enormous sums getting himself elected party president (and therewith, automatically, prime minister). Then in the 1974 House of Councillors election, feeling that the LDP was in danger of losing its majority, he mobilized a large number of corporations which poured money unstintingly into the election coffers. It was the disclosure of these financial operations that forced his resignation four months after the election. The Lockheed revelations later made it clear that enormous funds had been passed around during the two years between Tanaka's election as party president and the 1974 upper-house elections. When Tanaka was arrested, certain groups in the LDP resented Prime Minister Miki's authorizing it and feared the further spread of investigations. They moved into action with the "Down with Miki" campaign that intensified the political turmoil.

---

[2] Socialist Nishio Suehiro, for example, who held the posts of cabinet secretary and then vice–prime minister in the 1947–1948 socialist-conservative coalition cabinets, was convicted in the 1948 Shōwa Denkō scandal. He lost his seat in the 1949 elections, but in 1952 he came back to win in second place in his district (Osaka Second). In 1957 he was acquitted by an appeal court, and in 1960 he led the Socialist right wing out of the party to form the present DSP. Liberal Okada Gorō was defeated in 1955 after his arrest in the shipbuilding scandal; in 1958 he did not run, but in 1960 he came in second in his Hyōgo Third District. Liberal Katō Takemori, also arrested in the shipbuilding scandal, lost his upper-house seat in 1956, but won it back again in the very next triennial election, 1959.

[3] The indicted Lockheed candidates, Tanaka Kakuei and Hashimoto Tomosaburō, for example. In 1948 Ōno Bamboku continued to be reelected from his Gifu bailiwick despite his conviction in the Shōwa Denkō case. He not only kept his second position in the immediate postarrest election, but he went on to win first place in Gifu until the end of his political career. He was acquitted of the charges in 1957, nine years after his conviction.

More time is needed to unravel the full ramifications of the Lockheed case, and it is still too early to come to definitive conclusions about Tanaka's political crimes. Nevertheless the fact that he was arrested in July 1976 and then brought to trial came as a great shock. Tanaka was a dramatic personality, a true rags-to-riches success story who exemplified the principle that "money is omnipotent." The general public, saturated by the mass media in the information society that is Japan, watched the unfolding of the Lockheed drama with unabated fascination, and the case hung over the elections like a heavy cloud. Popular attitudes toward money and politics had clearly changed.

While the Japanese do have a tendency to resign themselves to corruption, at the same time they have a very fastidious side that strongly rejects it. Japanese political history is not without examples of people who have kept themselves untainted. They are often called "well-wall" politicians—that is, people who put so much of their own money into political activities that they eventually go bankrupt, have to sell off even their homes, and eventually are left with nothing but the well. Fujiyama Aichirō, for example, was a well-known business leader, at one time president of the Japan Chamber of Commerce, and a wealthy man in his own right, who decided to go into politics in a big way. In 1960, at the time of the U.S.-Japan Mutual Security Treaty riots, he was foreign minister. After spending a great part of his personal fortune trying to build a faction within the LDP, he finally decided in 1976 not to stand for reelection and left politics a much poorer man than when he started.

The Lockheed case intensified public criticism of big business and of the LDP, which had become complacent after its many years in power and insensitive to corruption. But even within the LDP a great deal of self-examination was taking place. As a result of the Tanaka case, the Miki government passed amendments to the Public Office Election Law and the Political Funds Regulation Law in July 1975; these have brought major changes to political financing. And in spring 1977, in the wake of the Lockheed scandals, the LDP voted to abolish factions and to reform the procedures for the election of the party president.

The deep-rooted collusion among business, the conservatives, and the bureaucracy is not, of course, so quickly eliminated—nor is vote-buying, nor the other forms of corruption that can all too often be seen at the grass roots in conservative constituencies. However, the revelations of the past few years have brought a decisive change in popular attitudes and in the relation between money and politics.

143

The LDP and Money

The LDP has been in office continuously for over twenty years. A key factor in its grip on power has been the financial support from the business community that enables it to win elections and to preserve its majority in the Diet. In return for its contributions, business expects the LDP to protect and promote its interests, and in particular to adopt policies favoring the business community.

Official contributions from business to the LDP during the 1970s have annually amounted to ¥10–20 billion,[4] but the total is much more. Through industrial associations and firms, business contributes political funds to the Kokumin Kyōkai (People's Association), which then passes on the money to the LDP.[5] In addition, corporations contribute money directly to LDP factions and to powerful individual politicians. These funds enable faction leaders to help their own candidates and to enlarge their factions in the Diet in hopes of winning the LDP presidency and therewith the prime ministership. The ability to collect large amounts of campaign funds is a sine qua non for the Japanese politician who wishes to lead a faction of any significance whatsoever.

The campaign contributions have naturally brought about a close relationship between LDP politicians and corporations. In the eyes of the opposition parties, this is "collusion between politicians and high finance," or "politics giving priority to big business."

Since the formation of the Miki government in 1975, however, business's political contributions have dropped drastically. There appear to be three principal reasons for the sudden shift. First, business earnings fell sharply during the protracted recession set off by the 1973 oil crisis. Second, severe restrictions were placed on corporate contributions to parties, factions, and individuals by the enforcement ordinances (passed in September 1975) for the amended Public Office Election Law and the Political Funds Regulation Law. Finally, because of the Tanaka and the Lockheed scandals, public criticism turned sharply against big business as well as against the LDP. In the face of this criticism, firms hesitated to go too far in assisting politicians

---

[4] During the period in question, the yen continued to increase in value against the dollar. In 1970 the rate was ¥360 to the dollar; by 1972, it had risen to ¥300 against the dollar. (As of this writing, the dollar has fallen to 200 yen.) At a rate of ¥300 to the dollar, these contributions are the equivalent of $33.3–66.7 million.

[5] Ostensibly a nonparty citizens' group to collect political funds, in effect the Kokumin Kyōkai is the LDP's fund-raising organization.

through campaign contributions. In addition, the new laws established fixed legal limits that could be exceeded only at serious risk.

The following sections examine in detail the political funding of the LDP and its five major factions during the 1970s.

1972. The year 1972 was highlighted by Tanaka's election to the LDP presidency in July and therewith his automatic election to the prime ministership and by the general elections in December. Political contributions during the year reached a record ¥54.5 billion, an increase of 37.8 percent, or ¥15.0 billion, over 1971.[6] Of this amount, LDP headquarters received ¥9.5 billion.

Nearly 87.9 percent of the LDP intake, or ¥8.32 billion, came from the Kokumin Kyōkai. During the half year immediately preceding the general elections, the Tokyo Banking Association, the Japan Iron and Steel Federation, and the Japan Automobile Industry Association each contributed between ¥120 million and ¥400 million to the Kokumin Kyōkai, which then passed on the donations in their entirety to the LDP.

In addition to what the party itself raised, the five main LDP factions raised ¥6.3 billion for their own use that year: the Fukuda faction, ¥1.7 billion; Ōhira, ¥1.4 billion; Tanaka, ¥1.3 billion; Miki, ¥1.1 billion; and Nakasone, ¥840 million. The factional total was less than the party total for that year. During the first six months of 1972, however, the factions collected ¥2.6 billion for the July 7 LDP presidential election, which greatly exceeded the party's income of ¥1.8 billion during that period.

Tanaka won the LDP presidency and soon became prime minister. But the electioneering began in the fall of 1971, and, starting in spring 1972, the four factions with candidates began to pass out large sums of money to national and local LDP representatives. Tanaka's war chest appeared to be the largest, and to the general public the 1972 LDP presidential election became the symbol of the "money is power" principle.

Rumors were rife. One faction was said to be secretly giving out Suntory whisky cases containing cash, in amounts ranging between ¥5 and ¥10 million, to build up support for the faction's candidate. How much each faction was offering was a subject of common gossip among Diet members, and it was quite apparent that the size of the contributions affected the number of supporters. Given the billions the Tanaka faction and the hundreds of millions the other factions are

---

[6] *Jichishō Seiji Shikin Shūshi Hōkōsho,* 1973.

believed to have spent, the actual funds used in this election were probably far greater than the amounts publicly declared. Fukuda Takeo, then a candidate, who became prime minister in December 1976, is quoted as saying afterward, "There was just so much money changing hands, I seriously considered resigning in the middle of the campaign."[7]

1973. In 1973 the LDP's income jumped to ¥18.6 billion. This doubling in an off-year, when there were only local elections but no general elections, was curious. It is safe to say that the majority of the funds were spent on preparations for the following year's House of Councillors election.

With the possibility that the LDP might for the first time lose its majority in the upper house, the LDP high command, from Tanaka on down, as well as top business leaders felt acutely that the conservative position was in danger. To cope with the situation, Tanaka invited a number of celebrities to run in the national constituency as LDP candidates and then persuaded large firms to take their campaigns in hand, thus skillfully turning their inherent competitiveness to the party's benefit. In the local constituencies with two or more seats, the party pushed hard with incumbent governors and other influential local notables.[8]

1974. The figure usually given for the LDP's expenditures in the 1974 Councillors election is ¥15 billion. But there is strong reason to believe that unreported funds, including those of the party, the factions, and the individual candidates, came to more than ten times that amount. It has been suggested that the contributions through the Kokumin Kyōkai in 1974 constituted no more than 5 to 10 percent of the funds used by the LDP in the elections. If this is correct, it means that the LDP had collected some ¥200 billion in 1973, and a great portion of it was used for the 1974 House of Councillors election.

This estimate is supported by the 1974 Home Ministry report on political funds,[9] which states that of the ¥18.9 billion collected by the LDP during the year, two-thirds was collected and spent during the first half of the year, when the bulk of the campaigning for the House of Councillors election took place.[10] The report goes on to state that

---

[7] This was widely reported in the press.

[8] In one-seat constituencies the LDP was expected to win easily; therefore such drastic measures were not necessary (see Table 5-4).

[9] *Jichishō Seiji Shikin Shūshi Hōkōsho, 1975.*

[10] The election was July 7, 1974, but the legal campaign period, when the heavy expenditures are made, is the preceding twenty-three days.

during the first half of the year the number of corporations and individuals making contributions of more than ¥10 million increased from twenty-four to ninety-four; of these, thirty-nine made contributions of ¥30 million or more, and twenty-four made contributions of more than ¥50 million. In addition to the more than ¥2.7 billion raised by the five major factions, large sums were also raised by individual candidates. These large-scale contributions to the LDP headquarters, its factions, and individual members, are exclusive of those made through the Kokumin Kyōkai.

1975. Because of public outrage over the brazenness of the election financing and the growing effect of the oil crisis in autumn 1973, the business world began to show an increasing reluctance to make contributions to the LDP. In the first half of 1975, the LDP's income dropped by more than ¥10.4 billion to less than one-third of that of the first half of 1974. The number of large contributions of ¥10 million or more dropped to thirty-seven. The electric power companies, like Tokyo Electric, and the banks completely stopped their contributions. Many who had regularly made contributions of ¥30 million or more suddenly dropped out of the ranks of large-scale contributors. These included the Tokyo Banking Association (¥440 million in 1974), the Japan Iron and Steel Federation (¥430 million in 1974), the Japan Automobile Industry Association (¥300 million in 1974), and the Japan Electric Appliances Industry Association (¥280 million in 1974).

On the other hand, in 1975 total contributions to the five major LDP factions came to ¥5.2 billion. While this did not equal the ¥6 billion of 1972, the year of the party presidential election, it did exceed the ¥4.8 billion collected in 1974. The factions actively collected funds in a political atmosphere that was heavy with talk of dissolution and a new general election. Big business, reacting against the Miki government's antibusiness policies, such as the revision of the Antimonopoly Law, made its contribution to the individual party factions rather than to party headquarters.

When the two revised election laws passed the Diet in 1975, it became clear that contributions from big business were coming to an end. Not only was there strong public criticism of the excessive funds used by the LDP in 1974, but there was also a great deal of self-reflection about this within the conservative camp itself. When it was learned that the LDP's 1973 income had increased sharply, President Kawamata of the Nissan Motor Company said, "It was an enormous sum, one that raises grave doubts as to its appropriateness."[11] Saka-mura Yoshimasa, a top-ranking LDP Diet member representing the Second District of Gumma prefecture, declared in August 1974 that he would no longer accept contributions from the business world. Saka-mura's finances were so typical among LDP Dietmen that his case deserves close examination.

Sakamura, who had been reelected four times, used to receive about ¥3 million per month from business enterprises. The greater part of this was used in his local constituency for customary donations on ceremonial occasions such as marriages, funerals, festivals, local meetings, and travel. It also went to pay the salaries or expenses of secretaries who acted as campaign leaders during elections and the expenses of his support organization. The remainder of the ¥3 mil-lion was used in a variety of political activities including campaign support within his district for candidates for local offices (prefectural, city, town, and village assemblies; governorships and mayoralties).

Sakamura published a full account of these funds and at the same time announced a three-point policy for the future: first, to switch over entirely to individual contributions; second, to get along on the funds raised by his supporters' organization in the constituency; third, to make public the accounting of his supporters' association. Saka-mura's change in fund-raising policy won public support and had an influence on other LDP Diet members. It is even possible that this swayed Miki's decision to announce his assets publicly in December 1974 after he was elected prime minister. However, no other LDP Diet member followed Sakamura's lead in refusing to accept contri-butions from the business world.[12]

Opposition Party Funds

The opposition parties can be divided into two groups on the basis of their support structures and financing. In the first group are the JSP and the DSP, which depend mainly on the major labor unions, the Sōhyō and the Dōmei, for organized support; in the second are the Kōmeitō and the Communist parties, which depend mainly on the mass membership of Sōka Gakkai in the one case and of the party units in the other. The two socialist parties are financed mainly by union dues, but the other two opposition parties derive their income mainly

---

[11] Widely reported in the press.

[12] In the end, Sakamura decided not to run a fifth time because of illness, and his wife ran in his place. She lost in the runner-up position.

from contributions by members and from the sale of official party publications.

These sources provide both funds and political support for the four opposition parties on a considerable scale. As of May 1977 the Sōhyō labor federation had a membership of 4.5 million and Dōmei 2.2 million; two other unions, the 1.3-million strong Chūritsu Rōren and the 70,000-member Shin Sanbetsu, have less clearly defined relations with political parties. The Kōmeitō's official membership is 141,000, and its party organ, *Kōmei Shinbun*, has a daily circulation of 850,000 and a Sunday circulation of 1.4 million. Its main supporting body, the Sōka Gakkai, claims the membership of 7.8 million families. The Communist party official membership is 380,000, and the party organ, the *Akahata* (Red Flag), has a daily circulation of over a million and a Sunday circulation of 3 million.

According to the Home Ministry report,[13] the Communist party's income in the first half of 1972 outstripped the LDP's for the first time. The JCP headed the list with ¥2.2 billion, followed by the LDP with ¥1.9 billion, Kōmeitō with ¥1.6 billion, the JSP with ¥206 million, and the DSP with ¥187 million. A closer look at the income and expenditure of the individual opposition parties for 1973 may be useful.

In 1973 the JCP had an income of ¥6.2 billion of which *Akahata* and other party publications accounted for 94 percent and party dues for about 3 percent. On the expenditure side, ¥2.6 billion went for supplies, ¥1.4 billion for printing and other expenses, and ¥1.0 billion for full-time staff.

The Kōmeitō's income for the same period was ¥3.8 billion, of which only ¥10,000 was reported as individual contribution; effectively, all its funds came from official publications and membership dues. The principal expenditures were ¥1.8 billion for official publications, ¥900 million for staff costs, and ¥500 million for regional branches.

The JSP's ¥700 million income came mainly from large-scale contributions of over ¥1 million each from individual unions in Sōhyō and the Federation of Synthetic Chemical Workers' Unions. Expenses amounted to ¥440 million for printing the party's semi-weekly publication *Shakai Shinpō*, and costs for full-time staff.

The income of ¥530 million received by the Democratic Socialists included contributions of over ¥1 million each from the Democratic Socialist Association, Hitachi Shipbuilding and Engineering Company,

---

[13] *Jichishō Seiji Shikin Shūshi Hōkōsho,* 1973.

and others. The party's main expenses consisted of ¥240 million for administration and staff costs.

In 1975, for the first time, the JCP's income for the entire year (not just the half-year, as in 1972), ¥11.6 billion, surpassed the LDP's ¥11.5 billion. Next came Kōmeitō with ¥6.5 billion, then the JSP with ¥1.7 billion, and finally the DSP with ¥779 million. The JCP's income boost had come from the increased *Akahata* readership and increased membership. If contributions to the five factions and to individual party members by the business world are included, the LDP certainly had the greater overall income, but the party headquarters' income fell ¥7.3 billion below the preceding year, thus bringing LDP party income well below that of the JCP. Imazato Hiroki, chairman of Nippon Seikō and a powerful figure in the business world, was shocked that "the LDP, the party of free enterprise, had fallen below the JCP in political funds for the first time in our political history. Steps must be taken to rectify this."[14] His statement revealed the growing anxiety among the backers of the LDP establishment.

Although the funding of particular opposition parties sometimes comes in for public criticism, it seldom becomes a major political issue. In the case of the LDP, there have been frequent instances of profit and corruption because it receives many corporate contributions that are made with the expectation of some benefit. In contrast, the opposition parties, with only a few exceptions, receive almost no corporate contributions and their financial backing is thus not directly related to expectations of favor. In their frequent attacks on the LDP, the opposition parties often argue that business contributions assure an intimacy and dependence that makes it impossible for the LDP to change its pro–big business policy. The opposition parties boast loudly that they do not take contributions from the business community. But however that may be, many individual opposition politicians do so.

The New Liberal Club used volunteers to raise funds for the 1976 lower-house elections. One method was to sell ¥1,000 or ¥3,000 tickets for the street campaign meetings. During the 1977 upper-house elections, the NLC sold jaguar T-shirts and held fund-raising parties. There are limitations to raising funds through volunteers, however, and, according to leader Kōno Yōhei, the NLC accepts corporate contributions "with moderation."

During the period from June 1976 to the end of the year the NLC had an income of ¥278 million and expenditures of ¥235 million. The income came from three sources: individuals, corporations, and

---

[14] This statement was widely reported in the press at the time.

loans. Apart from a clear profit of ¥39.6 million from fund-raising parties and three large contributions of ¥3.0 million each, ¥73.4 million (or 26 percent of the total) was raised from 5,500 individual contributions. Corporate contributions totaled ¥55.6 million from 140 companies. Among them were some large companies, like the Komatsu Company and the Seibu department store, but for the most part the contributors were small- and medium-sized companies. Another ¥100 million was raised through loans. The major expenditure was ¥150 million for the lower-house elections.

The 1977 House of Councillors election fund-raising operations brought in ¥450 million, ¥100 million from individual contributors, ¥200 million from corporations and other organizations, ¥100 million from the social gatherings and the sale of T-shirts, and loans. In May 1977 the NLC established its own fund-raising organization, the Shin Jiyūshugi Kyōkai (New Liberalism Association), but it has so far not been able to make any significant contribution to the NLC's coffers. For 1977 as a whole, the NLC raised ¥852 million, more than three times its 1976 showing.

The Kōmeitō and the JCP operate differently. Until the revision of the Public Office Election Law in 1975, both used their ample funds and organizational strength to distribute propaganda materials, such as posters and pamphlets, during general elections. The LDP and other political parties were not in a position to match the intensity of their efforts. The amended election law prohibits the publication of posters disguised as "extras," or special editions of party organs (a common technique), during the election period. In both elections since the law went into effect, however, the fund-raising capabilities of the JCP and the Kōmeitō enabled them to carry out a much more vigorous propaganda campaign of posters than any other party and still remain within the boundaries of legality.

By comparison, the propaganda capability of the JSP, the DSP, and the NLC lags far behind. The funding weakness of the second-ranking opposition party, the JSP, is particularly striking. Before the 1977 House of Councillors election the JSP withdrew its official recognition of the candidacy of Sasaki Shizuko because she could not raise the ¥100 million targeted for each candidate by the Osaka regional headquarters. This withdrawal demonstrated dramatically that the JSP and the labor unions supporting it were not able to raise sufficient funds to support their official candidates. Together with the case of Ogawa Hanji, an official LDP candidate, who had previously withdrawn his candidacy on the ground that he was unable to raise the necessary funds, the Sasaki case further strengthened the widespread public feeling that the House of Councillors election requires too much money.

Revision of the Public Office Election Law

The Public Office Election Law as amended in July 1975 had the support of the LDP, the JSP, and the DSP, but was opposed by the Kōmeitō and the JCP. The revision aimed at fair elections that would not cost excessive sums. It therefore applies very strict controls to activities before and during the election period.

The most distinctive feature of the revision may strike foreigners as odd: candidates for public office (including members of the national Diet and local assemblies, whether they are already in office or running for the first time) are forbidden to make any contribution to the voters in their electoral districts. The prohibition is not limited to the period before an election but is applicable at all times. The few exceptions to this rule are donations to political parties, to political organizations and their local branches, and to relatives and a limited amount of compensation for travel and living expenses to people participating in political meetings.

It is very expensive to be a Diet member. While a U.S. congressman or senator has a large staff paid by the U.S. Treasury, the Japanese Diet member is allowed only two legislative aides. Anything above that he must pay for himself or, more probably, raise money for. Routine expenses are very high, even if he is not so ambitious as to seek office space larger than the two small rooms assigned him in the Diet office building. If he does, then his expenses rise by a very substantial amount.

The Dietman also feels himself under pressure to cultivate his constituency in preparation for the next election. All members of the Diet, no matter what their party, have their own support groups (kōenkai).[15] Traditionally, the Diet member sends presents to his supporters or their relatives on special occasions such as celebrations, funerals, and so on. The most important are the garlands sent for the opening of new businesses and for funerals; the Diet member's name is written in especially large letters so that it will be remembered by the participants. Again, when supporters visit the capital to see the Imperial Palace or the National Diet Building, they are dined and given presents by their Dietman. And there are other small favors such as

---

[15] For a detailed explanation of this system, see Nathaniel B. Thayer, *How the Conservatives Rule Japan* (Princeton, N.J.: Princeton University Press, 1969).

farewell gifts to supporters' children traveling abroad, or help with getting into schools or jobs.

The cost of cultivating supporters in this way is a major burden and one that increases constantly as Diet members from the same district compete with each other in the size of the gifts they give. Unlike members of the opposition, who can count on some kind of organization already in existence, the LDP members have to create their own before the election. These supporters' organizations play a key role for the candidate, and therefore the investment in them is heavy. As in the case of LDP Dietman Sakamura cited above, the monthly cost of cultivating support back home, through donations and meetings, runs between ¥1 million and ¥3 million. For their part, supporters believe that since they work for the candidate during the election, it is quite proper that they should be recompensed. At times this comes close to being a forced contribution.

The Public Office Election Law's prohibition of such donations, which have always been the major cause of the high cost of elections, marked a new epoch. During the 1976 general election, the first carried out under the new law, both the candidates themselves and their supporters were confused by the ban on these deeply rooted customs. A great deal of evasive behavior was designed to get around the new laws and avoid discovery by the police. However, the new law was generally more welcome to the candidates than not; most of them had been suffering from the rising cost of donations. For an active politician, the cost of the routine office expenses, cultivation of constituents, supporters' organizations, and elections can easily come to between ¥2 million and ¥5 million a month.

The second revision of the law was the expansion of public management of elections. Candidates who received the legal minimum number of votes in the election were reimbursed a fixed proportion of the cost of promotional materials used during the campaign. Previously, the candidates or their parties had to pay all these costs, but under the revision promotion is now virtually cost-free to the candidate, except for posters using expensive special designs or colors. In return, posters with veneered wood or plastic backing are prohibited, and the number of posters is limited according to type of election.

Public management of elections has gone into other areas as well. For example, a fixed proportion of the cost of cars used by the candidate during the election campaign, including car rental, drivers' salaries, and fuel, will be borne by the Treasury. Parties can also place up to four newspaper advertisements during the elections free

of charge. Television programs, introducing the candidate and present-
ing his political views, have been at government expense since the
1971 House of Councillors election. Despite the improvements brought
about by the revised law, many members of both the government and
the opposition feel that the official election subsidies are still inadequate and that public management should be expanded.

A third feature of the revised law is the prohibition of election
literature in the guise of "extras" or special issues of party journals
during the official campaign period.[16] Although there have always been
very strict laws governing the number of pieces of election literature
that can be issued during the campaign, it was the practice to get
around these limits by issuing "extras" or special numbers of the party
journals. In this guise, there were effectively no limits. The Kōmeitō-
JCP competition became almost literally a "war of the handbills,"
much to the disgust of the other parties and the general public. The
new law, since it was specifically designed to meet this criticism,
naturally drew the opposition of the JCP and the Kōmeitō, who argued
that it placed restrictions on political activity and freedom of speech.

In exchange for the prohibition on party handbills, handbills for
individual candidates again became permissible. The Treasury provides a fixed subsidy to cover these costs.

Revision of the Political Funds Regulation Law

The Political Funds Regulation Law, which was revised in July 1975
concurrently with the Public Office Election Law, had originally been
promulgated in 1948 on instructions from the American Occupation
for the purpose of keeping the general public informed about the
income and expenditures of political funds and to prevent bribes and
concessions. The law was never effective, however, and because of
its many loopholes it had been known as the "sieve law."

Where the revised Public Office Election Law regulated the outflow of money from politicians more strictly than in the past, the
revised Political Funds Regulation Law was designed to regulate the
inflow of money and also to clarify the relationship between input and
outflow. Prior to the 1975 revision, there was no obligation for politicians or parties to report details of income received under headings
other than "contributions." It was therefore a simple matter to manipulate announcements of income and expenditure to mask suspicious
sums received from business.

---

[16] The official campaign period is usually twenty-three to twenty-five days, and
election activities are permitted only within that time.

The Report of Political Fund Income and Expenditure for 1975, made under the old law, showed that the Kokumin Kyōkai, the fund-raising organ of the LDP, had an income of ¥7.9 billion. But for no more than 0.1 percent of this was the source of the contributions clearly identified. The rest was listed as "membership dues and others," and no clear source was recorded. The Japanese media dubbed this the "0.1 percent clarification." In that year, the clarification ratio for the main LDP factions was 1.2 percent for the Fukuda faction, 0.5 percent for the Miki faction, and zero for the Tanaka and Ōhira factions.

The situation with regard to expenditure was not much different. Expenditures for political activities, meetings, or staff costs were listed as paid to individuals or organizations. But the Ministry of Home Affairs did not have the legal authority to investigate whether these names were falsified. Therefore the dominant faction could use the party funds for its own purposes, and the vague accounting provided by the party comptroller could not be challenged as illegal. As long as the accounting was consistent, no questions were asked about how the contributions from business were used to win votes in the party presidential elections.

Under the revised law, parties and their fund-raising organs are required to report in full all income and expenditures over ¥10,000, irrespective of whether it is a donation, membership fee, or something else. (The corresponding figure in the case of political factions or supporters' organizations is ¥1 million.) This has virtually eliminated the "0.1 percent clarification ratio." Furthermore, since in most cases supporters' organizations are "political organizations" in the definition of the law, they are required to report their revenues. By making use of the loopholes in the old law it was possible to create bogus supporters' organizations under the guise of fund-raising associations, but under the new law, when an organization fails to report its income and expenditure for two consecutive years, it is automatically removed from the registers of the Home Ministry and the regional Election Supervisory Committees. The new law has effectively curtailed the ability of political parties, factions, and individual politicians to manipulate income and expenditure and has made it mandatory to clarify the flow of all political funds.

The new law dealt a heavy blow to politicians, since the requirement of detailed reporting had the effect of severely curtailing contributions. First, the amount a donor can contribute to political parties, political funding groups, and candidates is limited to a maximum of ¥20 million a year for individuals. In the case of corporations, the figure varies from ¥7.5 million to ¥100 million, depending upon their capitalization. For companies capitalized at under ¥1 billion the maximum permissible annual contribution is ¥7.5 million, while for companies capitalized at from ¥5 billion to ¥10 billion, the figure is ¥30 million. In the case of contributions from labor unions, industrial and commercial associations, and religious organizations, limits on donations are determined on the basis of total membership or the previous year's expenditures, with a maximum of ¥100 million. In addition, contributions to factions or supporters' associations are permitted up to half this figure.

On top of these overall limits, a contributor may give only ¥1.5 million in any one year to a particular faction, supporters' organization, or candidate. Therefore factions or individual politicians who cannot depend upon a large number of firms or organizations to contribute somewhere in the neighborhood of ¥100,000 per month will find it impossible to raise the kind of funds they did before the reform went into effect. However, tax exemption has been allowed in order to encourage individual contributions.

The new law was to go into effect in January 1976 and, with the rumors of the impending dissolution of the House of Representatives, LDP dietmen rushed to raise as much from business circles as possible before the deadline. Last-minute business contributions to the LDP were reported to total ¥5 billion from thirty different industries, including ¥700 million each from the steel industry and the banks, ¥500 million from the automobile industry, ¥400 million from the construction industry, and ¥300 million from the electrical appliance industry.[17] With these funds the LDP was able to handle the 1976 lower-house election. However, raising the ¥5 billion election funds for the 1977 House of Councillors election—only one-third of the amount collected for the 1974 election—turned out to be very difficult.

With the funds from their factions and party headquarters curtailed, LDP dietmen scurried about from place to place to raise money in anticipation of a further drying up of the flow. Even though they managed, many complain that the new law will cut off the flow of political funds entirely. This feeling manifested itself in the anger against Miki, whose cabinet put the revised law into effect. Although much of the anti-Miki movement seemed to be an attempt to prevent any further revelations in the Lockheed scandal, an important underlying factor was the resentment among LDP members of his having made political fund-raising so difficult.

---

[17] *Yomiuri Shinbun*, December 27, 1975.

Public Attitudes toward the High Cost of Elections

Between the 1974 House of Councillors election and the two elections of 1976 and 1977, a popular slogan made the rounds, "Five wins, four loses"—that is, a candidate could win with ¥500 million but would lose with only ¥400 million. In fact not as many candidates spent ¥500 million or more on the campaign as generally believed. Because the LDP does not have the support of trade unions and its party organization is weak, candidates must rely primarily on their supporters' associations, and therefore their campaigns inevitably cost more than those of the other parties.

Most candidates must strain to the utmost to raise the enormous funds they need for elections. In addition to the cost of establishing and operating election offices in several different locations within their districts, they must pay for posters and billboards, for addressing and mailing hundreds of thousands of postcards appealing for votes, for last-minute telephone offensives, and for all staff and travel expenses to operate these programs. Often the supporters' associations bear these costs and do the work on a voluntary basis. The money value of this unpaid support cannot be fully calculated, but it certainly runs to hundreds of millions of yen. Therefore the "five wins, four loses" may be closer to the mark than it appears.

The upper-house national constituency elections are particularly expensive because of the size of the electoral district. Most official candidates of the five major political parties depend on national organizations to bring out their vote. The LDP utilizes the support of conservative business organizations and religious bodies; the Kōmeitō and the JCP allocate national candidates to district party units, which they depend on to drum up the vote. Both the LDP and the JSP run TV and movie personalities (tarento) for upper-house seats, in hope that they are sufficiently well known to win on their names alone, without needing the support of specific organizations.

Both the Kōmeitō and the JCP pay all the costs of their candidates' elections, providing, in effect, a party-managed campaign. In the case of the JSP and the DSP, most of the candidates belong to large industrial unions that supply the campaign funds. The LDP is supported by such pressure groups as the Military Pensioners' Federation, the Association of Post Office Heads, and the Japan Medical Association; by trade associations in construction, agriculture, and other areas; and by religious bodies such as the Seichō no Ie and the Risshō Kōseikai. While some of these groups offer both volunteer labor and financial help, in many cases the candidates have to fund their own election activities.

It is extremely difficult for a candidate who does not belong to one of the five main parties to win an upper-house seat in the national constituency because he will not have the support of a national organization. The elections in the prefectural constituencies of the upper-house and the 130 lower-house constituencies do not require as much money as the upper-house national constituency. However, because of extreme competitiveness election costs are higher in multimember districts than in single-member districts. The candidate depends heavily on his faction for his funds, and the 1976 House of Representatives election was a good example of a factional election. The factions play an important role in the local-constituency elections of the House of Councillors also, but with the dissolution of factions by the LDP in the spring of 1977—however much of a formality that might have been—and the decline in factional funds after the revised Political Fund Regulation Law went into effect, factional rivalry was not as extensive in 1977 as in previous elections.

As a result of the Lockheed scandal, the parties, Diet members, and the electorate all realized that costly elections make for financial corruption. Opinion varies, however, on where to place the blame. Some believe the election system itself is at fault; others blame the candidates for the heavy election costs. Those who blame the system seem increasingly of the opinion that the House of Representatives should shift to single-member electoral districts with proportional representation and that the House of Councillors national constituency should use a controlled registration system with proportional representation. In March 1977 Prime Minister Fukuda considered introducing controlled registration and proportional representation in the upper-house national constituency for the 1980 election, and the LDP has drafted a new public election law to this end. The JSP supports proportional representation for the national constituency, but both the JCP and the Kōmeitō are in strong opposition to it, and at this stage it is not possible to say what its chances are for 1980.

When Tanaka Kakuei proposed establishing a small-district proportional-representation system for the lower house in 1973, he ran into a buzz saw of opposition from the JSP, JCP, and Kōmeitō, which forced him to withdraw the plan. Electoral reform, particularly such fundamental ones as the small-constituency system or proportional representation, are life-or-death questions for the parties and are therefore difficult to bring about. However, the demand for some reform of the upper-house national constituency election, because of its excessive costs, cannot be ignored.

The revision of the election laws seemed to have some effect on the 1977 House of Councillors election. By comparison with the 1974 election, in which money played a significant part, the conspicuous flashing of money seems to have declined. As noted, some candidates even withdrew from the race for lack of funds. The LDP's war chest fell to ¥5 billion, one-third of the 1974 level of ¥15 billion, and candidates could no longer count on the factions for financial aid. Celebrities were also reluctant to run on the LDP ticket. At one extreme were independents who ran without campaign funds at all, like author Nakamura Takeshi, who, after the success of Aoshima Yukio in the 1974 election,[18] announced that he would use no facilities other than TV time and newspaper ads, which are paid for by the national Treasury. (He lost.) At the other extreme were candidates in the 1976 election like the New Liberals, who openly solicited contributions from the general public and used only these funds for their campaign along with whatever support the government was mandated to provide. Nevertheless, political funds for the entire year 1977 reached a total of ¥74 billion, second only to 1974's ¥81 billion.[19]

It is no exaggeration to say that the revision of the two election laws and the Lockheed scandal brought the problem of political funding to a head. The logical next step is a complete revision of the election system and a change in the attitudes of the electorate. The prospects for such sweeping change are, however, not clear. But in Japan, just as in the United States, the need for such a reform ranks high on the political agenda.

---

[18] Aoshima was a tarento, a composer and director, who won as a progressive independent in the second position in 1968. In 1974 he declared his candidacy but announced that he would not campaign, whereupon he set off ostentatiously on a European tour and returned only when the election was over. He came in third, with even more votes than he had won in 1968 (1.8 million to 1.2 million).

[19] Jichishō Seiji Shikin Hōkōsho, July 20, 1978, as reported in Yomiuri Shinbun, July 20, 1978.

7

The Significance of the Elections

Herbert Passin

For at least eight months during 1976 and 1977, Japan was caught up in election fever. If the media and the commentators are to be believed, vast issues were at stake. The questions confronting the electorate included the Lockheed scandal, the conflict between Prime Minister Miki and challenger Fukuda, getting the economy moving again, the conservative-progressive reversal, the reform of politics, ending bossism within the LDP, and the fate of the new political groups just entering the political scene. Journalists, politicians, political buffs, and much of the general public watched the ups and downs of daily politics for the slightest sign of change on any of these dimensions with the avidity of baseball fans lovingly poring over the daily statistics of their favorite teams, or of stockbrokers watching the ticker tape.

Again according to the media, vast issues were resolved. The elections were a "turning point," a veritable "landslide" bringing down the structure of postwar politics. "The LDP defeat," as one commentator wrote, speaking of the lower-house elections, "exceeded even the wildest expectations."[1] It was "shocking," "a great defeat," "a crushing defeat," depending on which newspaper or journal one happened to read. For the upper-house elections, the rhetoric was more sober: "The Popular Will Has Not Expressed a Clear Choice";[2] "The LDP Neatly Sidesteps the Reversal."[3] Even here, however, the sense of drama could scarcely be suppressed.

But were the elections in fact so dramatic? Or, to put the question in a slightly different way, what did they show, what changes did

---

[1] *Asahi Jānaru*, December 17, 1976.

[2] *Asahi Shinbun*, July 12, 1977.

[3] *Asahi Shinbun*, July 11, 1977.

they bring about, and what do they suggest about the future of Japanese politics?

The LDP Defeat

A look at the election results suggests that the changes were not very extensive, nor did the LDP really sustain a mortal blow. In the lower-house elections, the LDP vote share dropped by 5.1 percentage points (off 10.8 percent from the previous election) and its seat share by about 6.5 percentage points (off 11.8 percent). To be sure, this left the LDP seven seats short of a simple majority, but within a few days of the election enough independently elected conservatives joined the party to give it the necessary majority of 256 seats. And since two of the Lockheed-tainted candidates who won as independents considered themselves bound by party discipline, a working majority was never in question. The same general course of development took place in the upper-house elections as well. Although the LDP ended up just short of a majority, the opposition was unable to unite effectively to prevent LDP leadership of the house.

In terms of the conservative camp as a whole, then, there was virtually no change. In the upper-house elections, on the face of it, the LDP lost heavily in the national constituency, going down from 44.3 to 35.8 percent of the vote. But when the total conservative vote is added (that is, the 3.9 percent for the NLC and the 4.8 percent for the conservative independents), the total is 44.5 percent, almost as good as 1974 and even 1971.[4] In other words, popular support for conservative candidates in the national constituency elections held steady; it only redistributed itself slightly differently.

For the local constituency elections (see Table 5–2) the conclusion is even clearer: not only did the LDP hold steady, 39.5 percent (1977) and 39.5 percent (1974), but the conservatives as a whole went dramatically higher (counting in the NLC and independent conservatives), to 49 percent, a gain of 9.5 percentage points, or 24.1 percent, over 1974. It will also be noticed that all the opposition parties, except the DSP, lost shares compared with 1974—and the DSP gain was a bare 0.1 percentage point.

The lower-house elections tell the same story. The LDP 5.1 point vote decline is almost entirely accounted for by the breakaway NLC's 4.1 percent. If the independent conservatives are added, the conserva-

---

[4] The figure is actually higher than the LDP 1974 total of 44.3 percent, but if the conservative independent votes are added, the 1974 total would come slightly higher, 45.7 percent.

TABLE 7–1

Seats Won, by Party, 1969, 1972, and 1976 House of Representatives Elections

Party	1969 Number	1969 Percent	1972 Number	1972 Percent	1976 Number	1976 Percent	Seat Distribution (February 1978) Number	Seat Distribution (February 1978) Percent
LDP	288	59.3	271	55.2	249	48.7	256	50.6
JSP	90	18.5	118	24.0	123	24.1	120	23.7
KMT	47	9.7	29	5.9	55	10.8	56	11.1
JCP	14	2.9	38	7.7	17	3.3	19	3.7
DSP	31	6.3	19	3.9	29	5.7	28	5.5
NCL	—	—	—	—	17	3.3	17	3.4
Other	0	0.0	2	0.4	0	0.0	3	0.6
Independent	16	3.3	14	2.9	21	4.1	7	1.4
Total	486	100.0	491	100.0	511	100.0	511[a]	100.0

Dash (—): Not applicable.

[a] Five vacancies.

Source: Calculated from Nisihira, ed., *Naigai Senkyo Data.*

tive camp as a whole is left with a decline of less than one percentage point in votes.

None of this bespeaks the wholesale public desertion of the LDP trumpeted by the media just after the lower-house election. The redistribution of seats is somewhat less favorable to the LDP, but not as much as has been asserted. For the lower house, if the NLC's 17 and the several remaining independent conservatives are added to the LDP's 256, then the conservative total is 280, not as good as the 285 last time, but not too bad (see Table 7–1).

The upper-house elections come out about the same. The LDP went down from its slight majority of 126-123 on election day[5] to a minority position of 124-127.[6] But in a few months, because of deaths, by-elections, and resignations, both the government and the opposition held 125 seats each.[7] By January 1978, the government fell to a 123-125 ratio.[8]

[5] There were three vacancies resulting from death.
[6] One vacancy.
[7] Two vacancies.
[8] Four vacancies.

The Operation of the Diet

The changes are small, and they are certainly not of landslide proportions. Nevertheless, they are not inconsequential, and it would be wrong to disregard them. First, this was the first time in its history that the LDP failed to return a majority with its endorsed candidates. Its failure to win a majority in the upper house the following July only confirmed the feeling that it was on a falling curve. This affects the morale of the party and influences the decisions of voters who have not yet made up their minds. Second, the close division between government and opposition creates practical problems in the management of the Diet.

There are several reasons for this. First, by custom the speaker and the vice-speaker of both houses are required to resign from their parties on the theory that this assures their nonpartisanship. Their parties therefore lose their vote (except in the case of ties) and their inclusion in the party's roster for committees. Second, the number of seats a party can have on each standing committee is roughly proportionate to the number of seats it holds in each house (see Table 7–2). When the LDP majority was large, it always had enough seats to hold a majority on each committee. Third, according to Diet regulation, the chairman of the committee may not vote except to break a tie. Therefore the party that has the chairmanship normally loses one vote. When the LDP held a large majority on every committee, the loss of the chairman's vote was unimportant; there was always enough voting strength in reserve. But when the LDP holds a razor-thin majority, or is even in the minority, then the chairmanship may mean that the LDP will not have enough votes on the committee. Fourth, if, on the other hand, the party does not have the chairmanship, it cannot fully control the operations of the committee, even if it holds a majority.

As a result, the LDP does not control all committees of the two houses of the Diet, a control that is necessary for smooth operation of the government. Because there are sixteen standing committees per house, the LDP needs sixteen seats over and above a simple majority, that is, a total of 272 lower-house and 142 upper-house seats, to assure both a majority on every committee and its chairmanship. It does not have them.

In the absence of full Diet control, the LDP is forced to negotiate with the opposition parties to a degree never before required. This often means ad hoc coalitions on particular issues, tacit agreements, trade-offs, and compromises. At worst, the LDP may find its bills

TABLE 7–2
STANDING COMMITTEES OF THE DIET, FEBRUARY 1, 1978

Committee	House of Representatives					House of Councillors				
	Chairman	Number of members	LDP	Independent	Combined opposition	Chairman	Number of members	LDP	Independent	Combined opposition
Cabinet	LDP	30	15	0	14	LDP	20	9	0	10
Home	LDP	30	14	0	15	LDP	20	9	1	9
Legal	LDP	30	14	0	14	KMT	20	9	0	10
Foreign	LDP	30	15	0	14	LDP	20	9	1	9
Finance	LDP	40	20	0	18	LDP	25	11	0	13
Education	LDP	30	14	0	15	LDP	20	9	0	10
Social and Labor	LDP	40	20	0	19	JSP	21	11	0	9
Agriculture, Forestry, Fishing	LDP	40	19	1	19	LDP	25[a]	11	0	12
Commerce and Industry	LDP	40	19	1	19	LDP	21	9	0	11
Transportation	LDP	30	14	0	15	KMT	20	10	0	9

Communica-tions	JSP	30	15	0	14	JSP	20[b]	9	0	8
Construction	KMT	30	15	0	14	JSP	20	10	1	9
Budget	LDP	50	24	0	25	LDP	45	22	0	22
Accounts	JSP	25	10	0	10	JSP	30	15	0	14
Operations	LDP	25	12	0	12	LDP	25	12	0	12
Discipline	DSP	20	9	0	9	JCP	10	5	0	4

[a] One vacancy.
[b] Two vacancies.
SOURCE: Miyagawa Takayoshi, ed., *Seiji Handobukku* (Tokyo, February 1978), p. 148–60.

SIGNIFICANCE OF THE ELECTIONS

delayed so long within committee and in going from one house to the other that they die before the next Diet session or are even killed outright. The party must therefore operate with the constant possibility of stalemate.

While these inconveniences do exist, they are not sudden or of landslide proportions. They have been present, at least in the upper house, since 1974. Nor do they justify the heady anticipations about an opposition coalition to replace the LDP in office. The new situation does, however, force the LDP to come up with a new style of operation, one that requires more attentiveness to the opposition and new skills to deal with it. Small and incremental as these shifts may be, they often require very tedious and sometimes difficult adjustments.

Winners and Losers

If the election results do not add up to the "popular rejection" of the LDP, what do they add up to? What was the "awesome verdict of the people," to use a term dear to the hearts of many journalists? At the most elementary level, is it even clear who won and who lost?

For individual candidates, the meaning of "win" and "lose" is clear. Not that there are no ambiguities whatsoever. Two candidates in the Niigata Third District won their seats with a mere 8 percent of the vote.[9] What does this signify about the "popular will," other than that its effective representation is strongly affected by the quirks of the electoral system? And what does an 8 percent victory signify about whom the elected representatives represent? Do they represent their districts, in any significant sense, or do they represent only the 8 percent who voted for them? Again, in 41 percent of the lower-house districts, the difference between the lowest winner and the runner-up was less than 1 percent (see Table 4–3). In the Niigata Second District, for example, the LDP's Inaba Osamu, the incumbent and eleven-time winner, just barely nosed out his JSP rival, three-time winner and also an incumbent, Abe Sukeya, by ninety-three votes, to win the fourth seat in a four-seat district.

Nevertheless, in the case of individuals, "victory" is clearly defined: securing enough votes to be elected to a seat under the rules of the game. But in the case of the parties, the answer is by no means so simple. Did a particular party do well or badly? This depends not only upon absolute magnitudes but upon expectations—of the party, of the candidates themselves, of the public, and of the media. Al-

---

[9] Specifically, 8.8 and 8.1 percent.

though the LDP certainly lost somewhat, the opposition did not gain proportionately. Dividing the political spectrum broadly into conservative and progressive segments reveals that there has been virtually no change. That being the case, did the LDP win, or did it lose?

The JSP won a few seats in the lower house, but since the number of seats in that house was increased, the JSP's seat percentage remains about the same; in popular vote, it also remained about the same, losing no more than 1.2 percentage points (a decline of 5.6 percent from 1972). Was this a gain or a loss? It was a gain in seats but a loss in votes. Compared with 1972, the Socialists held reasonably steady; compared with 1969, however, there was a considerable gain. But the results remain below the party's historic performance and its highs of the early 1960s.

The KMT certainly had every right to be happy about its seat gains, but its overall performance was mixed. In the lower house its seat gain was dramatic—but only against 1972, not against 1969. Its vote gain was impressive, but in nine districts where it ran candidates the previous time, it lost votes this time. In other words, it simply returned, on the average, to an earlier position from which it had fallen off in the previous election. This is a good showing, but it is not clear evidence of the party's future possibilities. In the upper house, the KMT won the same number of seats as the previous time, but the popular vote was contradictory: a 2.1 point (or 17 percent) increase in the national constituency, which is certainly significant, but a 5.9 point (or 46.8 percent) drop in the local.

The DSP managed to improve itself marginally, not enough to cry victory but enough to ensure its continuation in place. Did it win, or did it lose?

The biggest loser was the JCP, which lost seats dramatically in both houses. But here again the outcome was not entirely without ambiguities: while the party lost seats in the lower-house elections, it held its vote share. However, the distribution of its vote was unfavorable. In the upper house, it lost both seats and votes, but its vote loss in the national constituency, which is a better indicator of true popular support than is the local constituency, was just under one percentage point, or about 10 percent of its vote.

Perhaps the only unambiguous winner in the lower house was the NLC, which turned in a performance much better than expected of a new party and ended up with a modest but firm parliamentary foothold. In the upper-house elections, however, the NLC did not do as well as expected, even though it amassed a respectable vote.

Public Opinion and the Elections

The problem is to determine what these, on the whole, quite small shifts signify with regard to public opinion. Elections, unlike referendums, are never single-issue contests. The voter's views on the various issues placed in consideration by the political parties may very well lead in contradictory directions. He may dislike the LDP's chumminess with big business but favor its foreign policy; he may like the KMT's position on environmental problems but not its sectarian affiliation. He may be a conservative but dislike the particular candidate available to him. Only the most determined party regulars will vote for a candidate they dislike in order to support the party.

Flirters and Floaters. Every public opinion sounding in Japan shows a large number of voters who do not support any existing party. At any given time, the so-called "floating vote"—that is, the don't knows, the undecided, and those who declare support of no party in public opinion polls—will run between 25 and 40 percent, and it appears, if anything, to be growing slightly. A substantial part of this group will not vote in elections at all, although usually more of them will vote in the more important lower-house rather than in the upper-house elections. The overall voting rate for the 1976 lower-house elections was 73.5 percent, for the 1977 upper-house elections, 68.5 percent.

Nonvoters constitute the largest or the second largest single grouping in the total electorate—the "No. 1" or the "No. 2 party," as the media describe it (Table 7–3). Since 1956, the nonvoters have typically been the largest group in the upper-house elections (except for 1974). The more nonvoters there are, the smaller the LDP vote share. The reverse, however, is no longer the case. It used to be that the LDP benefited from an increase in the voting rate. Now, however, much of the increase goes to the independents and minor parties, which make up the fifth largest group, just above the KMT in the local constituency and just below the national.

By election time, many of the undecided do vote, and all the parties make special efforts to pull in as many of them as they can. In 1976–1977 the floaters played a larger role than usual. Various indicators suggest that the LDP and the KMT drew about 70 percent of their votes from regular supporters, with the remainder from the floaters, that is, those who have no party identification at all, and from the "flirters,"[10] those who declare their support of one party

---

[10] I am indebted for this term to Professor Tanaka Yasumasa of Gakushūin University.

TABLE 7–3

DISTRIBUTION OF TOTAL ELECTORATE, 1977 HOUSE OF COUNCILLORS ELECTION

(percent)

Vote Disposition	Local Constituencies	National Constituency
Nonvoting	31.5	31.5
LDP	26.1	23.2
JSP	17.1	11.2
KMT	4.1	9.2
JCP	6.6	5.4
DSP	3.0	4.3
NLC	3.8	2.5
SCL	0.8 ⎫	1.8 ⎫
PFL	0.6 ⎪	1.8 ⎪
WP	0.0 ⎬ 5.5	0.2 ⎬ 8.9
Other	0.9 ⎪	0.3 ⎪
Independent	3.2 ⎭	4.8 ⎭
Invalid	2.3	3.8
Total	100.0	100.0

SOURCE: Calculated from Nisihira, ed., *Naigai Senkyo Data.*

but cross over to vote for another party at election time (Table 7–4). Dependence upon the floating vote is much higher among the other parties, particularly the DSP and the NLC.[11] A rough calculation would suggest that the LDP takes about 40 percent of the floating vote and the remaining 60 percent is divided among the other parties. This percentage, incidentally, is very close to the LDP's share of the national vote (Table 7–5).

The problem of floaters and flirters goes to the issue of the so-called protest vote. When a conservative voter, for example, wishes to express his discontent with the LDP, its policy, or its candidate, he may abstain from voting entirely or he may cast his vote for the candidate of another party. All the opposition parties have been, in varying degrees, beneficiaries of this protest vote. Since the JSP is the largest opposition party, it has usually been the largest beneficiary.

[11] See Naramori Rei, "Seiji-seitō nashi no dōkō," *Chōsa Geppō,* no. 255 (March 1977), for a detailed analysis of the floating vote in the 1976 lower-house elections.

TABLE 7–4

Composition of Party Vote, 1976 House of Representatives Election
(percent)

Party	Total Votes Won	Composition of Vote		
		Party supporters	Flirters[a]	Floaters[b]
LDP	100	68.6	10.7	20.7
JSP	100	66.4	11.7	22.4
KMT	100	71.8	13.5	15.2
JCP	100	53.4	18.0	28.6
DSP	100	47.4	27.5	25.0
NLC	100	36.5	32.4	31.1

[a] Those who regularly support one party, but voted for the candidate of another.
[b] Those who support no party.
Source: Naramori Rei, "Seiji-seitō nashi no dōkō," *Chōsa Geppō*, no. 255 (March 1977), p. 5.

TABLE 7–5

Share of Floating Vote, by Party, 1972 and 1976 House of Representatives Elections
(percent)

Party	1972		1976	
	Share of total vote	Share of floating vote[a]	Share of total vote	Share of floating vote[a]
LDP	46.9	46.9	41.8	41.3
JSP	21.9	23.4	20.7	22.1
KMT	8.5	4.6	10.9	5.1
JCP	10.5	9.7	10.4	11.8
DSP	7.0	8.0	6.3	6.1
NLC	—	—	4.2	5.6
Others and independent	5.4	7.4	5.8	8.0
Total[b]	100.2	100.0	100.1	100.0

Dash (—): Not applicable.
[a] "Floating vote" includes both floaters and flirters.
[b] Percentages do not add to 100 because of rounding of decimals.
Source: Calculated from Naramori, "Seiji-seitō nashi no dōkō."

But this is no longer invariably the case as it used to be in the past. Now, with so many opposition parties available, the protest vote— or more broadly, the anti-LDP vote—has more places to go, and this has cut into the JSP's former near monopoly. To take one example, many farmers expressed their discontent with LDP agricultural and rice-price policies by voting for the Communists rather than for the Socialists. Most farmers had no chance to vote for the other parties, even if they wished to, because except for the JCP the small parties ran very few candidates in rural districts. In the 1976 lower-house elections, all parties held about even or lost shares of the rural vote except the Communists, who improved theirs by 50 percent (see Table 4–5). But in the upper-house elections seven months later, it was the Socialists who were the big gainers in the rural districts, and the Communists' gain was much below their lower-house showing (see Table 5–9, semirural and rural columns).

Lockheed. In the light of these considerations, the verdict of public opinion indeed appears uncertain, as the newspaper headline put it. If there was any single issue that should have been clear-cut, it was Lockheed. The scandal lay like a black cloud over the political scene and contributed heavily to the general atmosphere of malaise, the disaffection with politics, and the growing sense of public outrage. The scandal took on some of the dimensions of a morality play, very much as Watergate did in the United States. The symbolism of former Prime Minister Tanaka Kakuei in front and Kodama Yoshiō, the ultra-rightist fixer, operating backstage was enough to keep the public glued to the TV screen and other media. And the remaining cast of characters—the All-Nippon Airways, the Marubeni Trading Corporation, self-made multimillionaire entrepreneur Osano Kenji— did nothing to detract from the already strong public suspicions about the "cozy" ties between the LDP and business.

No doubt Lockheed was a factor in people's minds, but it did not manifest itself clearly in their voting behavior. A voter might, for example, be appalled by Lockheed but nevertheless have no hesitation voting for the LDP candidate in his district, who was uninvolved, attractive, had a good Diet record, and looked after the interests of his district well. Undoubtedly in many cases the decision of a former LDP voter to shift to the NLC or the DSP candidate might be attributed to Lockheed. But the shift of a farmer from the LDP to the Communist candidate in his district may just as well have reflected not so much his feelings about Lockheed as his resentment over the LDP's holding the lid on the rice price. Moreover, almost as many flirters and floaters shifted their votes to the LDP, rather than away from it, despite Lockheed.

What is most surprising, however, is how little shift there was in districts where Lockheed might have been expected to have the greatest impact. In the six campaigns most directly affected, the scandal was not a salient issue for most of the voters. They made up their minds on other grounds.[12] The three officially endorsed Lockheed candidates all won their contests handily. Two of them (Katō Mutsuki, Okayama Second District, and Nikaidō Susumu, Kagoshima Third) came in first, as they had done in the previous election, and one (Fukunaga Kazuomi, Kumamoto Second) dropped from his previous third place to fifth place in winning his seat this time. Two of the three lost votes (19 and 6 percent, respectively), but fifth-place winner Fukunaga, who had gone down in the rankings, actually increased his vote, by almost 9 percent in numbers and 7 percent in share. These figures are hard to read as a rejection of the Lockheed candidates by their districts.

Three candidates, who were under indictment during the election period, ran as independents, and they are perhaps a more critical test case. Two of them won, Tanaka Kakuei (Niigata Third) holding his lead position handily, Hashimoto Tomisaburō (Ibaragi First) falling from first to third place (in a four-member district). Even though Tanaka's winning percentage went down from its previous 42 percent to 37 percent, he remained one of the top winners in the country. Media reports, which concentrated heavily on the Niigata Third, revealed that Tanaka's supporters rallied to their embattled leader out of loyalty, gratitude, and solidarity with one of their own folk under attack from outsiders—despite the fact that many were fully convinced of his guilty involvement. Hashimoto Tomisaburō, by contrast, although he held on to his seat, fell back considerably. The 28 percent drop in his vote may represent the Lockheed backlash in his district.

One of the "blacks" (indicted candidates), Satō Takayuki (Hokkaidō Third) did, in fact, lose. A four-time winner, he fell out of the winning ranks by one percentage point, dropping 19 percent of his vote. This 19 percent may represent the Lockheed backlash in his district. However, there were other factors, personal and local, completely unrelated to Lockheed, that were affecting his popularity. It should also be recalled that Hashimoto lost a larger percentage of his vote and still managed to win.

It can only be concluded that Lockheed may have been a factor, but not a large one.

---

[12] For details, see Blaker, Chapter 2 in this volume.

Incumbents and Newcomers. Another highly touted interpretation of the elections was the *shinkyū gyakuten*, or "overthrow of the old by the new." There is no question that many stalwarts of the past, including some of the big names and factional chieftains, particularly on the opposition side, "tasted the ashes of defeat," as the newspaper cliché put it. The LDP losers included at least thirteen former cabinet ministers, including three sitting ministers[13] and several high-ranking party officers. Even more spectacular were the opposition losers: the three heads of the main JSP factions[14] and other major leaders, and several leading members of the JCP's central executive committee.

It was not only the big-name incumbents that dropped off. In the lower-house elections, newcomers in general did better than they had in the past. Many observers, fully expecting a political turnabout, convinced themselves in the first flush of excitement that it had in fact happened. A cooler look, however, did not support these conclusions.

There was, to be sure, an increase in the proportion of new lower-house candidates elected, but the increase was small. The historical average for new lower-house candidates (that is, new candidates plus former dietmen in column 3, Table 5–11) over the past five elections, runs at a little over a quarter of the total winning candidates. In 1976 this figure went up to 33.5 percent, an increase of forty-two seats. While this is not unimportant, neither is it large. Moreover, in 1976 two special factors accounted for much of the replacement of the old by the new. First, more replacements than usual had to be made because of death and retirement, and they were naturally new faces. In 1972 there had been seventeen of these; in 1976 there were twenty-nine, an increase of twelve. Second, twenty more seats had been added to the House of Representatives, and they too had to be filled by new faces. These two factors alone account for thirty-two out of the forty-two new faces.

In the upper-house elections (Table 5–12), there is a reversal of the reversal. Both in the national constituency and, even more, in the local constituencies, incumbents actually increased their share of the winning seats.

The Young and the Old. Another prevalent stereotype was the replacement of older dietmen by younger candidates—in extreme form, the

---

[13] Amano Kimiyoshi, fifty-five, four-time winner from Tokyo's Sixth District, home minister; Maeda Masao, fifty-five, four-time winner from Nara Prefecture, director of the science and technology agency; Ōishi Buichi, sixty-six, ten-time winner from Miyagi Second District, minister of agriculture and forestry.

[14] See Curtis, Chapter 3 in this volume, for details.

TABLE 7–6

AVERAGE AGE OF REPRESENTATION, BY PARTY, 1976
HOUSE OF REPRESENTATIVES ELECTION

Party	Average Age in Years
LDP	57.9
JSP	55.9
KMT	45.0
JCP	48.8
DSP	52.8
NLC	45.2
Average, all representatives	54.9
1972 average	55.5

SOURCE: Compiled from newspaper and government reports.

youth "takeover" of the political system. On election day, December 7, 1976, *Asahi Shinbun* announced that "the voters demanded youth and progressivism." This image was no doubt abetted by the high visibility of younger faces among the newly formed NLC's candidates and by the increased number of KMT seat winners, since the KMT is on average much younger than the other parties (see Table 7–6).

But here again, the figures dispute the wishful stereotypes: there was no significant change in the average age of representatives. The proportion under fifty years of age, which was 30.1 percent in 1972, was 29.9 percent in 1976 (see Table 7–7). The average age of representatives shifted sideways from 55.5 in 1972 to 54.9 in 1976 (see Table 7–6). In the House of Councillors election, the reversal was reversed: those under fifty years old dropped from 38.9 percent in 1974 to 24 percent in 1977 in the national constituency; in the local constituency from 25 percent in 1974 to 15.8 percent in 1977 (see Table 7–8). The average age of the councillors rose between 1974 and 1977 from fifty-three to fifty-five in the national and fifty-six to fifty-eight in the local constituency.[15]

The Prime Ministership. The public and the press also watched the election closely to see how the Miki-Fukuda conflict in the LDP would

[15] Nisihira Sigeki, ed., *Naigai Senkyo Data—Mainichi Nenkan Bessatsu* (Tokyo: Mainichi Shinbunsha, 1978), p. 16.

TABLE 7-7

AGE DISTRIBUTION OF WINNERS, 1969, 1972, AND 1976
HOUSE OF REPRESENTATIVES ELECTIONS

Age Group	1969 Number	1969 Percent	1972 Number	1972 Percent	1976 Number	1976 Percent
25–29	4	0.8	1	0.2	3	0.6
30–39	39	8.0	30	6.1	37	7.2
40–49	107	22.0	117	23.8	113	22.1
50–59	160	32.9	155	31.6	193	37.8
60–69	135	27.8	143	29.1	123	24.1
70 and over	41	8.5	45	9.2	42	8.2
Total	486	100.0	491	100.0	511	100.0

SOURCE: Calculated from Nisihira, ed., *Naigai Senkyo Data*, p. 11.

turn out. Although it seemed obvious from the start that since Miki's faction was only fourth in size, he could be turned out of office any time a suitable combination of factions was put together, there was some feeling that the elections would make a difference. The issue was not who would get more seats—although that plays an important role

TABLE 7-8

AGE DISTRIBUTION OF WINNERS, 1971, 1974, AND 1977
HOUSE OF COUNCILLORS ELECTIONS

Age Group	1971 National	1971 Local	1974 National	1974 Local	1977 National	1977 Local
30–39	3	0	4	4	2	3
40–49	11	19	17	15	10	9
50–59	24	18	20	26	23	33
60–69	8	31	10	25	14	19
70 and over	4	7	3	4	1	12
Total	50	76	54	76	50	76

SOURCE: Calculated from Nisihira, ed., *Naigai Senkyo Data*, p. 16.

in intraparty maneuvering. No great change here was likely, because of the nature of the multimember constituency system. (In the event, the Miki faction lost two seats; but so did every other faction except Nakasone's [see Tables 7–9 and 2–9].) But if the LDP did well under Miki's leadership, he would have been entitled, by custom as well as by political prudence, to remain on as prime minister. If, on the other hand, the party did poorly, he would have been expected to take the responsibility and resign. This situation therefore had the odd effect of giving the anti-Miki groups a stake in the party's doing poorly. Miki publicly committed himself to an LDP victory of more than 272 seats. Even though this was less than the number of LDP seats in the outgoing House, it would be enough to control the House and its committees. On the eve of the election, he reduced this estimate to 265 seats. When the party fell so far below not only his optimistic but his pessimistic predictions, Miki promptly resigned and Fukuda took over. This issue was therefore resolved by the election, but it was not an election issue.

New Political Forces

The successful emergence of the NLC raised the possibility in many minds of a more effective impact of the large undecided vote. Vari-

TABLE 7–9

LDP FACTIONAL DISTRIBUTION IN BOTH HOUSES

Faction	Councillors[a]	Representatives[b]
ex-Tanaka	27	46
Fukuda	31	53
Ōhira	19	41
Miki	9	34
Nakasone	6	33
Funada	3	8
Shiina	0	16
ex-Mizuta	0	9
Ishii	0	4
Other	5	0
None	24	23
Total	124	260

[a] Immediately after elections, July 10, 1977.
[b] As of July 11, 1977.
SOURCE: Compiled from newspaper reports.

TABLE 7–10

Tokyo Metropolitan Assembly Elections

Party	July 1977 Votes	Percent votes	Seats	Percent seats	Previous Election Seats	Percent seats
LDP	1,832,205	35.4	56	44.4	51	40.8
JSP	771,419	14.9	18	14.4	20	16.0
KMT	748,327	14.5	25	19.8	26	20.8
JCP	722,497	13.9	11	8.7	24	19.2
DSP	174,300	3.4	3	2.4	2	1.6
NLC	515,763	10.0	10	7.9	—	0.0
SCL	67,976	1.3	0	0.0	—	0.0
PFL	32,251	0.6	0	0.0	—	0.0
Other parties	100,227	1.9	0	0.0	—	0.0
Independents	213,268	4.1	3	2.4	2	1.6
Total	5,178,233	100.0	126	100.0	128	100.0

SOURCE: Compiled from reports in *Asahi Shinbun*, July 12, 1978.

ously referred to as the floating vote, the protest vote, the disillusioned vote, the turned-off (*shiraketa*) generation, the *non-poli* (nonpoliticals), the nonvoters, they were expected to make some kind of distinctive mark. There is no doubt that the NLC received much support from these groups, but in no sense could the NLC be described as *the* party of the *non-poli*.

The success of the NLC stimulated a number of other groups dissatisfied with the existing parties to make a try. The most notable of these was the SCL.[16] When founder Eda Saburō suddenly died, his son Eda Satsuki, in the characteristic Japanese dynastic manner, leaped into the breach and won a thumping victory in the upper-house national constituency, coming in as the second-place winner with 1.4 million votes. But Eda could not pull anyone else along with him; he was the SCL's sole winner. In fact, he accounted for 96.4 percent of his group's total vote. Even with the adhesion of Den Hideo, the first-place winner in the national constituency, and two followers, the future of this group is very unclear at this time. It did not make a good showing in the Tokyo Metropolitan Assembly elections held the same day as the upper-house elections, in part undoubtedly because it did not have enough time to organize (see Table 7–10).

[16] For details, see Curtis, Chapter 3 in this volume.

A second effort came from slightly further to the left, the Progressive Freedom League (PFL), which was based on independent, somewhat new-leftish types. The PFL took one seat in the upper-house national constituency. That it was not a rising star was clear in its failure to go any place in the Tokyo metropolitan elections. For a party claiming to base itself on the urban masses, this was a particularly bitter blow.

Another nonstarter was the Japan Women's party. For all its fanfare and the flamboyance of its leader, it was out of the running from the start and stayed that way (see Table 5–3). So far at least, Japanese women's consciousness has not reached a level that produces many women legislators. Although women voters have outnumbered men by over 2 million during the past several years, and their voting rate is higher, they do not aggregate their votes for women candidates. All successful women candidates (except for one independent) were from the regular parties; not a single one came from the Women's party. In the national constituency elections of the upper house, where the chances for aggregating a national women's vote were at their highest, the Women's party's highest winner came in seventy-seventh in a field of 102 (only the first fifty win). The highest woman winner was not from the Women's party but from the KMT, Kashiwara Yasu, who came in sixteenth.

Campaign Issues

Although there were presumably major issues at stake in the national election, the parties were singularly lacking in programs. Except for the opposition's ability to score a point on Lockheed, and the optimistic announcements that one or another variety of anti-LDP coalition government was in prospect, no party clearly tackled the issues confronting the country with anything like a distinctive program. In fact, what might have been the divisive issues turned out to be nonissues. Almost nobody spoke seriously about basic problems of foreign policy, U.S.-Japanese relations, the Mutual Security Treaty, or Japan's own security forces. On the basis of declared ideology and program, these should have been the principal issues. Nor did the important economic issues facing the country fare any better. Inflation, recession, trade liberalization, and the trade surplus were not entirely absent, but they were present largely as platitudes, more or less the same things being said by all of the candidates regardless of party. On the basis of their campaign statements alone, it would have been difficult clearly to distinguish the candidates' parties, except that the opposition candidates self-righteously attacked the LDP for its economic performance and the LDP took a defensive posture. As for proposals to break out of the impasse, there was little to choose from among them. On foreign policy issues, the opposition parties appeared to be muting their historic positions, particularly in regard to the U.S.-Japan Mutual Security Treaty.[17]

One is therefore tempted to conclude that despite the formal platforms, which suggest vast disagreements in principle and ideology, the parties were in substantial agreement on these issues and differed only on matters of degree—a little more here, a little less there. But matters of degree are scarcely the stuff of which vast political changes are made, and the excitement of the election was to be found more in the nuances and in the game of politics itself rather than in the substantive issues raised for public consideration.

Political Developments

Clearly, LDP rule has not yet collapsed in the way that many observers expected or hoped. In spite of the steady downward slide, the LDP still remains a giant among pygmies at the national level, even though only the largest among equals in the local urban constituencies. Nevertheless this does not mean that nothing at all has happened. There is obviously a big difference between an LDP with a commanding lead and an LDP with only a bare majority or a plurality. The real question is whether the present position is the bottom of the curve or only a brief pause on a continuing downward trend.

In the eighteen years between the 1958 and the 1976 elections, the LDP share of the national vote declined from 57.8 to 41.8 percent, a total of 16 points, or 28 percent.[18] The decline in seats has been less dramatic, but nevertheless inexorable: 12.8 points, or about 21 percent (see Table 4–1). The disaggregated figures are more meaningful, however. The LDP has always been stronger in the rural areas than in the large cities (see Tables 4–5 and 5–9). On a continuum from rural to urban electoral districts, LDP support goes down with every upward degree of urbanization.

During the past twenty years two important trends have affected politics. First, there has been an enormous shift of population from rural to urban areas and, with it, a shift of voters. At the end of

---

[17] For a detailed explanation, see Curtis, Chapter 3 in this volume.

[18] The figures refer to votes cast for LDP-endorsed candidates in the House of Representatives elections and do not include the votes for independently elected conservatives, many of whom joined the LDP after the elections. The trend for the upper-house elections is about the same, although the details differ because of the different constituency structures of the two houses.

World War II, almost half the labor force was in agriculture and almost 60 percent of the population in rural areas. Today, the figures are respectively about 9 percent and 13 percent. The reorganization of voting districts in accordance with population still lags dramatically —some rural districts elect three times as many Diet members per population as urban districts do[19]—largely because the LDP majority has been able to slow down redistricting, since it is clearly disadvantageous to itself. Nevertheless the shift of weight toward the urban areas has been steady. In 1969 rural areas returned 85 parliamentary seats, or 17.5 percent (of which 70.6 percent went to the LDP), while metropolitan areas returned 102 seats, or 21.0 percent (of which 39.2 percent went to the LDP). But in 1976 rural areas returned only 51 seats, or 10 percent of the total (of which 58.8 percent went to the LDP), and the metropolitan areas 134, or 26.2 percent (of which 29.1 percent went to the LDP) (Table 7–11). Even if the LDP were to hold on to its share of the rural vote, the LDP vote would inevitably decline because the rural share of the national vote is shrinking.

But the LDP has not even been able to hold its share of the rural vote. Between 1969 and 1976, while the overall rural share was shrinking slightly, the LDP rural vote declined from 70.6 to 58.8 percent, or by about 16.7 percent. In all other categories (semirural, intermediate, urban, and metropolitan), the decline has been even greater. Despite its overall decline, however, at the national level the LDP retains a clear plurality in every type of electoral district.

Correlatively, the opposition parties have increased their strength in all types of districts, but particularly the urban and metropolitan ones. As a result, eight prefectures plus many cities have come under opposition control. While this has created some problems for the LDP, particularly in the national capital, Tokyo, which has a progressive governor, they have been manageable.[20] Since the end of World War II, largely because of the American Occupation's reforms, local autonomy has become much stronger, with increasing budget shares and decision-making areas coming under local, as against central, control.

Another important development has been the pluralization of political life already referred to. Since the start of Japan's postwar drive for economic growth, and particularly during the last ten years, the size, power, and activity of interest and pressure groups has in-

---

[19] For example, Hyōgo Fifth District elects 3.5 times as many per voting population as Chiba Fourth.

[20] In April 1979, however, the progressives lost all the gubernatorial and mayoral elections they contested.

TABLE 7-11

LDP Seat Share, by Degree of Urbanization, 1969, 1972, and 1976 House of Representatives Elections

Type of District	1969				1972				1976			
	Total	Per-cent[a]	LDP	LDP percent	Total	Per-cent	LDP	LDP percent	Total	Per-cent	LDP	LDP percent
Metropolitan	102	21.0	40	39.2	114	23.2	36	31.6	134	26.2	39	29.1
Urban	67	13.8	38	56.7	78	15.9	45	57.7	80	15.7	40	50.0
Intermediate	92	18.9	61	66.3	143	29.1	85	59.4	145	28.4	78	53.8
Semirural	140	28.8	89	63.6	106	21.6	71	67.0	101	19.8	62	61.4
Rural	85	17.5	60	70.6	50	10.2	34	68.0	51	10.0	30	58.8
Total	486	100.0	288	59.3	491	100.0	271	55.2	511	99.9	249	48.7

Note: Degree of urbanization is based upon the proportion of the labor force engaged in the primary industrial sector (see Table 1–3).
[a] Percent of total electorate.
Source: Calculated from Nisihira, ed., *Naigai Senkyo Data.*

creased dramatically. This is evident in the proliferation of environmental movements, consumer groups, and civic movements of all kinds.

Of equal significance is the increased self-assertiveness of interest groups that have always been considered conservative supporters of the LDP alliance—fishermen, doctors, dentists, and farmers. The farm bloc, organized and powered by the national farm cooperatives and supported in the councils of government by Diet members dependent upon them for reelection, is now a major factor. It is no longer surprising to see truckloads of farmers, arrayed in a type of battle dress usually associated only with radical students, demonstrating before the Diet or the LDP headquarters or marching through the streets of Tokyo to demand higher rice subsidies, to oppose lower tariffs for citrus fruits or beef, or to support some other cause. The government's difficulty in responding to foreign pressure for greater liberalization becomes evident when the powerful pressure groups deploy their forces in demonstration, protest, petition, and threat. One reason for the LDP rural decline is that farmers have discovered the value of a protest vote. In many districts, it has become increasingly common for the local agricultural cooperatives, or some factions among them, to withhold endorsement of the LDP candidate as a way of registering protest or of forcing the LDP to some more favorable course of action. Another way is to cast a protest vote for another party.

In Japan, as in all the developed industrial countries since the late 1960s and particularly since the oil shock of 1973, a growing clamor of criticism has been directed against capitalist industrial society and rapid economic growth. This trend, coming from a wide variety of sources, has seriously eroded the postwar consensus on catching up with and overtaking the West. Business, once highly admired for its achievements and its ability to manage, has become tarnished by a series of scandals, environmental pollution, and its failure to cope with the continuing stagflation. The trinity of business, LDP, and bureaucracy has lost both stature and self-confidence. The LDP has been the victim of this trend both because it was part of the establishment trinity and because it has been in power for so long that it is blamed for what goes wrong. The result is the feeling that political corruption is on the increase, that corruption is the "inevitable" consequence of being in office too long. Whether corruption has in fact been increasing is difficult to judge, but there is no question that public awareness of corruption has increased.[21] Although Lockheed was the most spec-

---

[21] On this question see Katō, Chapter 6 in this volume.

tacular scandal, it was not the only recent case. The pall of corruption has been hanging over the political scene since the 1974 upper-house elections, and how much the reforms in the political financing laws will do to dispel it is not yet clear. Meanwhile, corruption continues to contribute a quantum of dissatisfaction to the current political mixture.

That the LDP is not in the most desirable position is beyond doubt. What happens next, however, is by no means a foregone conclusion. For while the LDP has been ebbing, the opposition has not been waxing proportionately. It has not been able to take full advantage of the LDP weakness, partly because it is divided and partly because Japanese voters seem to calibrate their protest votes very carefully so as not to risk too drastic a change. The main beneficiary of the votes lost by the LDP has not been its principal challenger, the JSP, but rather the smaller parties who have no chance to take over. The Communists lose votes in the big cities, which means they lose seats; their gains, however, come in the rural areas where they clearly have no chance to win. The KMT, the DSP, and the NLC all received small increments of votes hewed off the LDP block. But the JSP has also been losing votes, and these too have been going to the smaller opposition parties.

In the middle 1960s, when the LDP was riding at its highest, it was possible to see portents of impending changes in the pattern of local voting.[22] The LDP seemed to be holding its national dominance but losing its position in the cities. Today, when the LDP has reached the lowest point in its history, a reading of local political trends suggests that a new turning point, this time in the other direction, may be in the making. Although during the last decade the opposition has wrested a number of governorships and mayoralties from the conservatives,[23] this tide now seems about to turn.

Another straw in the wind is the elections for local assemblies that took place at the same time as the upper-house elections in 1977. In Tokyo, the coalition supporting progressive Governor Minobe (JSP, JCP, and KMT) lost its majority, going down from seventy seats, or 56 percent of the total, to fifty-four seats, or 43 percent (see Table

[22] For one such prediction, see Herbert Passin, "The Future," in Herbert Passin, ed., *The United States and Japan* (Englewood Cliffs, N.J.: Prentice Hall, 1966), pp. 147–53.
[23] As of February 1, 1978, the opposition held nine of Japan's forty-seven prefectural governorships (as against three for neutrals and twenty-three for the LDP); and three of the nine principal mayoralties (as against three for neutrals and three for the LDP). In April 1979, however, local elections went about as predicted here.

TABLE 7–12

PUBLIC OPINION POLL: DO CONSERVATIVES OR PROGRESSIVES
MAKE BETTER ADMINISTRATORS?

Response	Tokyo	Osaka	Kyōto	Okinawa	Yokohama
Conservatives	27.1	25.5	33.3	20.0	22.3
Progressives	21.8	17.1	18.8	26.0	25.2
Cannot say	37.9	38.7	32.5	29.3	33.5
Don't know	13.2	18.7	15.4	24.7	18.9

SOURCE: *Yomiuri Shinbun* poll conducted in five areas that have recent experience with progressive governments—Tokyo Metropolis, Osaka Prefecture, Kyōto Prefecture, Okinawa Prefecture, and Yokohama City—May 13–14, 1978; reported in *Yomiuri Shinbun*, May 29, 1978.

7–10). Governor Minobe has already ruled himself out of the next race, and the latest results suggest very strongly that the next governor is unlikely to be a progressive.[24] Recent local elections in other parts of the country have been along the same lines, and the results strengthen the impression that much of the bloom has worn off the progressive local governments and that local voters no longer give them the high marks they used to. A recent survey shows a high degree of dissatisfaction and even disillusionment with local progressive governments, pluralities favoring a return to conservative rule, and a widespread feeling that conservatives make more reliable administrators than progressives (see Table 7–12). A newspaper headline following the upper-house and the local elections of 1977 is symbolic: "The Love Affair Is Over/Citizens Desert the Progressives."[25]

Perhaps an even more striking straw in the wind, particularly for those who remember the 1960s and the student rebellions that continued into the early 1970s, is the change in political attitudes among Tokyo University freshmen. Eda Satsuki, leader of the Socialist Citizens League and a prominent student activist at Tokyo University's liberal arts college in the 1960s, stated, "When I was a student on the Komaba campus, it was a very shameful thing to express support for the LDP, and it needed courage to do so."[26] The majority of politically

---

[24] Since these lines were written, the Tokyo gubernatorial election has been held (April 8, 1979). The conservative candidate won the election, and the KMT switched its support from the progressive to the conservative candidate.

[25] "Hatsukoi ga sameta hi/Jūmin no kakushin-banare," *Yomiuri Shinbun*, May 29, 1978.

[26] Reprinted in *Asahi Evening News*, August 14, 1978.

articulate students supported either the Communist party or the new left groups. Even today the JCP controls the formal apparatus of student government at Japan's leading university. But a survey conducted during the summer of 1978 showed that 62 percent of the entering freshmen who declared support of any party favored the conservatives (LDP and NCL) and that support for the JCP had declined sharply (see Table 7–13). Also noticeable was a slight decline in the *non-poli* proportion, which is usually highest among university students.

It is therefore by no means certain that the LDP will undergo another serious decline. But whether it holds steady or even improves slightly, in the coming period it will hold a little less than a safe majority of seats and at best only a bare majority. But this is not good enough to assure stable management of the Diet.

Japan is entering an era of *de facto*, and perhaps even *de jure*, coalition government. The recent period has provided some preliminary experience in this novel situation for the LDP. How well it will

TABLE 7–13

TOKYO UNIVERSITY FRESHMEN POLITICAL PARTY SUPPORT

Party Supported	1978		1977	
	Percent of total[a]	Percent of those who support parties	Percent of total	Percent of those who support parties
LDP	16.8	45.2	6.5	23.2
JSP	6.8	18.4	4.2	15.2
KMT	6.7	1.8	1.2	4.4
JCP	1.3	3.5	6.4	23.2
DSP	2.4	6.5	3.1	11.3
NLC	6.2	16.6	6.5	22.7
SCL	2.3	6.1	—	—
PFL	0.7	1.9	—	—
Other parties	0.0	0.0	3.1	0.0
None	62.8	—	69.1	—
Total	100.0	100.0	100.0	100.0

Dash (—): Not applicable.
[a] There were 2,468 freshmen in the survey.
SOURCE: Compiled from reports in *Asahi Evening News*, August 14, 1978, based on reports in the *Tōdai Shinbun*, the Tokyo University student newspaper.

manage depends on many factors that cannot be fully anticipated, particularly the balance of political forces at any particular time.

If, as seems likely, the LDP continues to be much larger than any of its competitors, it should be able to form coalitions, even though informally, with the more centrist opposition parties—the NLC, the DSP, and the KMT. Even if a formal coalition is not feasible (and it seems unlikely for the coming period), negotiations and agreements on particular issues should be possible. Agreements with the JSP are likely to be more difficult, but not entirely impossible if they are tacit and need not be publicly acknowledged by the JSP.

Throughout the period of LDP single-party control, the opposition parties have been able to take extreme positions that entailed no responsibilities. Essentially they have been able to take a posture critical of the LDP government without having to offer any practical programs of their own except, of course, in local government. Today, however, as the prospects of greater participation in national decision making become more realistic, all the opposition parties, one way or another, appear to be adjusting toward more flexibility and pragmatism. These adjustments are necessary to win a wider base of popular support, whether the opposition parties are thinking of forming coalitions to take the reins of government away from the LDP or of forming coalitions with the LDP.

Despite these adjustments, there is no guarantee that they will lead to the formation of a genuine opposition coalition, and perhaps not even of a new "middle force" that is ardently sought by some political elements. The growth of the opposition, whether of the opposition as a whole or of the centrist elements alone, is hampered by the recent fissiparous tendencies that have resulted in the birth of the NLC from the body of the LDP, of the SCL from the JSP, the PFL from the new left and the *non-poli,* and the Japan Women's party from the women's liberationists. These not only whittle away at the established left parties, the JSP and the JCP, but also contribute to such a multiplicity of parties that the LDP, for all of its loss of votes, still remains far ahead of the pack. Today six major parties are contending for the voters' support, and there are several minor groups, some of which may rise to more significant dimensions.

Whether these particular groups prove durable or eventually fall apart, their very appearance bespeaks the growing pluralism of Japanese political life and the growing unwillingness of assertive interest groups to continue indefinitely to subordinate their own interests to any presumptive "larger interest." They demand attention, and the new compromises that lie ahead will have to take their interests into account. But the fragmentation also suggests that some larger regrouping of political forces may be in the making, at least of the centrists. If this were to be achieved, whether formally or informally, Japanese politics might be simplified into a right, center, moderate left, and extreme left, with the greatest strength lying in the right and center. Such a regrouping would open up possibilities for the alternation in power of right and center or of well-balanced coalitions. If the hold of present organizational boundaries could be loosened entirely, there might well be a drastic restructuring, with a very much reduced true conservative right, a center constituting a clear majority of the electorate, and a small left. In such a case, Japanese politics would become a new ball game.

APPENDIX

Japanese Ballots, 1974

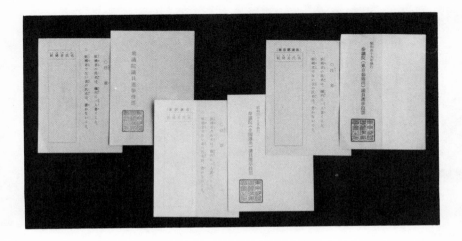

The outside of ballots used for national elections in Tokyo in 1974. The left-hand sheet in each group reads: "1. Write the name of one candidate within the column. 2. Do not write in the name of anyone who is not a candidate." The right-hand side identifies the election; from left to right: House of Representatives; House of Councillors, national constituency; and House of Councillors, Tokyo constituency. The characters within each square read: Tokyo Election Administration Committee.

CONTRIBUTORS

MICHAEL BLAKER is senior research associate and director of the Project on Japan and the United States in Multilateral Diplomacy at Columbia University's East Asian Institute. He is the author of *Japanese International Negotiating Style*, a work also published in Japan, and editor of *Japan at the Polls: The House of Councillors Election of 1974*, and *The Politics of Trade: U.S. and Japanese Policymaking for the GATT Negotiations*.

GERALD L. CURTIS is director of the East Asian Institute and professor of political science, Columbia University. He is the author of *Election Campaigning Japanese Style* and editor of *Japanese-American Relations in the Seventies*. He has written numerous articles in English and Japanese on Japanese politics and international relations.

NISIHIRA SIGEKI is director of training at the Institute of Statistical Mathematics, Tokyo. He is the author of *Nihon no Senkyo* (Japanese Elections), *Daisan Nihonjin no Kokuminsei* (National Character of the Japanese People), no. 3, and *Seron Hanei no Hōhō* (Methods of Reflecting Public Opinion).

KATO HIROHISA is a political writer on the *Yomiuri Shinbun*, a Tokyo newspaper, and author of *Seitō Shiji Nashi-sō* (The Non-Party Supporters).

HERBERT PASSIN is a staff member of the East Asian Institute and professor of sociology, Columbia University. He is the author of *Society and Education in Japan* and editor of *The United States and Japan*, and he has written numerous books and articles in English and Japanese on social change, changing values, and the role of intellectuals in Japan.

INDEX

(Page numbers in italics designate tables.)

Advertising. *See* Campaign advertising
Age
    of candidates/dietmen, 173–75
    of councillors/representatives, 5
    of JSP leadership, 53
    of KMT candidates, 64
    of LDP candidates, 39
Ainu Liberation League, 118
All-Nippon Airways, 15, 171
Amami-Ōshima District, 4
Anpo. See U.S.-Japan Mutual Security
    Treaty
Antimonopoly Law, 147
Aomori First District, 73
Aoshima Yukio, 159
Asai, Vice-Chairman KMT, 64
Association of Post Office Heads, 157
Asukata Ichiō, 121

Ballot, 100 n.12, 105
"Black officials," 23 n.20, 172

Campaign advertising, revised election
    law and, 151, 152, 153
Campaign funding. *See* Elections, fi-
    nancing of
Campaign issues. *See also* Lockheed
    bribery case
    of election (1977), 117–18
    foreign policy/domestic policy, 178–
      79
    opposition party agreements and,
      71–72
Candidates. *See also specific candidates*
    analysis of new and incumbent,
      173–76
    career background of JSP, *51–52*
    competition rate of, 44
    contributions to voters and, 152
    defined, 6

    description of, 1977 elections, 128–
      29
    DSP, 54–57, *58*
    "going down together," 93–94
    JCP, 67, 68
    JSP, 44–47, 49–50
    KMT, 59–60, 64, 65–66
    LDP strategy and, 30, 31–34, 41
    opposition parties', 69–73, 103
    running in all districts, 26, 122
    selection of, for 1976 election, 21–
      25
    success rate of, *45*
    tarento ("talents"), 128–29, 159
Centrist policies. *See* Political parties,
    centrist policies of
Chūma Kōki, 31
Chūritsu Rōren (labor federation), 55,
    149
Clean Politics League (Kōmei Seiji
    Renmei), 62
Coalitions. *See also* Political parties
    anti-LDP, *69*, 73, 78
    DSP, 58
    JCP/JSP, 76–77
    LDP campaign funding and, 144–
      48
    LDP and opposition, 163–64, 185–
      87
    Miki and, 15
Communist party. *See* Japan Commu-
    nist party (JCP)
"Competition rate," 86–87
Conservatives. *See* Kōmeitō (KMT);
    Liberal Democratic party (LDP);
    New Liberal Club (NLC)
Constitution, JSP opposition to amend-
    ing, 83
Corruption. *See* Lockheed bribery case;
    Political parties, scandal
Councillors. *See* House of Councillors

Democratic Socialist party (DSP/Min-shushugi Shakaitō), 44, 47
    business support of, 55–57
    campaign funding and, 148, 149–50, 151, 157
    campaign issues and, 75, 76, 77
    candidate selection and, 54–57, 103, 107
    characteristics of, 106–107
    election results and
        1976, 54–58
        1977, 161, 167
    electoral opposition cooperation and, 69, 70, 71, 73
    "floating" voters and, 169, 170
    formation of, 49, 78
    unions and, 54–55, 79
    voting percentages of, 27, 28, 29, 30, 43, 82–83, 85, 88, 122
Den Hideo, 79, 128–29, 136, 177
Densely inhabited districts (DIDs). See Electoral districts
Diet. See also House of Councillors; House of Representatives
    analysis of new/incumbent members in, 173–76
    committees in, 42, 163, 164–65
    composition of, 3–5
    operation of, after elections, 163–66
    upper house in, analysis of, 115–17
    seats in
        election of 1976 and, 35, 44, 46, 54, 59, 60, 62–63, 66, 67, 69, 82–84, 179
        election of 1977 and, 119, 121, 122, 123, 125, 126–27, 128, 130–31, 132, 137–38, 161–62, 167
        elections and, 4–5
        European party comparison and, 110
        party distribution of, by size of constituency, 93–100
        population density and, 100, 101, 102
        won in 1969, 1972, 1976
            by LDP, 181
            by party, 27
Districts. See Electoral districts
Dōmei labor federation. See also Unions
    campaign agreements and, 70–71, 73
    campaign funding and, 148–49
    DSP and, 54–55, 57, 79
    JCP and, 67

Economy
    domestic, as campaign issue, 77
    as election issue (1977), 118, 178–79
Eda Saburō, 70, 79, 177
Eda Satsuki, 136, 177, 184
Education
    of JSP candidates, 53
    of KMT candidates, 64
    reform of, and NLC, 20–21
Elections. See also Political Funds Regulation Law; Public Office Election Law; Voting percentages; names of individual political parties
    conclusions concerning (Blaker), 38–42
    corporate money/NLC and, 19–20
    financing of, 6
        industry and, 156
        LDP contributions and, 144–48
        LDP factions and, 37
        LDP "money politics" and, 74
        limits on, 155–56
        opposition party funds and, 148–52
        scandal and, 141–43
        union support and
            DSP, 55
            JSP, 49–52
        high costs of, public opinion and, 157–59
Electoral districts. See also names of specific districts
    classification of, 6–9
    densely inhabited (DIDs), 91–93, 100
    distribution of seats in, 93–100
    LDP votes and, 36
    metropolitan
        JCP and, 66, 67
        JSP and, 46–47
        KMT and, 59, 60
        LDP and, 41
    number of, 4
    party voting percentages by, 86–89
    redistricting of/LDP and, 180
    redrawn (1976), 26
    rural
        JCP and, 67
        JSP and, 46–47
        KMT and, 59, 60
        LDP and, 33, 34
    semirural
        JSP and, 46–47
        LDP and, 34
    semiurban
        JCP and, 67

JSP and, 47
KMT and, 59, 60
LDP and, 41
urban
  dividing of, 95
  election results and, 43
  JCP and, 66–67
  JSP and, 46–47
  LDP and, 31–32, 41
voting rate/urbanization and, 89–93
Electoral reform, 158–59
Electoral system
  features of, 3–9
  flaw in Japanese, 26
Electorate, defined, 5. See also Voters; Voting percentages
England. See United Kingdom
Enterprise-based campaign. See Kigyō gurumi
Etsuzankai (support group/Tanaka), 18

Factions. See also Political parties
  in both houses/LDP and, 176
  campaign funding and LDP, 144–48, 150, 155, 157
  ending of LDP, 158
  JSP leadership and, 53–54
  LDP election results (1976) and, 37–38, 39
  Miki's, 15
  NLC formation and, 19
  in upper house/LDP and, 115
Farmers, rice price/voting patterns and, 171, 182
Financing of elections. See Elections, financing of
Fishing zones, as campaign issue, 117
"Flitters" (uncommitted voters), 168–71. See also "Floating" voters
"Floating" voters (uncommitted), 13–14, 80, 108. See also Independents
  election results and, 28–30, 39, 168–71
  NLC and, 176–77
France, 2–3
  parties in, compared with Japanese, 109–112
Fujiyama Aichirō, 143
Fukuda Takeo, 16, 39
  campaign funding and, 145, 146, 155
  electoral reform and, 158
  faction of, 37–38
  Miki conflict and, 175–76

Fukunaga Kazuomi, 16
Funada Naka, 16

Germany
  government changes in, 2
  parties in, compared with Japanese, 109–112
Gifu First District, 72, 73
"Going down together" (tomo-daore) candidates, 93–94
"Gray officials," 23 n.20

Hara Bumpei, 129
Hashimoto Tomisaburō, 16, 22, 142 n.2, 172
Hiroto Kōichi, 129
Hori Shigeru, 16
House of Councillors. See also Diet
  age requirement in, 5
  analysis of new and incumbent members in, 173–76
  composition/functions of, 115–17
  election methods and, 3, 5
  high cost of elections and, 157–58
  LDP defeat proportions in, 161, 162
  local constituencies of, urbanization and, 8
  lower house and, 136–37
  speaker in, 133, 136, 163
  unrepresentativeness and, 138
House of Representatives. See also Diet
  age requirement in, 5
  analysis of new and incumbent members in, 173–76
  election methods and, 3–5
  electoral districts of, classified, 6, 7, 9
  high cost of elections and, 158
  LDP defeat proportions in, 161–62
  power of, 115–16
  upper house and, 136–37

Imazato Hiroki, 150
Independents, 6, 80, 108, 109, 129–33, 159, 161. See also "Floating" voters
Industry (primary), voting patterns and, 93
Italy, 2–3
  parties in, compared with Japanese, 109–112

Japan Communist party (JCP/Nippon Kyōsantō), 20, 44, 47, 49, 80, 103, 109, 186
  campaign funding and, 148, 149, 150, 151, 157
  campaign issues and, 75, 76–77

Japan Communist party (*continued*)
  characteristics of, 107, 108
  election results and
      1976, 66–68
      1977, 167
  electoral opposition cooperation
      and, 69–70
  European parties and, *110*, 111
  "floating" voters and, *170*, 171
  the national vote and, 26
  proportional representation opposition and, 158
  student support of, 185
  unions and, 67–68
  voting percentages and, 27, 29, 30, 31, 43, 84, *85*, 89, 90, 93, 122, 123
  "war of handbills" and, 154
Japan Medical Association, 157
Japan Socialist party (JSC/Nihon Shakaitō)
  campaign funding and, 148, 149, 150, 151, 157
  campaign issues and, 74, 75, 76, 78
  candidate endorsements and, 44–47, 49–52, 103
  characteristics of, 108–109, 186
  coalitions and, 186
  decline of, 41, 167
  decline of, analysis of election results (1976) and (Curtis), 44–54
  electoral opposition cooperation and, 69, 70, 71–73
  European parties and, *110*, 111
  "floating" voters and, 169–71
  the national vote and, 26
  proportional representation and, 158
  as rival to LDP, 2
  unions and, 49–52
  voting percentages and, 27, 29, 30, 43, 46, 82–83, 88, 89, 91, 101–103, 119–21, 122–23
Japan Teachers' Union, 51–52, 67, 68
Japan Women's party (WP/Nippon Joseitō), 136, 178, 186. *See also* Women
Jiten (runner-up), defined, 58

Kakushin Kyōdō (united-progressives), 68
Kashiwara Yasu, 178
Kasuga, Ikkō, 69
Katō Kan, 135
Katō Mutsuki, 16, 172
Kawamata, President Nissan Motor Co., 147–48

Kigyō gurumi (enterprise-based campaign), 56–57
Kodama Yoshio, 15, 171
Kokumin Kyōkai (People's Association), 144, 145, 146, 147
Kōmeitō (KMT/Clean Government party), 44, 47, 49, 109, 174
  campaign funds and, 148, 149, 150, 157
  campaign issues and, 74, 75–76, 77
  candidates of, 59–60, 64, 65–66, 103
  characteristics of, 107–108
  election results and
      1976, 59–66
      1977, 167
  electoral opposition cooperation and, 69–73
  European parties and, *110*, 111
  "floating" voters and, 168, *170*
  the national vote and, 26
  proportional representation opposition and, 158
  Sōka Gakkai and, 59, 60, 62–66, 78, 79
  voting percentages and, 27, 28, 29, 30, 43, 84, *85*, 88, 90, 93, 119, 121
  "war of handbills" and, 154
Kōno Kenzō, 129, 133, 135, 136
Kōno Yōhei, 19, 40, 105–106, 133, 150
Kotchian, Carl, 14

Liberal Democratic party (LDP/Jiyū-Minshutō), 44, 49, 52, 53
  campaign funding/factions and, 144–48, 150, 157
  campaign issues and, 74, 75, 76, 77, 78, 79
  candidate selection of, 21–25
  constitutional amendment and, 83
  decline of, 13, 109, 179–86
  defeat proportion, 161–62
  Diet operation and control by, 163–66
  election results and, 25–26, 31–38, 40–42
  European parties and, 109–112
  faction dissolution and, 158
  factions and election results, 37–38, *39*, 176
  "floating" voters and, 168–71
  formation of NLC and, 18–21
  future of, 183
  as majority party, 1–3
  Miki's faction/Lockheed and, 15–17
  the national vote and, 26

opposition party cooperation and, 70, 72, 73
proportional representation and, 158
scandal and, 142–43
voting percentages and, 27, 28, 29, 30–31, 43, 81–82, 87, 89, 91, 101, 103, 119, 122–23, 133–35
Lockheed bribery case, 158, 159
analysis of, 14–18
as campaign issue, 74, 78
election results and, 25, 36–37, 38–39, 171–72
LDP candidate selection and, 22, 23, 142–43
LDP decline and, 182–83
NLC formation and, 19
Lower house. See House of Representatives

Marubeni Corporation, 15, 16, 171
Matsumoto, Vice-Secretary-General KMT, 64
Metropolitan districts. See Electoral districts
Miki Takeo, 143
campaign funding and, 145, 155, 156
election forecast and, 25–26
faction of, 15, 37–38
Fukuda conflict and, 175–76
Lockheed scandal and, 15–17, 142
Military Pensioners' Federation, 157
Minobe, Governor, 183–84
Miyamoto, Chairman JCP, 76–77
Miyata Satae, 54–55
Mutual Security Treaty. See U.S.-Japan Mutual Security Treaty

Nakamura Takeshi, 159
Nakasone faction, 176
campaign funding and, 145
Miki and, 37–38, 39
Narita, Chairman JSP, 71, 76–77, 119–21
National Railway Workers' Union, 51–52, 68
New Liberal Club (NLC/Shin Jiyū Kurabu)
campaign funding and, 150–51, 159
candidate selection strategy of, 21, 22, 103, 105–6
characteristics of, 105–6
creation of, 18–21, 79, 105, 186
election results and
1976, 26–31, 36, 39–40

1977, 161–62, 167
"floating" voters and, 169, 170, 176–77
voting percentages and, 43, 84–86, 89, 93, 119, 135–36
Niigata's Third District, 17–18
Nikaidō Susumu, 172
Nishimura Eiichi, 38
Nishimura Shōzō, 57
Nishio Suehiro, 142 n.2
Nishioka Takeo, 19–20
Nuclear processing, as campaign issue, 117–18

Ogawa Hanji, 151
Ohira Masayoshi, 16
campaign funding and, 145, 155
faction of, 37–38
Okinawa, 4
Okita Saburō, 136
Ono Bamboku, 142 n.2
Opinion polls. See also Public opinion
actual vote and, 105
on conservative/progressive administrators, 184
"floating" voters and, 80 n.2
Lockheed scandal and, 17
NCL and, 20
on popularity of Miki, 26
Tanaka's election and, 18
uncommitted voters and, 13
Osaka, 43, 60, 67

Parties. See Political parties
Political Funds Regulation Law, 143, 144
revision of, 154–59
Political parties. See also Coalitions; Elections, financing of; Factions; names of individual parties
candidate selection and, 21–25
centrist policies of, 77–78, 80, 135, 186–87
characteristics of, 105–9
compared with European, 109–12
distribution of seats in Diet and, 93–100
election issues and, 117–18
opposition, cooperation of, 69–73
scandal and, 141–43
Political pressure groups, 157, 180–82
Political support groups
bogus, 155
Etsuzankai/Tanaka, 18
restrictions on, 152–53
Population
density of, electoral districts and, 9

Population (*continued*)
    shifts and LDP decline, 179–80
    vote distribution and, 100–5
Prefectures
    classified, *8*
    defined, 5
Progressive Freedom League (PFL/ Kakushin Jiyū Rengō), 129, 136, 178, 186
Progressive local governments, decline of, 184
Public Office Election Law, 143, 144
    revision of, 151, 152–54
Public opinion. *See also* Opinion polls
    the elections and, 168–76
    high cost of elections and, 157–59

Reform. *See* Electoral reform
Representatives. *See* House of Representatives
Rice prices, farm vote and, 171, 182
Risshō Kōseikai (religious pressure group), 157
Rural districts. *See* Electoral districts
Russia. *See* U.S.S.R.

Sakamura Yoshimasa, 148
Sasaki Shizuko, 151
Satō Takayuki, 16, 22, 37, 172
Scandals. *See* Lockheed bribery case; Political parties
Seats in Diet. *See* Diet, seats in
Seichō no Ie (religious pressure group), 157
Seirankai (right-wing group), 122
Self-Defense Forces, 2
Semirural districts. *See* Electoral districts
Semiurban districts. *See* Electoral districts
Shibata Mutsuo, 68
Shiina Etsusaburō, 16
Shin Jiyūshugi Kyōkai (New Liberalism Association), 151
Shin Sanbetsu (labor federation), 149
Shinkyū gyakuten (overthrow of old by new), 173
Shōwa Denkō, 141 n.1, 142 n.2
Social Democratic League, 79
Socialist Citizens League (SCL/Shakai Shimin Rengō), 70, 79, 136, 177, 184
Socialist party. *See* Democratic Socialist party; Japan Socialist party
Society to Think about a New Japan, 70, 76

Sōhyō labor federation, 54, 55, 73. *See also* Unions
    campaign funding and, 148–49
    JCP and, 49–50
    JSP and, 67–68
Sōka Gakkai (Value Creating Society)
    campaign agreements and, 70
    campaign funding and, 148, 149
    KMT and, 59, 60, 62–66, 78, 79
Support groups. *See* Political support groups

Takeiri, Chairman KMT, 64, 71
Tanaka Kakuei
    campaign funding and, 145, 146, 155
    as candidate, 22–23
    election of (1976), 17–18, 36
    electoral reform and, 158
    faction of, 37–38
    Lockheed and, 16, 19, 142–43, 171, 172
Tarento ("talents"/candidates), 128–29, 159
Television, campaigning and, 154
Tokyo, 43, 60, 67
    Governor Minobe and, 183–84
    JSP election results in, 47–48
Tomo-daore. See "Going down together" candidates
Tsukawa Takeichi, 99

Unions. *See also* Dōmei labor federation; Sōhyō labor federation
    campaign agreements and, 71
    campaign funding and, 148–49, 151
    DSP and, 54–55, 57
    JCP and, 67–68
    JSP and, 49–52
United Kingdom
    government changes in, 2
    Parliament of, 138
    parties in, compared with Japanese, 109–12
United-progressives. *See* Kakushin Kyōdō
Upper house. *See* House of Councillors
Urban districts. *See* Electoral districts
Urbanization
    degree of, electoral districts and, 6–8
    voting rate, by degree of, 89–93
U.S., election issues and, 117–18
U.S.-Japan Mutual Security Treaty, 71
    as campaign issue, 75–77, 178–79
U.S.S.R., North Pacific fisheries and, 117

Value Creating Society. *See* Sōka Gakkai
Voters. *See also* Electorate; "Floating" voters; voting percentages
  age requirement for, 5
Voting percentages. *See also individual party for specific party percentages*
  in 1976 election, 25–38, 43, 46, 58, 60–*63*, 66, 67, 81–86
    competition rate and, 86–87
    by degree of urbanization, 89–93
    by electoral district, 86–89
    by size of municipality, 100–5
  in 1977 election, 118–22, 132–33, *169*
    per councillor, 129
    general overview of, 133–36
    LDP defeat proportions, 161–62
  by size of constituency, 123, *124*
  by urbanization, *125*–28, 130–31, *137*
  LDP decline and, 179–80

"War of the handbills," 154
Women. *See also* Japan Women's party
  as candidates, 129
  candidates/voters, 178
  as JCP candidates, 68
Women's party. *See* Japan Women's party

Yamamoto Kōichi, 72
Yano, Secretary-General KMT, 64
Yasui Ken, 133, 135
Yokoyama Nokku, 129, 136

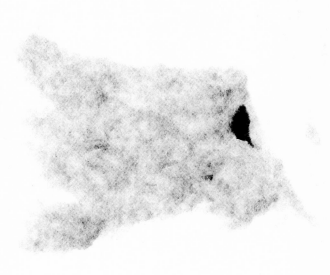

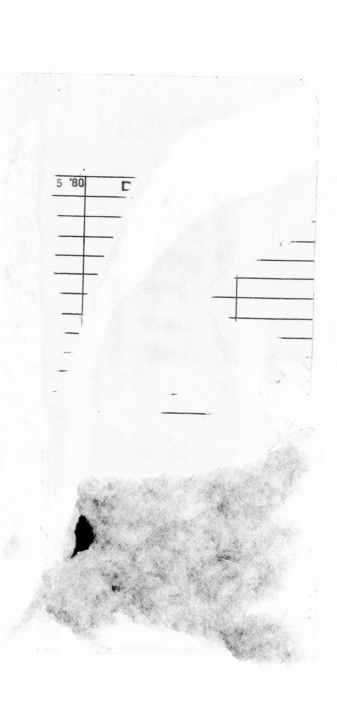

5 '80

Contents of

Japan at the Polls: The House of Councillors Election of 1974

Edited by Michael K. Blaker

Published by the American Enterprise Institute
$3.00

PREFACE   *Michael K. Blaker*

1   THE HOUSE OF COUNCILLORS: PROMISE AND ACHIEVEMENT   *Herbert Passin*

Origins/ Checks and Balances/ The Broader Interest/ Representation/ Stability and Continuity

2   THE 1974 ELECTION CAMPAIGN: THE POLITICAL PROCESS   *Gerald L. Curtis*

Party Policies and Postures/ Choosing the Candidates/ Candidate Endorsement in the Local Constituencies/ Conclusion

3   THE OUTCOME OF THE 1974 ELECTION PATTERNS AND PERSPECTIVES   *Michael K. Blaker*

The Changing Electorate/ Analysis of the Results/ Party Performance/ Implications

APPENDIX: Statistical Data

INDEX

AEI's *At the Polls* Series

In addition to this volume, the following titles have been published by the American Enterprise Institute as part of the *At the Polls* Series, a collection of studies dealing with national elections in selected democratic countries.

Israel at the Polls: The Knesset Elections of 1977, Howard R. Penniman, ed. (333 pp., $6.75)

Germany at the Polls: The Bundestag Election of 1976, Karl H. Cerny, ed. (251 pp., $4.75)

India at the Polls: The Parliamentary Elections of 1977, Myron Weiner (150 pp., $3.75)

Ireland at the Polls: The Dáil Elections of 1977, Howard R. Penniman, ed. (199 pp., $4.75)

Italy at the Polls: The Parliamentary Elections of 1976, Howard R. Penniman, ed. (386 pp., $5.75)

Scandinavia at the Polls: Recent Political Trends in Denmark, Norway, and Sweden, Karl H. Cerny, ed. (304 pp., $5.75)

Australia at the Polls: The National Elections of 1975, Howard R. Penniman, ed. (373 pp., $5)

Japan at the Polls: The House of Councillors Election of 1974, Michael K. Blaker, ed. (157 pp., $3)

Canada at the Polls: The General Elections of 1974, Howard R. Penniman, ed. (310 pp., $4.50)

France at the Polls: The Presidential Election of 1974, Howard R. Penniman, ed. (324 pp., $4.50)

Britain at the Polls: The Parliamentary Elections of 1974, Howard R. Penniman, ed. (256 pp., $3)

This series also includes *Britain Says Yes: The 1975 Referendum on the Common Market* by Anthony King (153 pp., $3.75).

Studies are forthcoming on 1977 elections in Greece and Australia; 1978 elections in Colombia, France, New Zealand, and Venezuela; 1979 elections in Canada, Britain, Italy, and Sweden; the 1977 and 1979 elections in Spain; and the elections to the European Parliament in 1979.